Captain Thomas Faulden
a true Cavalier

A Family Historian's Dream Fulfilled

REG POSTLETHWAITE

Published by
Robert Boyd Publications
260 Colwell Drive
Witney, Oxon OX28 5LW

First Published 2010

ISBN: 978 1 899536 98 6

Printed and bound by
Information Press, Southfield Road, Eynsham
Oxford OX29 4JB

Dedicated to the memory of

Our loving son

IAN REGINALD POSTLETHWAITE (1964-1973)

Who fell at Read, when he sallied

Out to capture some conkers.

`O Pomfret, Pomfret! O thou bloody prison Fatal and
Ominous to noble peer! Within the guilty closure of thy
Walls Richard the Second here was hack'ed to death; and,
For more slander to thy dismal seat, we give to thee our guiltless blood to drink'

Shakespeare `Richard III Act III, scene 3.

Richard II confiscated the Lancastrian inheritance of Henry Bolingbroke, Son of John of Gaunt and banished him
from the country. When Henry returned, he sent Richard II to his death at Pontefract from where the body travelled
to London with the head exposed for all to see.

`I love Pontefract Castle
Why, 'tis in all our histories.'

Dr. Johnson

Contents

List of Illustrations

Appendices

Forward

It is the fervent hope of most family historians that they will find someone or something in their ancestry which is of real interest so that they are not merely recording a list of names and dates. Unfortunately for most of us we come from very ordinary stock with perhaps only a marriage which never took place as a highlight. We would therefore envy Reg Postlethwaite's fortune in having been born into the family he writes about.

He was fortunate to be part of this particular family with such fascinating people as ancestors, but that is as far as luck goes. Gathering the tremendous amount of detail and information has cost many years of sheer hard work, tenacity and determination. Even the quickest glance at the list of references shows he has left few stones unturned.

Whether the local history or the family history research came first is unimportant. What the research has shown is the human side of the history taught us at school. Events are seen and related by participants in those events, who knew personally other actors in the drama. What we read is how real people felt, acted and reacted in difficult circumstances and we can applaud their courage. Who, walking around the seemingly impregnable Pontefract Castle has not been thankful that they did not have to storm or defend it. These people did those things.

The Civil War, Pontefract, Family History - and indeed spying - will never seem the same again.

Maisie Morton
Hon. President, F.H.& P.S. Sec. Yorkshire Archaeological Society
October 1991

Acknowledgements

My greatest debt of gratitude in writing this account, is owed to two of my closest friends whom I met among scores of others whilst pursuing our mutual interest in family history.

Fred Hughes and Roy Hudleston, Chairman and President/Editor; founder members of the Cumbria Family History Society, have by their interest and encouragement inspired me to produce this study.

Roy, besides researching at the Public Record Office and transcribing P.C.C. wills for me, read and corrected my first draft, for which I am most grateful.

I also wish to thank Maisie Morton for her kind Forward and the Archivists and staff of the Record Offices of Lancashire, at Preston; of Cumbria at Carlisle, Kendal and Barrow; of Yorkshire at Claremont, Wakefield, Sheepscar and The Borthwick Institute; and the librarians and staff of the Halifax, Rawtenstall and Manchester Central libraries, for their help and patience which I have enjoyed and benefited from over many years.

Last, but not least, my thanks are due to my mother for providing a loving family and stimulating my interest in history; to my dear and long suffering wife Jennie and family, who have endured with cheerfulness and fortitude (apart from altruistic suggestions that I might work better in the loft or in the garden shed) my two fingered typing.

Introduction

I first became interested in my ancestors at the age of eleven when my mother told me what little she knew of her great grandparents whose photographs she had then recently inherited when her father died in 1947.

Thomas Jackson (1806-1883) was a farmer at Wilmans, Grindleton, W.R.Yorkshire and his wife Ann had died from a stroke whilst feeding the calves: their headstone lies in Holden Independent Chapel yard. The seed had been sown and I was disappointed not to discover more information, when I secretly removed the pictures from their frames and in 1948 I wrote a school essay entitled `My Ancestors were Farmers'.

As my interest in history grew so did my curiosity about what part, if any, my ancestors had played in local or even national events but like most ordinary people I never imagined that the mysteries of the past could be rediscovered.

When I first began researching and I discovered that the names of my own insignificant family WERE recorded and yes some of them HAD left wills, it was a very exciting experience. After this initial euphoria and the discovery of many ancestors however, it was a number of years before I was forced, by frustrating experience, to conclude that discovering what individuals had actually done during their lives was not as easy as I had naively begun to hope.

A question to which I eagerly sought an answer was. Were they Cavaliers or Roundheads during the Civil War) I found very difficult, if not impossible to discover.

Most 19th century family papers have perished long ago so what chance had those of 200 years earlier. Even many parish registers of the Civil War period, if perfectly kept, and most were very imperfectly so, have like most paper records been lost or destroyed by fire or more likely by damp or mice over the years. The muster rolls, commissions, letters, government and family papers &c., that have survived, relating to the Civil War, are the official ones in the P.R.O. or others in important family archives, very few of which reveal biographical information about the ordinary people or infantryman / pikeman of the period whom I imagined some of my family to have been.

When I discovered that my ancestor Jeremiah Postlethwaite (1674-1738) was a staunch member of Tottlebank Independent Chapel near Ulverston for many years and named after the eldest son of the one time Parliamentary Governor of Carlisle, Colonel Roger (Praying) Sawrey, of Broughton Tower, who was a great supporter there, I felt confident in the knowledge that Jeremy shared the Colonel's Puritan ideals but whether his father John, who was also a member there, or his grandfather John, followed the Colonel during his Civil War experiences, remains yet to be discovered.

I was thrilled when I discovered that my ancestor Lawrence Breres (1616-1662) Yeoman of Whittle-le-Woods, near Chorley, Lancashire was a Royalist. The Royalist Composition Papers[1] gave me marvellously full details of his small estate and also revealed that `he deserted his own house, went and lived six weeks in a King's garrison,' (for which action he was later fined £10 as a delinquent) but whether this was the Latham House siege, near Wigan or the siege and battle of Preston, any further precise information about his involvement remains as yet tantalizingly obscure. The same source however, did tell me that Lawrence had travelled down to London to take the National Covenant.

My great uncle x7 Thomas Stackhouse (1626-1663) was a Lieutenant of horse at Dunkirk[2] and later Captain of horse at Tangier[3] where he took part in many exciting battles and skirmishes against the Moors and he was very likely with his Tangier commander and close friend Colonel Sir Tobias Bridge when he was in the Parliamentary Army[4] but once again details of his career during that period remain to be discovered.

It was not until I found, through the Dictionary of National Biography, the quite fantastic unique first-hand account of part of his Civil War exploits `The Siege of Pontefract Castle' [5] by our relation Captain Thomas Paulden of Wakefield [6] that I could shout eureka!! And his account forms an important part of my story.

My understanding of the background history of the period has been greatly enhanced by that masterful work by David Underdown, `Royalist Conspiracy in England 1649-1660' [7] to which I owe so much.

Pontefract Castle before it was destroyed following its last siege in 1649.

The author at the remains of the Great tower, Pontefract Castle.

CHAPTER 1

Radcliffe, Paulden and Knowles

It had long been my ambition to discover a relative who took part in the English Civil War, to know that some member of our family was personally involved in that great struggle between King and Parliament, because the mid-seventeenth century, is I believe, like Hartley Coleridge, not only one of the most exciting and colourful periods in our history but one in which we still feel passionately involved. Many years of fruitless research passed, however, before I found someone in whose story we could delight.

Our eleventh great uncle on my mother's side Henry Radcliffe, woollen draper of Wakefield and cloth maker of London, as he describes himself in his will dated 25 Oct 1658,[1] made scores of bequests to his relations and friends, the first being to his brother John Radcliffe (c1573-1662) gentleman of Light Birks, Clapham near Settle, Yorkshire, who was our direct ancestor. Henry gave John the messuage and tenement on which he lived at Light Birks, plus £20 for his better maintenance and he forgave the £20 that John owed him.

The majority of clothiers and merchants declared for the Parliament during the Civil War because they were independent both in spirit and religion and they also lived in towns, which were less under the sway and control of the nobility. Henry Radcliffe, however, belonging also to the gentry, was a Royalist, `having traded with and adhered to, the late King's party' for which he was fined £70 in September 1650.[2] Despite his loyalty to the King he must still have felt love and respect for at least one Roundhead captain, his nephew Roger Radcliffe, son of his brother John, to whom he left £20. To his good friend and cousin William Paulden of Wakefield he bequeathed £10, and this is the reference which led me to discover the subject of my study, William's third son THOMAS PAULDEN.

Gregory Paulden (1556-1613) Thomas' grandfather, was descended from a family living in the West Riding from very early times.[3] John de Paldene was an assistant steward to Henry Earl of Lincoln and sold cattle for him in Pontefract market in the period 1296-1305.[4] John de Palden was fined 6d for unjust detention at Clitheroe in 1324 [5] and another John de Paulden of Cowling paid his poll tax in 1379. [6]

Halifax has, from time immemorial, been a great centre of the woollen industry and in the sixteenth century the town issued licences to 'broggers' to deal in small parcels of wool collected from dales farms and villages. Gregory Paulden, who later became a chapman (dealer), probably started out in his youth as a 'brogger' when he would travel widely to buy raw wool, put it out for spinning and weaving and then sell it in the markets of Halifax and Wakefield.

On one of his regular journeys through the dales he must have met and fallen for the charms of Jannet Knowles, a daughter of one of his customers living at Long Preston and after the custom of the time a suitable dowry would be agreed before they were married in about the year 1577. Gregory perhaps did business and was a good friend of William Hall of Settle, who bequeathed him XXs in his will of 1609.[7]

In 1588, as the Spanish Armada sailed to attack Elizabethan England, Gregory was paying 1s annual rent for his property in Halifax[8] and in 1591 he gave £6.13s.4d in money and 6s 8d in lands, out of his property in Kirkgate, Wakefield to help establish the Grammar School there.[9] His business must have prospered, because only the very rich gave more, led by the Savile family, great Yorkshire land owners.

From 1598 until the time of his early death in 1613, Gregory combined with his brother in law James Knowles, clothier of Wandons Green, Fulham near London, in taking out a number of twenty-one year leases on several large closes of land in Wakefield Old Park.[10] These belonged to Sir Richard Gargrave of Nostell Priory and the notorious land speculator Sir Lionel Cranfield, Lord High Treasurer and soon to become 1st Earl of Middlesex.[11] Cranfield and his crony Sir Arthur Ingram were typical grasping, unscrupulous merchants, familiar to and satirised by Ben Jonson in his successful contemporary play Volpone.[12]

Ingram, whose father came from Yorkshire, had already gained control of the extensive manor of Halifax from the indebted Waterhouse family. By agreeing to buy and then pretending to find fault with their title, he frightened off other buyers and so obtained the property for much less than its true value.

Sir Arthur Ingram c.1565-1642. From a portrait by George Geldorp at Temple Newsham, Leeds.

Another local family in decline was that of Peter Frobisher, spendthrift nephew and heir of the great explorer Sir Martin Frobisher.[13] Ingram bought up his estate at Altofts near Wakefield to enable him to pay off his debts.

Ingram and Cranfield were joint predators in the rapid decline of Sir Richard Gargrave who had already pawned his jewels to Cranfield. The Old Park of Wakefield was a large tract of land granted by Queen Elizabeth to Sir Thomas Gargrave, Speaker of the House of Commons and Vice President of the Council of the North, for his loyal services during the great rebellion of 1569.[14] Sir Richard Gargrave, his grandson, who inherited a large estate – it was said (no doubt with some poetic licence) that he could ride on his own lands from Doncaster to Wakefield - gambled and spent his fortune and by middle age was reduced to travelling with the pack horses. He died in a hostelry with his head on a pack saddle.

The biters were bitten but only moderately I'm sorry to say, when Cranfield wanted to buy the Old Park from Sir Richard Gargrave, offering £2,500. The twenty-one year leases held by Gregory Paulden and James Knowles had to be cleared and bought out and Sir Richard and Cranfield complained bitterly when after long negotiations, (Sir Richard entertained James Knowles several times at his house in Westminster) they were forced to pay £440 to James Knowles; more than double what he had paid to Sir Richard Gargrave in 1604 despite the fact he had already enjoyed six years of the lease.[15]

In 1613 Gregory, whose first wife Jannet had died, married Rosamond, widow of William Horsefall of Harewood, who was descended from the Oates family of Shibden Hall, Halifax.[16] Only months later at the age of 57 on 9th December 1613 Gregory made his will [17] leaving 13s 4d to his daughter Ann Dobbie, who must have received her dowry and £50 to his daughter Dorothy still unpreferred. William his only son, was made sole executor and heir. Roger Radcliffe, Dean of Doncaster and Pontefract and Minister of Horbury near Wakefield, brother of Henry and my ancestor John, was a witness and is described as 'my landlord'. Gregory's well-formed signature denotes a good education.[18]

Rosamond, who had lost two husbands within two years, soon had to face another problem. A suit in Chancery was brought against her for a debt of £89 10s by Thomas and Robert Harrison of York.[19] They claimed that their father Thomas Harrison, of the City of York, Alderman, had made a loan of £180 to William Horsefall, Rosamond's first husband and as he had died intestate, she as administrator of his estate was responsible for the £89 left unpaid.

Rosamond responded by asserting that all the money had been repaid for her husband by his brother John Horsefall and the bonds for the loan had been cancelled but not collected. She went on to say that her husband William Horsefall was very well known in the country as having a good estate with sufficient ability to have paid any such debt but he had never mentioned anything of the like to her and she asked that Robert and Thomas Harrison should be subpoenaed to appear and show the uncancelled bonds. They, for their part, threatened to take action against her at common law. We do not know if Rosamond lost the suit but a proposed third marriage to John Nichols (a marriage licence was taken out) [20] did not take place and in those practical, not to say, mercenary times this may have been because she had become so much less eligible (£89 representing approx.£10,000 in today's money). On the other hand ill health may have overtaken her because on 18 January 1620 we find her making her will at Halifax.[21] Her many bequests included:

> `to my sister Grace Howarth my Russet gowne, my white petticote, my hat and band lyned with velvet which I were of the work days, a pair of hose and shoes with a work day donning of lynnen clothes and also a coverlette and a blankett'

To her daughter Ann Hauke she gave:
> `one iron range and a round table in the house where Francis Drake dwelt.'

This was to be a portentous reference as Nathaniel Drake, who belonged to the same family as Francis, took part in and wrote about the first two sieges of Pontefract castle - where much of the drama of our story takes place.[22] And yet another member, Toby Drake, witnessed her will. Rosamond must have been very ill as she died soon afterwards.

To return to James Knowles, who, following in true Dick Whittington tradition, (or indeed that of his contemporary Sir William Craven) [23] country boy from Long Preston in Craven, had become a rich merchant of Wandons Green, Fulham, London. James, making his will on 17 March 1614 [24] possessed a fortune of over £3,000 and like Sir William he did not forget his birthplace, leaving over £1,000 to build and maintain alms houses for ten poor people with a chapel attached, to beautify the parish church and to build a workplace and provide work for the poor of the parish. Having no sons to carry on his name he bequeathed money for a plaque to be placed in Long Preston church bearing the inscription:

JAMES KNOWLES
I may be dead by name
yet I hope to live by fame

He left £100 to the town of Wakefield, where he had served his seven year apprenticeship:

> *'for the use of two apprentices to follow the trade of buying woollen cloth and selling it at Blackwell Hall, London.'*

James had enjoyed good fortune and success in business but he must have suffered greatly in family matters, having lost at least four children in their infancy and also their mother.[25] Despite having married again James made his nephew William Paulden his heir and sole executor, responsible for carrying out the many difficult and arduous bequests in his will.

One other of the many bequests in James's will was £20 to his nephew William Moon son of his sister Richard Moon of Long Preston. This reference provides a further link with our family as Richard was nephew of my direct ancestor Elizabeth Preston née Moon of Stackhouse, Giggleswick, and descended from a brother of Richard Moon, the last Prior of Bolton (Abbey) Priory in Wharfedale.[26]

CHAPTER 2

The English Civil War 1642-49

In most of the conflicts which have divided nations against themselves, one side or other has been so wicked, or both so worthless, or the points at issue so personal or valueless, that the recital of their progress and results, merely amuses by variety of incident, or disgusts by sameness of depravity; but in the principles of the fortunes of the Cavaliers and Roundheads, we still experience a real and vital concern. The warmth of passion, though abated, is still not extinguished, we feel as if our liberty, our own honour and religion, were involved in the dispute.

Hartley Coleridge

William Paulden, nephew of James Knowles and son of Gregory Paulden, was also a chapman and no doubt carried on his father's business in the woollen and clothing trade. Being comfortably off he took an interest in his old school and he was elected a governor of Wakefield Grammar School on 30 September 1624 [1] and he continued in office until the beginnings of the Civil War in the 1640's. William was a parent governor and it seems probable that all four of his sons William (1618-1648), Timothy (1622-1648), Thomas (1625-c1706) and Gregory (1629-?) all born at a house in Silver Street which later became the George and Crown Inn, were educated there.

Both William and Thomas went up to Cambridge, William to Jesus College in 1634 where he took his B.A. degree in 1637-38 and his M.A. in 1641 and Thomas to Clare College on 18 June 1641 [2]: this later date I find highly significant owing to three not un-related happenings. First George Villiers, Duke of Buckingham and his brother Francis entered Trinity College, Cambridge in 1641 and were there for something less than two years, being eager to join the King's forces when he raised his standard at Nottingham on 22 August 1642. Secondly, a visit to Peterhouse by the eleven years old Prince of Wales with the Duke of Buckingham on 21 March 1642 and thirdly a visit on 23 March by the King himself, when he was entertained at Trinity.[3]

After the assassination of their father in 1628 the Villiers boys had been brought up with the Prince of Wales and the King had treated them like his own sons.[4]

How could these events fail to impress the young undergraduate from Wakefield and I feel sure that Thomas's reported `unflinching loyalty and devotion to both King Charles I and his son Charles II'[5] either began or was greatly enhanced at this time, and also perhaps his friendship with the Duke of Buckingham.[6]

The President of Thomas' college in 1642 was an old boy of Wakefield Grammar School and a distant relative of his, Barnabas Oley (1602-1686) a zealous Royalist who, when the University sent its plate to the King at Nottingham to be converted into money for his use, was entrusted with its care and owing to his skill and because he knew all the highways and byways between Cambridge and that town it was safely brought to the King's headquarters, this despite the troops of Cromwell who were sent specific orders to intercept him.[7]

Thomas' mother was Susan daughter of Edward Bynnes, Yeoman of Horbury who died in 1598 and in 1600 his widow Alice married the Rev. Richard Lister of Wakefield: in the back of the parish register there is an interesting copy of a licence to eat meat during Lent:

`given to Alice the wife of Richard Lister, Clerk who now sojourneth wth her son William Paulden, by reason of her old age and her stomach so cold not able to digest cold meat and fish. Given by James Lister, vicar of Wakefield 8 February 1631.'[8]

William Paulden, (now described as gentleman after inheriting a goodly sum from his uncle James Knowles) was high constable of the Wapontake of Agbrig and Morley from 1638 until 1641,[9] when he applied for, and was granted, release. Which, arriving at this juncture must have come as a great relief to him considering his Royalist sympathies and the great national and local unrest which was about to develop into civil war.

The list of those refusing to take the 1641 Protestation oath (to be faithful to Parliament) in the Wapentake of Agbrigg, included William Paulden, Gent, followed by his son Timothy Paulden. James Lister, Vicar of Wakefield, William's wife's step-father was also one of the several local clergy amongst this list of zealous Royalists.[10]

In January 1643, when Sir Thomas Fairfax, the Parliamentary General, had captured Bradford and the Leeds, many Royalists soldiers fled to Wakefield and Pontefract. The Earl of Newcastle, Royalist commander in the north, ordered all his forces to retire to York. The Wakefield garrison quitted the town about midnight and the 'malignants' - as the Roundheads called the Royalists - Mr. Paulden, Nevile and Reynor and the rest conveyed what goods they could to Pontefract from whence the next night they fled to York with thirty carriages, leaving two hundred men to keep the castle.[11]

In 1649 William Paulden, the elder, was fined £91 6s 8d as a Royalist delinquent [12] and that, apart from being mentioned in a letter dated October 1652,[13] is the last we hear of him: he would after all be about seventy years of age and hardly fit for soldiering. Family honour, however, was secure in the hands of his sons.

The three eldest sons, being now about 24, 22 and 20 years old respectively, joined the Royalist Army immediately upon the outbreak of hostilities; and I suspect their first commander to have been Sir William Savile of Thornhill Hall, leader of the King's forces in the Wakefield area. Very soon afterwards, however, probably owing to Sir William's death (whether from wounds or natural causes is unknown), they became part of the Northern Horse under the command of Sir Marmaduke Langdale, [14] their beloved general for most of the war. They fought in many battles and skirmishes including Naseby, where Thomas was captured and Marston Moor: in both battles they fought gallantly but were defeated by superior numbers.

They had, however, been successful at Melton Mowbray, Ferrybridge and the brilliant relief of Pontefract Castle during the first siege in March 1645, and they were regarded as a superior force of gentlemen cavalry.[15]

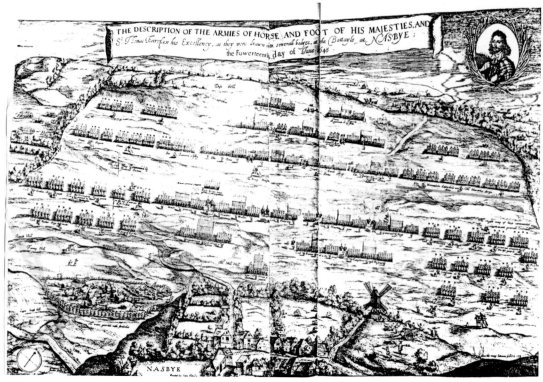

Langdale's Horse at the battle of Naseby.

'Skirmishing', drawing by Stephen Beck.

CHAPTER 3

The Siege of Sandal Castle

Early in 1645 Lord Fairfax, commander of the Parliamentary forces in Yorkshire, entrusted the siege of Sandal castle near Wakefield and just six miles from Pontefract, to Sir John Savile of Lupset, who was half uncle to Sir William Savile, the Royalist. Colonel Bonivant and his Royalist garrison, who were greatly outnumbered, completely surprised the besiegers whilst they were at prayers; they threw open the gates and totally defeated them, killing 42 and capturing 50.

News of the exploit was sent to those shut up in Pontefract castle which was also closely besieged and there was much co-operation between the two garrisons at this time, both for information and morale.[1] Capt. John Benson of Sir John Ramsden's company left Pontefract castle where he had been since the commencement of the war and went to Sandal castle, taking his own man and two soldiers with him and here he remained until the siege was over. On Friday 23 May 1645, Captain Washington and Lieut. Wheatley left Pontefract castle by night for Sandal, where their safe arrival was notified by a great bonfire, which was answered by another from Pontefract and some days later they returned.

In June, however, three hundred dragoons blockaded Sandal and the besieged were in much distress for want of fodder for their horses. On 20 July Pontefract castle was forced to surrender and the next day the Roundhead commander, describing their po-

Sandal Castle

sition as hopeless, demanded that Sandal Castle follow suit. The garrison replied that they would not submit only on the King's authority; this dispatch was signed by ten officers amongst whom were William and Timothy Paulden, Thomas's elder brothers.[2] The total garrison was one hundred officers and men, described by the Parliamentary Post as:

> 'a pack of as bold and desperate fellows as any that were in all that country or perad-venture in the kingdom.'

Soon, however, four great batteries of large guns were brought to destroy the castle and several breaches were made in the walls forcing the defenders to surrender on honourable terms.

The first part of the Civil War was virtually ended with the Parliamentary forces under Thomas Fairfax and Oliver Cromwell in control of the country. The scattered Royalists though beaten were constantly meeting and plotting to raise arms and men for a rising in the forlorn hope of putting the King on his throne again.

In 1647 Thomas Paulden was attending meetings of loyal gentlemen at the house of Rev. George Beaumont, M.A. vicar of South Kirkby, (cousin of Sir Thomas Beaumont owner of Sandal Castle at the outbreak of Civil War and Governor of Sheffield Castle when it was besieged) five miles from Pontefract and privately enlisting troops of both horse and foot.

He and his brothers seem to have been the sole confidants of the Royalist colonel John Morris to whom Colonel Robert Overton, the Parliamentary governor of Pontefract, had promised to betray the castle; but the removal of Overton to Hull rendered the plan impracticable.[3]

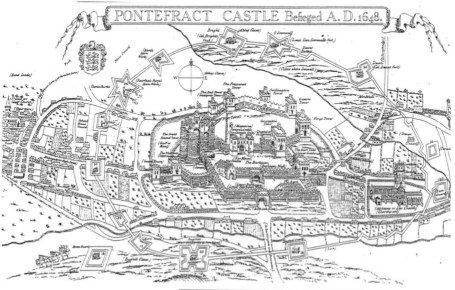

Pontefract Castle A.D. 1648.

Signature of Gregory Paulden.

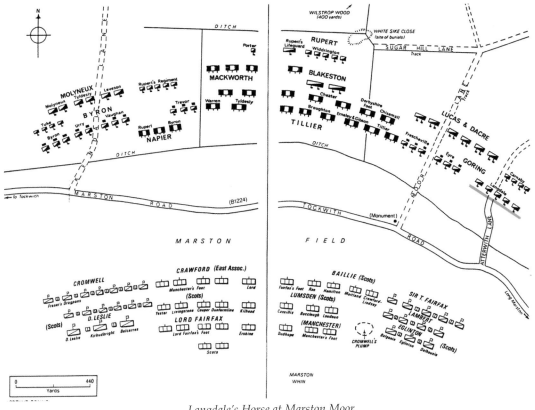

Langdale's Horse at Marston Moor.

Lady Ann Savile.

Pontefract siege medal.

Cromwell's friend and chief Intelligence Officer, Secretary of State John Thurloe.

King Charles I at his trial in January 1649.

Death warrant of Charles I.

*Major-General John Lambert (1619-1684), com-
mander of the Parliamentary forces in the north until
Cromwell's arrival during the second civil war. He
took possession of the Castle in March 1648-49 and
became M.P. for Pontefract as Lord Lambert.*

*Oliver Cromwell (1599-1658) unfinished
miniature, painted by Samuel Cooper about
six years after Marston Moor, is the most
vivid likeness.*

Colonel John Morris.

from the original Picture in possession of Sir Mark Masterman Sykes, of Sledmere, co. York. Bar.

Colonel John Morris.

Sir Thomas Fairfax, later Baron Fairfax (1612-71) known as 'Black Tom'.

Examples of Pontefract siege coins.

As the Pontefract garrison ran short of money they struck siege coins in the name of King Charles I, bearing the motto 'dum spiro spero' - `Whilst I breath I hope' and after King's death on 30 January 1649, they proclaimed his son King Charles II, producing coins inscribed `post mortem patris pro filio'-`after the death of the father we are for the son' which became the motto for the town of Pontefract. [4]

Cavalry combat: apart from the fact that most wear cuirassier armour, this is a good representation of a fight between two bodies of horse during the Civil War (engraving by Jaques Callot from Miseres et Malhueures de Guerre (1633).

'Siege operations', drawing by Stephen Beck.

'Roaring Meg'. Probably the only surviving mortar of the Civil Wars. It was made in the Forest of Dean for Colonel John Birch, and was employed against Goodrich and Raglan Castles. It can be seen in the Churchill Museum, Hereford. (S.B.Webb)

CHAPTER 4

The Third, and last, Siege of Pontefract Castle

The Royalists, the Pauldens among them, made an unsuccessful attempt at a surprise on Pontefract castle on 18 May 1648. Thomas himself relates the story in a letter he wrote to an un-named friend and fellow Yorkshireman [Could it have been the Leeds historian Thoresby?] from London in 1702 when he was in his seventy eighth year and living in poor circumstances:

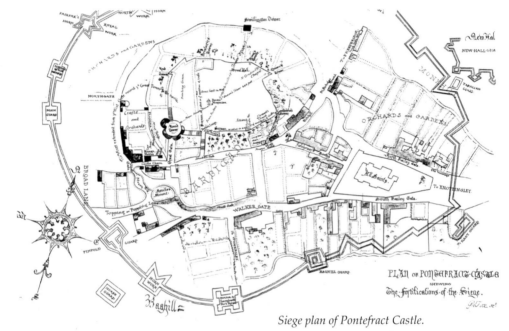

Siege plan of Pontefract Castle.

The foundations of St. Clement's Chapel inside Pontefract Castle where Captain William Paulden was buried, (1984) (HF)

Sir William Savile when a soldier in the King's army.

On 29 Sept 1642 Lord Fairfax, Mr Belasis, Sir William Savile and other leading figures in Yorkshire, endeavoured to make an association of neutrality and sent heads thereof to Parliament, but in vain. [1]

George Villiers, second Duke of Buckingham.

Frontpiece to The Earl of Clarendon's History of the Great Rebellion.

Charles II

Sir Richard Willys – (traitor to the Royalist cause) portrait by William Dobson at Newark-on-Trent.

George Monk. An unfinished sketch by Samuel Cooper.

Steps leading down to the magazine where Col. Morris imprisoned the guards after asking for refreshments.

The powder magazine, used also as a prison. (both H.F.)

Pontefract with All Saints Church; beyond is the Castle and St Giles' Church, drawn in 1830 by N.Whittock.

The New Hall; often used as an outpost by the besieged at Pontefract castle. The windmill stands on the spot where Thomas of Lancaster was beheaded.

Two prisoners scratched their names on the wall of the prison at Pontefract Castle.

Pontefract Castle. An account how it was taken, and how General Rainsborough was surprised in his quarters at Doncaster, Anno 1648.

Sir,

I received your letter, wherein you tell me, that the late news of Prince Eugene's surprising the Marshall Villery in his quarters at Cremona, put yourselfe and somme of your friends in mind of the surprise of General Rainsborough, at the siege of Ponte-fract Castle in the late civil wars of England. And I being the only person now living, that was an actor in it, you are pleased to desire a particular account of it., which as far as I know, was never yet published. I appeal to you, and all that know me, if ever I had the vanity to boast of it, or so much as mention it, but sometimes at the request of a friend, as I do now at yours; tho' I had rather Refuse to comply even with your desire at this time, than be thought so vain as to make any comparison (other than with small things with great) between such a particular action in our own country, and so publick an glorious an on, as that of Prince Eugenes, on the stage of Europe; which failed by one Accident of having been yet more glorious.

But this I might say without vanity, that our Design was Honourable, not to kill a General in the midst of his army but to take him prisoner, & thereby to save the life of our own General, Sir Marmaduke Langdale, then a prisoner, and condemned to die, under whose command we had served in the precedant war.

It may not be unacceptable to you being a Yorkshireman, to know the most minute particulars of this enterprise, we being all Yorkshire men who took a share in it. And first let me tell you how we took the castle, which was a garrison for the parliament, as they called the government then established in a small part of the House of Commons and a very small number of the Lords sitting at Westminster.

`Pontefract, commonly called Pomfret-Castle, was thought the Greatest and Strongest Castle in England. It was the ancient Inheritance of the Dukes of Lancaster, called, The Honour of Pomfret: And it had the Honour to be the last Garrison in the War begun in 1642, that held out for the King.*

In the year 1648 the first War being over, we, that had served the King in it, submitting to our common Fate, lived quietly in the Country, till we heard of an intended Invasion by Duke Hamilton: Then we met frequently, and resolved to attempt the Surprising this Castle, of which Colonel Cotterel was Governor for the Parliament, having under him a Garrison of an hundred Men, most of them Quartered in the Town of Pomfret, and in no Apprehension of an Enemy.

The Design was laid by Colonel Morice, (who in his Youth had been Page to the Earl of Strafford) my two Brothers, who were Captains of Horse and my self Captain of Foot, and some others. We had then about Three hundred Foot, and Fifty Horse, of our old Comerades, privately Listed.

We had secret Correspondence with some in the Castle, Among the rest, with a Corporal, who promised, on a certain Night, to be upon the Guard, and to set a Centinal, that would assist us, in Scaling the Walls by a Ladder, which we had provided and brought with us. But the Corporal happened to be drunk at the hour appointed, and another Centinal was placed, where we intended to set our Ladder, who fired upon us, and gave the Alarm to the Garrison. They appearing upon the Walls, our Men retired in haste, leaving the Ladder in the Ditch; whereby the next Day they within knew, that it was no false Alarm, but that there had been a real Attempt to surprise the Castle.

They took not a Man of us ; our Foot dispersed themselves in the Country; and half our Horse marched to Sir Marmaduke Langdale, who had then taken Berwick and Carlisle. The rest, being Twenty or Thirty Horse, kept in the Woods, while we sent Spies into the Castle, and found that our Confederates within were not discovered, nor our design betrayed, but only failed by the Corporal's being drunk.

The Ladder being found the next Morning, made the Governor call the Soldiers out of the Town, to lodge in the Castle: in order to which, he sent Warrants into the Country, for Beds to be brought in by a Day appointed.

We had notice of it, and made use of the Occasion. With the Beds came Colonel Morice, and Captain William Paulden, like Country Gentlemen, with Swords by their sides; and about Nine Persons more, dressed like plain Countrymen, and Constables, to guard the Beds, but arm'd privately with Pocket-Pistols and Daggers.

Upon their Approach, the Draw-bridge was let down, and the Gates opened by our Confederates within. Colonel Morris, and those who were with him, entered into the Castle. The Main-Guard was just within the Gate, where our Company threw down the Beds, and gave a Crown to some Soldiers, bidding them fetch Ale, to make the rest of the Guard drink; and as soon as they were gone out of the Gate, they drew up the Draw-bridge, and secured the rest of the Guards, forcing them into a Dungeon hard by, to which they went down by about Thirty steps; and it was a Place that would hold Two or Three hundred Men.

Then Captain William Paulden made one of the Prisoners shew him the way to the Governor's Lodg-ing, where he found him newly laid down upon his Bed, with his Cloaths on, and his Sword, being a long Tuck, lying by him. The Captain told him, the Castle was the King's, and he was his Prisoner; but he, with-out answering any thing, started up, and made a thrust at the Captain, and defended himself very bravely, till being sore wounded, his Head and Arm cut in several places, he made another full and desperate Push at the Captain, and broke his Tuck against the Bed-post; and then asked Quarter, which my Brother granted; and he, for the present, was put down, among his own Soldiers, into the Dungeon.

Notice was immediately sent to me, lying hard by, of the Taking of the Castle; upon which I marched thither with about Thirty Horse, and, it being Market-Day, we furnished our selves with all manner of Provisions from the town.

There came speedily to us, in small parties, so many of our old Fellow-Soldiers, that our Garrison at last was increased to Five hundred Men, which at the rendring of the Castle afterwards, were reduc'd to One hundred and forty.

We found in the Castle a good quantity of Salt and Malt, with Four thousand Arms, and good store of Ammunition, some Cannon, and two Mortar-pieces. We expected a Siege very suddenly, and got what Provision of Corn, and Cattle, we could, out of the Country.

Particularly in one Sally, having notice that there were at Knotingly, three Miles from the Castle, Three hundred head of Cattle, bought up in the North, going into the South, under a Guard of two Troups of Horse, and Half a dozen Foot, with Half-pikes to drive the Cattle. We faced the Troops that guarded them, while our Foot drove the Herd towards the Castle; then we followed, and kept betwixt them and danger, the Enemy not daring to Charge us, and so we came all safe with our Purchase into the Castle. This, and other Provisions, we got in, by several parties almost every Night, enabled us to keep the Castle above nine Months, though we had not one Months Provision, when we were first Beleaguer'd.

For in a very short time after, we were besieged by Sir Edward Rhodes, and Sir Henry Cholmondly, and Five Thousand regular Troops: But we kept a Gate open on the South-side of the Castle, which was covered by a small Garrison, we placed in an House called New-Hall, belonging to the Family of Pierr-point, being about a Musquet-shot or two from the Castle.

Some time after, We heard, Duke Hamilton was beaten at Preston in Lancashire, and Sir Marmaduke Langdale taken Prisoner, and brought to Nottingham Castle. He was General of the English at Preston, who behaved themselves bravely, and, in truth, did all that was done there. He had also, as I said, been our General; we had his Commission for taking the Castle, as he held the Prince of Wales's, and we were resolved to run any hazard to release him; for it was commonly given out, that they intended to bring him before Pomfret-Castle, and to Execute him in our sight, if we would not immediately surrender.'

Timothy Paulden, who had gone north with Langdale, was later killed at Wigan while serving as major of horse to Colonel Mathew Boynton under the command of the Earl of Derby: being shot as he crossed a stream there, as they retreated south after the 1651 battle of Preston.

The Doncaster Raid

`It being like to prove a tedious Siege, General Rainsborow was sent from London by the Parliament, to put a speedy end to it. He was esteemed a Person of great Courage and Conduct, exceeding zealous and fierce in their Cause, and had done them great Service by Land, and also at Sea, where he was for a time one of their Admirals. His Head Quarters were for the present at Doncaster, being Twelve Miles from Pom-fret, with Twelve hundred Foot; a Regiment of his horse lay Three or Four Miles on the East of Doncaster, and another at the like distance on the West.

Captain William Paulden, who commanded all the few Horse in the Castle, laid a Design to surprise him in his Quarters at Doncaster; not to kill him, but to take him Prisoner, and exchange him for our own General, Sir Marmaduke Langdale; and it was only his own fault that he was killed, and not brought Prisoner to the Castle.

The Design seemed the more feasible, because the General and his Men were in no Apprehension of a Surprise; the Castle being Twelve Miles off, closely besieged, and the only Garrison for the King in England.

In order to execute this our purpose, Captain William Paulden made choice of Two and twenty Men, such as he most confided in. At Midnight, being well horsed, we marched through the Gate, that was kept open, over the Meadows, between two of the Enemy's Horse-Guards, whom, by the favour of the Night, we passed undiscovered.

Early the next Morning we came to Mexborough, a Village Four Miles West above Doncaster, upon the River Don, where there was a Ferry-boat. There we rested, to refresh our selves and our Horses, till about Noon.

In the mean time we sent a Spy into Doncaster, to know, if there was any Discovery of a Party being out, and to meet us, as soon as it was dark, at Cunsborough, a Mile from Doncaster; which he did, and assured us, there was no Alarm taken by the Town, and that a Man would meet us at Sun-rise, it being then the beginning of March, who would give us Notice if all was quiet. Thither the Man came accordingly; the Sign he was to bring with him, to be known by, was a Bible in his hand.

Captain Paulden then divided his Two and twenty Men into Four Parties; Six, were to attack the Main-Guard upon the Bridge; Four were ordered to General Rainsborow's Quarters; and the Captain, with the remaining Six after he had seen the Four enter the General's lodgings, was to beat the Streets, and keep the Enemy from assembling.

We presently forcing the first Barricades, and the Guards there dispersing into the Country, all the rest succeeded as we wish'd; the Main-Guard was surprised, we entring the Guard-Chamber, and getting between them and their Arms, Bid them shift *for their Lives; the same was done to the Guard upon the Bridge, their Arms being thrown into the River.*

The Four that went to General Rainsborough's lodging, [Captain William Paulden his Lieut. Alan Austwick, his Cornet Michael Blackburne and Marmaduke Greenfield [2]] *pretended to bring Letters to him from Cromwell, who had beaten the Scots; they met at the door the General's Lieutenant, who conducted them up to his Chamber, and told him, being in Bed, that there were some Gentlemen had brought him Letters from General Cromwell. Upon which, they delivered Rainsborow a Packet, wherein was nothing but blank paper. Whilst he was opening it, they told him, he was their Prisoner, but not a Hair of his Head should be touched, if he would go quietly with them. Then they disarm'd his Lieutenant, who had innocently conducted them to his Chamber, and brought them both down Stairs. They had brought a horse ready for General Rainsborow, upon which they bid him mount; he seem'd at first willing to do it, and put his foot in the Stirrup; but looking about him, and seeing none but four of his Enemies, and his Lieutenant and Centinal (whom they had not disarm'd) standing by him; he pull'd his Foot out of the Stirrup, and cry'd Arms, Arms. Upon this, one of our Men, letting his Pistol and Sword fall, because he would not kill him, catcht hold of him,* [by his waistcoat] *and they grappling together, both fell down in the Street. The General Rainsborow's Lieutenant catching our Man's Pistol that was fallen, Captain Paulden's Lieutenant, who was on Horseback, dismounts and runs him through the Body, as he was cocking the Pistol. Another of our Men run General Rainsborow into the Neck, as he was strugling with him that had caught hold of him; yet the General got upon his Legs with our Man's Sword in his Hand; but Captain Paulden's Lieutenant ran him through the Body upon which he fell down dead.*

Then all our Parties met, and made noise in the Streets, where we saw Hundreds of their Soldiers in their Shirts, running in the Fields to save themselves, not imagining how small our number was. We presently marched over the Bridge, the direct way to Pomtfret Castle, and all safely arrived there; carrying with us Forty or Fifty Prisoners, whom we had met by Eight or Ten in a Company. We took no Prisoners at Doncaster; nor were any kill'd, or so much as hurt there, but General and his Lieutenant, and they very much against our Will, because our main Intention was defeated thereby, which, I told you, was to exchange and redeem our own General Langdale; who however, the very Night before, had fortunately made his own Escape, and lived to see King Charles the Second's Restoration, and to be made a Peer of England for his eminent Services in the War.'

The Parliamentary party described Rainsborough's death as a horrid deliberate murder and used it as anti-royalist propaganda.[3]

Rainsborough's body was buried at Wapping and the funeral was marked by a great public demonstration by the Levellers, One thousand five hundred horse and fifty coaches followed his funeral cortege and his widow Margaret was granted £200 a year pension.[4]

From another source we learn more details of Langdale's escape. Lady Ann Savile, now widow of Sir William, who had died at the tragic age of thirty two, was left pregnant with five young children under the age of eleven; but despite her domestic preoccupations she is described as:

> `a person of incomparable affection to his majesty, of singular prudence and of great interest and power by the adherence of many persons of honour, ability and loyalty unto her and particularly my Lord Langdale. The excellent Lady Savile employed all her thought, and no-one had a better head, to contrive the means of Langdale's escape, as she had already done with good success, those for surprising Pontefract castle and surprising Colonel Rainsborough in his quarters.'* [5]

Nor did her usual good fortune fail her, for she found out such a subtle method of bribing the guards and invented so feasible a way of escape that Sir Marmaduke got out of prison with little difficulty to himself and not much censure to his keepers. Langdale lay hidden in a haystack for some weeks in the open air and when the rebels were at last weary of hunting for him, he got to London to Mr. Barwick's with the help of that holy man and excellent divine Mr. Barnabas Oley, who disguised him in the habit of a clergyman. [6]

Barnabas Oley, fined £80 as a Royalist,[7] was a preacher to the garrison in Pontefract castle as was the Rev. Francis Corker, vicar of Bradford, whom we shall meet anon, but in stark contrast to the zealous Royalist Barnabas Oley, Rev. Francis Corker was to become a traitor.

Moat and gate-posts at Thornhill 1993.
(Photo from Margaret McCollum)

The Siege of Thornhill Hall

It was well that Lady Ann Savile had left her home at Thornhill Hall, near Dewsbury and gone to live at Rufford in Nottinghamshire before events reported to the Speaker in a letter from Sir Henry Cholmondely, Parliamentary commander of the forces besieging Pontefract castle, when he wrote on 18 July 1648:

> `Whilst I was attending the enemy towards Nottingham, they drew out two hundred of their foot from Pomfret and possessed themselves of Thornhill Hall, where they began to fortify, which, being of itself defended by a moat was soon made strong enough to be maintained till cannon should be brought against it. Upon Sunday morning last my own regiment of horse and Col. Fairfax's regiment of foot marched up close to the house.'[8]

Colonel Charles Fairfax, brother to the General, also wrote, saying:-

> `We possessed ourselves of the church and the Parsonage house (a stone caste from the house) without opposition, sent them the summons to which we have the answers and replies here enclosed.'* [9]

To the Governor of Thornhill Hall-

> *Sir, -We thirst after no man's blood, but desire that God will scatter the people that delight in warre. I do therefore as here commanded for settlement of these parts, and prevention of insurrection and tumults demand of you the hold, wherein you now are, together with your arms to be forthwith delivered into my hands for the use of King and Parliament. If this motion be rejected, expect hostilities, and the Lord look upon each of us according to the sincerity of his heart, as we desire our peace to the greatest honour both of God and King.*
>
> C.FAIRFAX

Thornhill Hall: 16 July 1648.

From Thomas Paulden to Colonel Fairfax, Commander-in-Chief of Thornhill Town:

> *Sir, -In answer to your demands I return we are equally with you desirous to prevent Christian bloodshed, But to your demand of the house we answer that we may not part with our loyalty, but together with our blood: we were commanded hither by our lawful superiors, and may not in honour or duty part hence without their order. But if you please to suffer a messenger from us to go to the Governor of Pontefract Castle, at his return you may expect to have a further answer from Sir, your servant,*
>
> THOMAS PAULDEN.

Colonel Charles Fairfax.

Captain Paulden's request was denied in a reply the same day:

    'Sir, I am Engaged to make good my proffer, the rendition of that house will forfeit no loyalty, thoug(h) blood be precious, yet we cannot condescend to so long a cessation as to expect any answer from Pontefract, but a speedy surrender.

    From my quarters at Thornhill 16 July 1648, To the Governour of Thornhill Hall.

                C.FAIRFAX.

Which refusal received this riposte: - from Thomas Paulden to Col. Fairfax.

    Sir, - You may not expect anything here, but what you can win with your sword, until I receive further commands from my superiors, -Yours, THOMAS PAULDEN.

    Cholmondely and Fairfax had more than three times as many men as Paulden but still needed reinforcements before they were able to make inroads into his defences. Lieutenant General Cromwell sent four troops of horse and two of dragoons.

Fairfax's letter to Parliament continues:-

    `We fell on the work, entered the barns, stables and malthouse within the fold, but without the moat. It was a very sharp dispute betwix one and six. We spent most of our ammunition, viz, four barrels of powder, and sent presently to York and Leeds for more. We have about twelve men slain and thirty wounded, whereof a few of them mortally.

    On Monday we cut off their fresh water, then set workmen to draw off the moat: and on Tuesday towards night completed the work and so sent them a last summons.'

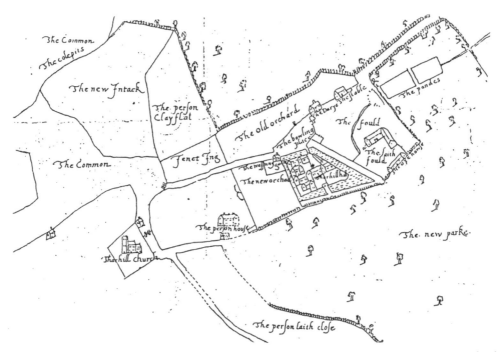

Thornhill Hall and Surroundings, 1602. Plan by Christopher Saxton.('Colepits' would be bell pits, 'Laith = barn, 'person' = parson) [10]

The odds against the Thornhill garrison were overwhelming and on 18 July Thomas Paulden agreed to a parley, asking that hostages should be sent whilst it took place and according to Fairfax it was decided:

> `That they should deliver to Sir Henry Cholmondely and me the house and arms: only the governor and Major Bonifant to have their horse and swords and the common soldiers to march away only with their apparel. -An hour before their march merely by accident fire took hold of their powder, blew up part of the house, slew four or five of theirs but none of our men, and miserably scorched about seven or eight more and the same flame hath consumed all the buildings. The breach was on their part for not rendering the powder, but chiefly for that one of them took out a pistol and many marched with their monies: therefore it is confessed some lost their clothes, for which cause the Governor and Bonifant refuse to render themselves prisoners according to the engagement.*

Thornhill, 22 July, 1648.   C.FAIRFAX. [11]

As I find no mention made elsewhere to loss of clothes, perhaps this is the incident referred to by Robert Howcott in July, 1660 when he petitioned for the office of Surveyor, Waiter or Solicitor in the Custom House, London. He said that his father lost £800 in the tiege of Leicester and that he was at the last siege of Pontefract castle which was surrendered on condition of the soldiers marching out without molestation, but when they had got forth a mile they were all stripped naked! [12]

A Royalist report of the surrender of Thornhill Hall says that Captain Paulden proffered a parley because of a letter from Sir John Ramsden, chief constable of the division of Morley, urging their cessation of hostilities.

Part of Sir Henry Cholmondely's letter to Thomas Paulden says:-

> ` -be assured that the blood of those that dye, in the slaughter, a work we abhor, if you do not enforce it, will be required at your hands and all of them that advise you.'

With the following reply from Capt. Paulden:-

> 'Sir, - To infer your conclusion that the blood spilled will be required at our hands before you prove that. We ought not to defend our rights and the King's with our blood, is very bad logic, and your rhetoric not so pregnant as may persuade us to assent to so dishonourable conditions upon so small reason, but in order to the tenderness we have of Christian blood, if you please to appoint two of the like condition with ours mentioned in my letters to Sir Henry Chalmondely, and send us hostages we shall embrace a parley.
>
>   Your servant, THOS. PAULDEN.

July 18, 1648. To Col. Fairfax. These present.[13]

Whatever the details of the ending of the Thornhill Hall siege, Capt. Thomas Paulden was soon back fully involved in the major one of Pontefract, and we read more of his own account.

The Third and Last Siege of Pontefract Castle. Abstracts from Thomas Paulden's Account in Clarendon [14]

> 'almost eaten up and we so straightened that the Foot were ready to mutiny for want of ``Many times did we sally out to discomfit the Enemy and when the town of Pomfret was meat. Our forces were nigh Four hundred Horse and Eight hundred Foot whereof Three hundred Horse went away to Doncaster to quarter there. It was resolved by a Council of War to fall upon the Enemy at Ferrybridge, when we heard they were marching away to York with most of their strength. Our intelligence proved false when we found them not quitting the town but in a posture to receive us, in the confusion we attempted to break into their barricades but was repulsed with loss of about one hundred men killed and many wounded. My brother Will had his horse kill'd under him and another horse shott; my brother Tim was shot in the shoulder and the bone broken and in the hand and his horse shott in three or foure places, but carryed him off. There were very few of the party there was not either shott or their horses and some ten or twelve kill'd outright by pistols and two drakes.
>
> But some 4 or five days afterwards we recovered some part of our reputacon at a pass called Olerton Boate, about five miles from Pomfret, where we fell upon two of the enemies troops which was off General Fairfax his lifeguard, who was accounted the best horse in the Army & had a boast never to have beene beaten. Our numbers & theirs were neere upon an equall and the dispute was very sharpe, they worsting us in the two first charges, but in the third we broake them, routed them, killed, took & drowned most of them, tooke both their colours, woundede Brown who commanded them, desperately in the body. Sir Richard Byron commanded the Reformados in this action & my brother the rest. On 9 Sept. 1648 the enemie brought down some foot within Carbine shott of the Castle & there made a barricade & planted 3 foot colours & brought a horse guard upon the south-west side of the castle & placed them upon Bag-hill. The next day we made a sally with 100 foot & 40 horse (which my brother commanded), towards their horse guard. The foote entered their barricade kill'd some, took others & their 3 colours, & beat them upp to the market place; our horse likewise beate their horseguard but catch'd few. they running away betimes. Five or 6 days were spent in getting corn which was then shorne & ready for getting in, which daily occasioned some skirmishing. After getting the corn within our reach, we made a sally with 30 horse (commanded by my brother William) upon their horseguard and surprized them, took 30 prisoners & 40 horse.''

There was a fair amount of honourable communication between the enemy commanders concerning the exchange of prisoners, burial of the dead and even the granting of passes for personal or important business.

William Paulden wrote desiring leave for the bearer, a drummer, to pass to Wakefield on necessary business for his brother the famous Captain Thomas Paulden.[15]

Colonel John Digby wrote from the castle respecting Mr. Ellis and thanking Colonel Fairfax for granting the civilities desired by Captain Paulden: Mr. Ellis wanted a pass for himself, his sister and a servant.[16]

The garrison did, however, take many substantial men prisoner, whom they took to the castle and detained there, till large sums of money were paid for their release: Sir Arthur Ingram, eldest son and heir of Sir Arthur the unscrupulous merchant, who had become the richest man in Yorkshire; was carried off from his own house at Temple Newsham near Leeds, and for his ransom he was forced to pay £1,500.[17]

Captain Thomas's 1702 Account continues:

> `About three months before the surrender on 9 Nov. 1648 having but lately received an order from his majesty, the Prince of Wales, to keep it, we refused to deliver it up.'

After defeating the Scots Army at Preston and Wiggan, Cromwell sent Major General Lambert against us and we were close shut up without hope of relief and our provisions very near spent which put us upon capitulating; they threw papers over the walls offering favourable conditions except for six persons, to be named after articles of surrender were signed by the Governor.

Soon after, Cromwell himself, arrived at Pontefract and he spent a month before the castle, (until forced to go south for political reasons), when he wrote:

> - For the governour of Pontefract Castle
> 'Sir,
>
> Being come hither for the reduction of this place, I thought fit to summon you to deliver your garrison to me. Those gentlemen and souldiers with you may have better terms, than if you should hold it to extremity. I expect your answer this day, and rest,
> Your Servant,
> O. CROMWELL.' [18]

November 9, 1648.

Colonel John Morris's reply questioned the Lieutenant General's power to perform any conditions they might agree, without the authority of Parliament, which prompted Cromwell into prosecuting the siege with renewed vigour.

Thomas Paulden's account continues:-

> `Cromwell planted two new batteries of large guns, with which he beat us from our guns and his mortar piece blew up a great part of our buildings; sharp fever began to rage among us whereof many died including the truly wise and courageous Captain William Paulden my brother who was buried in the Chapel of St. Clements in the castle, by the Rev. Mr. George Beaumont with much grief. The garrison had been reduced from 500 to 100 men, many of them sick and unfit for duty.
>
> The Governor, Colonel Morice, hereupon call'd the Officers of the Castle together; and we unanimously promised, we would never agree to deliver any Person up, without his consent.
>
> Upon this Promise, our Governor sent Six Officers out of the Castle, to Treat with the same Number named by Major General Lambert. Of our number I was one. When

we met we told them, That we came to Capitulate about the Surrender of the Castle, but they could not expect that we would deliver our selves up for Execution. Upon which, Colonel Bright,[19] *the first of their Commissioner, told us, That he had Authority, from Major General Lambert, to engage, That none of us, that Treated, should be any of the excepted Persons: We told him, That perhaps the Governor might be one of them: He answered, That he did not believe the Major General did so much look upon the Governor, as some that had betray'd the Castle to us, when it was taken. So we parted for that time, without concluding any thing.*

At our return to the Castle, we acquainted the Governor with all that had passed. - - I told him that he was likely to be one of those to be given up. Upon which he resolved we should go out and conclude, saying generously, that if he was excepted, he would take his Fortune, and he would not have so many worthy Gentlemen perish for his sake.

Upon this, I desired the Governor to send somebody else in my place, for I had promised solemnly, I would never consent to deliver him up; - - So they went out, and concluded, and Signed the Articles; and after Signing of them, they brought to us, in the Castle, the Names of the excepted Persons, whereof the Governor was the First: Allen Austwick, W. Paulden's Lieutenant, [who died in 1665, and was the son of Thomas Austwick, Mayor of Pontefract, who died a volunteer in the castle in March 1648] *as one of those that killed Rainsborow; Blackborne, Captain Paulden's Cornet; for the same Reason; Major Ashby, Ensign Smith and Sergeant Floyd, These three had been our Correspondents in the Castle when we Surprised it.*

We were not obliged to deliver up these Excepted Persons, but they had liberty to make their Escape if they could, which they attempted on Horseback the next Evening, by charging through the Enemies Army. At that very time their Guard unluckily happened to be relieving, so that the Number was doubled they were to break through.

The Governor, and Blackborne charged thro', and escaped; but were taken in Lancashire, about ten days after, (seeking for a Ship to pass beyond Sea) [They were taken before Colonel John Sawrey and Colonel Thomas Fell of Ulverston] *and brought to York.'* [where from a high window they once again managed to escape but Blackborne broke his leg in the fall and Colonel Morice refusing to forsake a friend they were both retaken and executed without Court Martial].

The only surviving son of Colonel Morris was christened Castillian, in memory of his father's famous enterprise, and he grew up to become Town Clerk of Leeds and an attorney at Pontefract.

`Smyth was kill'd in the Attempt. Austwick, Ashby and Floyd, were forced back into the Castle where they hid themselves in a private Sally-port (which we had cover'd, designing to take the Castle again by it, when there should happen a fair Opportunity.) Thence they made their Escape the next Night, after the Castle was surrender'd, and lived till after the King's Return.*

Major General Lambert, Commander-in-Chief of the Parliamentary forces in the North, who had entered the siege on 4th December 1648, took possession of the castle on 24th March 1648/49.[20]

`*Thus ended the Siege of Pomfret-Castle, which was soon after demolished; (by petition of the townspeople who had suffered greatly during the hostilities; two hundred dwelling houses having been destroyed and many people killed) so that now there remains nothing of that magnificent Structure, but some Ruines of the great Tower, where, the Tradition is, King Richard II was murthered.* [Had Shakespeare helped to rekindle local tradition?]

We kept the Castle, till after King Charles the First was Martyr'd: When we solemnly proclaim'd King Charles the Second in it; and did not deliver it up till almost two Months after.'

CHAPTER 5

Thomas and his brother Gregory as Secret Agents

Thomas' 1702 Account continues:

`I my self followed the Fortune of King Charles in his Exile, and was sent into England on several Occasions for his Majesty's Service. I was once betray'd and brought before Cromwell; but I denied my Name and nothing could be proved against me: However he sent me to the Gatehouse in Westminster, from whence I made my Escape, with our old friend Jack Cowper, by throwing Salt and Pepper into the Keeper's Eyes; which, I think, has made me love Salt the better ever since; as you, and all my Friends know I do, with whom I have eaten many a Bushel.*

I went beyond the Sea; and, upon King Charles the Second's Restauration, returned into England accompanied with my old Companion, Loyalty, and the usual Companion of that, Poverty. The first never quited me, the other, by the Favour and Bounty of the Duke of Buckingham, was made tolerable.

And having now survived most of my old Acquaintance, and, as I verily believe, All, who had any Part in the foregoing Story, being in the 78th Year of my Age, I am glad to have had this Occasion of shewing my ancient Respects and Friendship for you, by obeying your Commands in this Particular; though you will not let me have the Honour to Mention your Name otherwise, than as a Yorkshire Man, and a Lover of them, who had faithfully served King Charles the Second, as you yourself had done.

After all, perhaps it will not be thought amis, by our Countrymen of Yorkshire at least, that I have lived on until this time; if for nothing else, yet for this, that when the Memorable Action at Cremona shall hereafter be spoken of, with the Honour it deserves, this Attempt at Doncaster may not be altogether forgotten by Posterity.

> *Sir, I am*
> *Your most faithful*
> *Humble Servant.*

> THOMAS PAULDEN.'

London, March 31, 1702.

So ends Thomas's own account of his exploits in his letter to an unknown friend - apparently one of rank and distinction - who had wished to be reminded of the Pontefract siege after hearing about the daring of Prince Eugene in Marlborough's wars.

Six months after the end of the siege Thomas was writing to his mother, Mrs Susan Paulden, from Brussels on 23 Sept.1649:

`Dear Mother. - I have sent many letters but never received any from you, but one from my father, and one from Greg; which I much wonder at, unless they have miscarried. In my father's you desired to know of my health, which has continued reasonable well (God be praised) and my arm grows stronger, only I have lost most of the hair of my head, which I think was occasioned by my sickness. I was scarce recovered on when I left England, but it now begins to grow again. I can give you very little hopes of seeing you in England in that condition we was hoped for, unless the business of Ireland prosper, which we are confident is not so desperate as our enemies report it. The King is safely arrived in Jersey where I believe he will stay, expecting the issue of Ireland. My Lord Montrosses design for Scotland goes on, with whom I had hopes to have gone, but that Colonel Gilbee is raising a regiment under the Duke of Loraine, and we are in hopes of getting some employment under him (if it goes on) the certainte whereof you shall know in my next. I am sorry to hear of the unfortunate death of Morris and Blackburne, and of Mrs. Morris being distracted. I desire to know whether Capt. Clayton have paid the money or not. If he have I desire we may have it if possible, for that money we brought over with us is almost spent, our lying so long at sea being exceeding chargeable, and travelling after the Court, before we could possibly resolve of settling ourselves, else the place we are now in is as cheap as England. I pray remember me kindly to my sister Susan and very many thanks for her care and paines with me in my extremite, which at this time is all the acknowledgement I can make; my love to Greg: Mal: my cooz Gascoigne and all with you, to all my friends at New Hall. Thus begging my father's and your blessing and prayers I rest, your dutiful son
ROB: JACKSON.' [1]

Despite the use of a false name, it is clear that Thomas had not yet been recruited as a Royalist conspirator, for he had only just recovered from his wounds and illness brought on by the long siege and the privations of war.

For the sons of the minor gentry, of whom Thomas was one, there was little chance of employment at home and, for many like him the choice was between exile and an empty future, governed by enemies. There would be a strong temptation to look for excitement, and employment, in one of the armies of Europe or as a professional conspirator. [2]

Whether Thomas served in any European army we do not know but the opportunity to serve as a Royalist agent appears to date from about October 1652 when he writes to his father, again using an alias:-

`Sir,- I must beg your pardon that I have not hitherto acquainted you with my resolution but the reason was till now they was very uncertaine and I was unwilling to trouble you or them till I was more assured of my underertaking which is this. I am promised from a person of great quality (whom I cannot here name) to have a particular care taken of me and now in order to it I am preparing myself for France. I hope I shall be there within a month at furthest if you please to give me your leave which I hope you will not deny me when I tell you that it is a fortune which many men of far greater condition than myself would be glad to meet with and besides I know no other way of living by which I can possibly subsist myself above half a year longer and this which is

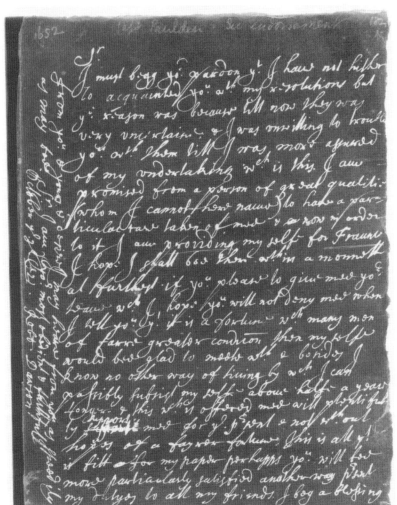

Endorsed 'Capt. Tho. Paulden under a borrowed name given me by his aged sister 1710. This Capt. T.P. wrote an acct. of Pontefract Castle in 1702 - he was killed at Wigan.' - It was his brother Timothy that was killed at Wigan.

The Marquis of Montrose (1612-1650)
Captain-General in Scotland.

offered me will plentifully support me for the present and not without hopes of a fairer fortune. This is all that is fit for my paper perhaps you will be more particularly satisfied another way present my duties to all my friends. I beg a blessing from you and yours and I desire I may hear from you as speedily as may be. Sir I am your most obedient and faithful

ROBT.DAWSON.

October 3rd (52) [3]

The person whom Thomas cannot name is almost certainly Sir Edward Hyde, Secretary of the King's Council, later to become Earl of Clarendon and grandfather of Queen Ann; to whom Thomas was sending intelligence regarding the strength of the Parliamentary forces under the command of Sir William Lockhart, at Dunkirk, with whom his relation Lieut. Thomas Stackhouse was serving and for which he was receiving payment on the King's account in 1652-54.[4]

After serving a successful apprenticeship in his new calling Thomas was employed in returning to his native Yorkshire and making contact with members of the Sealed Knot; a secret society making plans to restore the King.

Though many plots were hatched, in various parts of the country, the main reason why none succeeded was the counter espionage work of John Thurloe, Cromwell's master spy, whose virtual control of the Post Office during the Commonwealth sealed the fate of all Royalist aspirations. His experts intercepted, deciphered and copied Royalist correspondence before sending it on its way. He knew of most plots even before many of the participants and he encouraged many schemes so that he could catch those responsible red-handed.

Francis Corker - Royalist Traitor and Double-Agent

One of the most important Royalists entrapped by Thurloe was one Francis Corker, vicar of Bradford, who joined the Royalist forces at Pontefract when puritan Bradford was besieged by the King's Army in December 1642; he served as scoutmaster under Langdale and claimed to have been the King's chief guide on his northern expedition, he was in several battles and received some wounds, had two horses killed under him and took several prisoners. [5]

He was chaplain to Sir John Ramsden's regiment in Pontefract garrison and he was later imprisoned as a Royalist agent. Together with the Rev. George Beaumont he was taken by General Lambert to be executed before the walls of Pontefract castle on 19 Feb. 1649; for holding secret intelligence with the enemy and refusing to reveal his cypher and the name of his friends.

Beaumont was hanged but - in his own words - Corker 'unhappily escaped' as he explained later 'I could have died in the best cause and with a clear conscience.' [6] He settled secretly in Sussex where he taught school and acted as a curate under the assumed name of John Symonds but in 1656 he was captured for the third time and taken before Thurloe, who threatened him but then under promise of security and reward, reported to be £400 a year, he was persuaded to become a double -agent.

For three years he travelled widely among his Royalist `friends' and he became one of the Government's most prolific sources of information; writing long detailed letters every week to Thurloe through his deputy Samuel Morland.[7]

The men who carried on the northern conspiracy were, as in all such affairs, of two kinds. The lesser agents enlisted men, distributed commissions, collected arms and horses, maintained communications with London and the exiles, and generally obeyed orders. Behind them were the men of wealth and rank, landowners accustomed to local leadership; these made the real decisions, but usually kept discretely in the background. Men like Thomas Paulden, the Rev. Charles Davison and John Cooper, from the Pontefract garrison, were characteristic of the first kind. Lord Byron, Lord Belasyse and Sir Marmaduke Langdale were examples of the second.[8]

Thurgarton between Nottingham and Rufforth, the home of the substantial Royalist Sir Roger Cooper, was a centre of conspiracy and many visitors including Thomas Paulden and his younger brother Gregory - who had also become an agent - Charles Davison and of course John Cooper but a meeting there broke up in disorder, with arms being thrown into a pond, when a rumour spread that they were betrayed.

In September 1656 Edward Hyde asked Langdale to help in a renewed design but few of his old supporters were willing to risk their necks again. Several of the lesser agents - Scott, Cooper and the Paulden brothers - were repeatedly sent into England but little progress was made. Langdale made the mistake of enlisting another of his old clients, Thurloe's spy Francis Corker, who was soon handing over all Langdale's letters to his employer and giving full details of the people on whom he relied.[9]

At the Restoration Corker claimed to have betrayed not more than five persons but his letters tell a different story. He claimed to have little knowledge of Dr. Hewitt, who tried to bring about a rising in Sussex; yet one letter consists almost wholly of information obtained from him and Dr. Hewitt was beheaded.

Take the case of Paulden, whom he mentions frequently. In one of his letters Corker informs Morland:

> `...where Paulden, One of the greatest enemies to Secretary Thurloe's person, is lodging'

And suggests that Mr. Secretary should send particulars whether he should be taken alone or with some of his comrades; Paulden was taken and imprisoned in the Tower.

In one letter he lists fifty-three active Royalists in Yorkshire, many of them who were with him in Pontefract. Most of his letters gave information about Charles Stuart and the Cavaliers and their intended movements to and from abroad and of plots in which many lives were lost.

Yet after being imprisoned once again at the Restoration, as a suspected Thurloe agent, his appeals were successful and he was pardoned under the Act of indemnity and restored to his benefice at Bradford.

Of all the Royalists that turned traitor, Corker had the least scruples about denouncing his comrades. Intelligence gushed from him both verbally and in writing. If the evidence of Thurloe's papers had been available in 1660 it is inconceivable that he would have been pardoned but he was undeservedly given the benefit of the doubt.

Most of Corker's letters are undated but here are some brief extracts relating to Thomas and / or Gregory Paulden:

`Cooper went away to Flanders on Monday last, Hopton this day and Paulden on Monday next, all of them for blank commissions to make Col. Generals for each county.'

`I have found the lodging of Paulden, when he is in town, which is not constant by reason he is two or three nights together some times in the country. He lies at one Aplin's, a taylor's house in Blackfriers and he brags he hath and escaping place in his lodging.'

`Davison sent yesterday £5 to Paulden in the Tower, so I believe Dr. Hewitt and he enrich themselves upon Charles Stuart's account.'

`This last week Paulden and another was with the Duke of Buckingham at Windsor, he told them that there is a petition for his release but if unsuccessful he would endeavour to escape. He acquainted them with the manner of it and they me, desiring my assistance in it. Paulden suspects Roscarrock and he Mr. John Stanhope.'

`Paulden, who goes by the name of Hobbs, is not yet come to town, though we have letters, that he is upon his journey; and then we shall know the result of all. By my most diligent search I cannot as yet find anything more of the footsteps of Sir Langdale (sic), what I hear of him, or any other news, wherein Paulden informs us or any other, I will faithfully inform you.'

`At length Paulden and Aldborough (who hath been long expected) are now returned but with cold news for the Cavalier Party; they say that Charles Stewart's design for England is for some time absolutely laid aside.'

CHAPTER 6

Events Leading to the Restoration

Extracts mainly from the *Calendar of Clarendon State Papers* also help to reveal the part played by the Paulden brothers in Royalist conspiracy.

3 June 1657 - Hyde to the King:
  - `On his arrival on Friday night, found Grigg and his brother newly arrived from England with three horses for the Duke of Gloucester; they say that some will shortly come for the King; they not only have brought no money but have borrowed £20. Some propositions which Grigg brings will keep till the King comes: a ship has already come away resolved to put into these parts, he has brought some letters of old dates, which show the probability of confusion with Cromwell and the Fifth Monarchy Men, who are like to make mad work. Tom Paulden saw the soldiers who have come over to France, and says there are not more than 4,000 for Lockhart to command.'

17 June 1657
  - `Lockhart Governor of Dunkirk asked to enquire whether there is not one Paulden at Calais.'

12 February 1659 Rumbold [Secretary of the Sealed Knott] to Hyde:
  - `a number of Royalist supporters including Mr. Paulden and Capt. Binns, were last week freed from the Tower by suing their habeas corpus, in spite of Thurloe and some of the Council wishing to put Halsall on trial.'

4 March 1659 - Hyde to Cooper - [inter alia]:
  He asks if it is true that he is to have some office about the Duke of Buckingham - and with his conclusion he asks to be commended to Greg and his brother.

12 June 1659 - The King to John Barwick:
  - He desires him to encourage his two friends to proceed in their negotiations with Redman and Clobbery.
  Endorsed by Hyde - Grigg.

April [?] 1659 Cooper to Hyde:
  - `Greg would still have been a prisoner had it not been for the last bounty of the King sent through writer.'

Hyde to Langdale at Brussels, from Bruges:
- `I am glad to direct this immediately to yourself at Mr. Tompson's where Tom Paulden assures me you lodge.'

24 June 1659, London - George Thomlinson [i.e. Greg Paulden] to Sarah Thomlinson [i.e. Hyde]:
- full of all political intrigues of Fairfax, Lambert and Parliament and Cromwell.

8 July 1659 - Hyde to Cooper:
` - has given information to Lord [sic] Langdale of anything Cooper says. Parson Corker, who Hyde saw but once two or three years ago, and of whom Charles Davison had a great opinion, may be trusted by Tom Paulden, Grig Paulden and Cooper. Perhaps he is an honest man, but Hyde has heard that he has from time to time given intelligence to Thurloe. Their friends should be made wary of him; wished he could be sent on some sleeveless errand some distance from London for a month or two, without arousing his suspicions.'

1 July 1659 - Greg to Hyde:
- `the great ones are much displeased with a letter from Monck.'

11 August 1659 - Earl of Ormond [Royalist leader in Ireland] to Hyde:
`The King is pleased with the arrangements brought by Paulden, and will be ready by noon tomorrow. He approves of sending Paulden back with the assurance of his being ready to follow, and resolves to go to Calais.'

28 July 1659 - Brussels, Hyde to Ormond at Trevuerre:
- `I was alarmed at the note from Grigg Paulden, sent for him and found all well. Encloses a letter from Mordaunt to the King. The day holds and all was well on Wednesday morning when Grigg came away; he has brought a little note in cypher for arms to be ready embarked when they advise of the port. The King need not be here before Tuesday, Ormond this day will dispatch Grigg again if the King thinks fit and that he may let their friends know his Majesty's resolutions, and take orders with Baron to be at Bulloigne, with the news, money, and other preparations.'

2 November 1659, London - Jo:Thornton [Cooper] to Mr. Greg:
Coles [Hyde] - Acquainted Grigg with Hyde's commands; hears that letters are stopped - Lambert goes north tomorrow to reduce or reconcile Monck.

21 November 1659 - Hyde to John Barwick:
- [Sir Richard] Willis [Leader of the Sealed Knott and therefore the most effective traitor of all] not to be trusted - negotiations with Monck - Col. Redman to be restored in Ireland - is glad to find Col. Clobbery a principal Councillor with Monck - money to be paid to Grigg.

21 November 1659 - Hyde to Cooper:
  - `no letter this week from Cooper or Greg.'
20 December 1659 - Hyde to Cooper:
  - `chide Grigg for not writing this week.'

Dr. John Barwick [1] and John Otway

One of the very few churchmen to risk their estates and their lives in the Royal cause and also one of their leading intelligence agents, was that zealous prebendary of Durham and Fellow of St. John's College, Cambridge, Dr. John Barwick from Witherslack in Westmorland.

He was one of the principals who helped to secure money and plate for the King from Cambridge University at the outbreak of the war in 1642, despite Cromwell's attempts to intercept them. Helped by Gregory Paulden, John Cooper, Rumbold and Mordaunt, we also know he sent over £1,728 to the King between April and June 1659.

Barwick was the most successful agent in the complicated game of angling for support from prominent Army men and his most useful contact with them was fellow Westmerian and ex Sedbergh scholar, John Otway, born at Beckside Hall, Middleton, and like Barwick an excluded Fellow of St. John's College. In a poignant example of divided family loyalties, one of Otway's brothers in law, Colonel Daniel Redman yet another Westmerian from Kirkby Lonsdale, served under Henry Cromwell in Ireland but was purged by the Rump Parliament. And a second, who married Otway's sister-in-law, was Colonel John Clobbery who commanded a regiment in Scotland under General Monk, was one of his most trusted men, and also his kinsman. The vitally important influence of Barwick and Otway on Redman [2] and Clobbery [3] to eventually persuade Monk to support the Restoration can not be overestimated.

A letter of Barwick's reveals how central was his role with the principals whom were responsible for making way for the Restoration.

John Barwick to the King :
  `- for the two businesses whereof I gave your Majesty an account of by Mr. Paulden, they are both managed by one instrument, whom I believe to be both discrete and honest, one Mr. Otway, a councillor of Grey's Inn, formerly in arms for his late Majesty [he took part in the second siege of Pontefract castle] and always faithful and true in his principles. He is very intimate with both of them, corresponds with them and is employed by them in all affairs as concerns their estates, and is nearly allyed to both of them, the one having married his sister, the other his wife's sister.'

Otway, after receiving a special request from the King, went to Edinburgh to try Clobbery in July 1659 and received a sympathetic hearing, John Evelyn, the diarist, also helped to make converts, Barwick and Otway were authorised to continue their efforts through Clobbery by Sir John Grenville, now leader of the King's cause.

Lord Mordaunt and Sir John Grenville had received the King's commission to lead the Royalists restoration efforts after the dismal failure of the Sealed Knott group.

26 July 1659 - Lord Mordaunt to Harthill Baron:

> `Sir Richard Willis and other leaders of the Knott, have for some time resolved to destroy this vast preparation. None of these gentlemen have looked towards providing money, arms or horses. They made many excuses, including getting in the harvest, and blamed anyone but themselves.'

The many risings for the King were frustrated, because, as was suspected at the time but only proved much later, several of the Royalist agents, including Sir Richard Willis [one of the leaders of the Sealed Knott], were acting as double-agents for Cromwell's master spy, John Thurlow.

26 September 1659 - Hyde to Barwick:

> - `I must recommend Greg: Paulden to your care, that when you have any money to dispose of, he may receive £20. He is a very good youth, and deserves well of his Majesty. If you see him, pray let him know that I have received two or three letters from him; but he gives me no advice, how mine should reach him, which he should do.'

Thomas Paulden and John Cooper had been imprisoned after the March rising but escaped overseas once again; some time later Greg and they were involved in a design against Hull, the most important garrison port in the north. This was wrecked by their contact there, who visited a kinsman, a servant of Richard Cromwell's wife at Hampton Court and aroused suspicion by his conduct which resulted in his immediate imprisonment.

The Paulden brothers continued to frequent the conspiratorial underworld in London but Greg was caught and imprisoned in December and was held for thirteen months on suspicion of high treason. The opening of Parliament in January 1659/60 saw opposition to arbitrary imprisonment and Gregory was released in February on writ of Habeas Corpus.

16 December 1659 - Col. Philips [one of the Royalist leaders in Devon] to Hyde:

> - if anything is to be done suddenly in that county, Rumbold can furnish necessary commissions. He asks what Clobbery and Otway think of Monk. And recommends him to assist Greg Paulden with money.

27 January 1660 - Mordaunt to the King's Secretary, Sir Edward Nicholas:

> - He complains of attempts to discredit him with the King. Every man here rails if his own opinion be not accepted. Jealousy of Broderick, Scott, Paulden and Cooper: the Council is composed of people too considerable to suffer communications with persons of so little reputation [he means men without title, estates or money].

It is not to be wondered at that members of the nobility were jealous of the sons of minor gentry who had become important because they were the King's couriers.

30 January 1660 - Barwick to Hyde:
- `I divided £20 between Greg Paulden and Sir Theophilis Gilbee [He commanded a regiment at Edgehill and Naseby, knighted at Newark 1645; agent for Langdale]. *Perhaps Otway comes with his brother Clobbery in Monk's army.'*

13 April 1660 - Greg Paulden to Hyde:
`*Lambert escaped. The General and Council of State, ordered the streets to be chained up last night.'*

After Cromwell's death in September 1658 his son Richard proved too weak to lead the country and the Army took control; General John Lambert made a bid for power but was foiled when 1,500 of his horse elected to follow their old commander Colonel Daniel Redman [3] and so cleared the road from Scotland for the passage of General Monk who was persuaded, after long and tedious negotiations, to support the return of Charles II.

As we have seen, John Barwick played no little part in restoring the King; in fact the services he rendered to the Royal cause were immense.

During the Interregnum he was betrayed and sent to the Tower for two years and four months where he was on the point of death owing to his overwork in the Royal cause. His great friend John Otway prepared for his funeral, but he miraculously recovered and was released without trial in August 1652. He attended Dr. Hewitt on the scaffold, (receiving from him a ring with the motto `Alter Anstedes' which he wore until his death) and after the Restoration he refused a bishopric but accepted the Deanery of St. Paul's, which he enjoyed for so little time, before dying of pleurisy in 1664.

He made many bequests; including several important ones to his native village of Witherslack and £40 to his old school at Sedbergh; and *...the immortal writings of the King's father, as no improper pledge of his love and gratitude to his dearest friend Mr. John Otway, who declined no labour nor danger, that the King's Son might be restored to his throne. To Mr [Barnabus] Oley, Mr James Cookson and Mr John Kirkby a mourning ring of 20s, my special friends...21 Oct 1664.* [4]

Charles's departure from Scheveningen in Holland to regain his kingdom, May 1660.

CHAPTER 7

The King restored to his Own again

At the Restoration, as he watched the cheering crowds, King Charles made his famous remark – 'It is certainly a mistake that I did not come back sooner, for I have not met anyone today who has not professed to have always desired my return.' [1]

Many thousands asked to be rewarded for their great losses incurred whilst supporting the Royal cause, but few were satisfied as King Charles lacked the resources and the will, after being assailed continuously with spurious or greatly exaggerated claims.

Monk was created Duke of Albemarle and granted large tracts of land which included the Honour of Clitheroe and Grenville was created Earl of Bath. Clobbery was knighted with a pension of £600 a year; Otway was knighted and became Vice-Chancellor of the Palatine of Lancaster and the King's Attorney General there.[2]

For the lesser mortals who had served their purpose, like the Paulden brothers, rewards were few indeed. As Thomas recorded in his letter:

`I returned into England with my old companion Loyalty and the usual companion of that Poverty' [3]

He must have felt some bitterness, especially towards the turncoats, like Col. Henry Ingleby for example, who claimed in a petition of July 1660 that Capt. Paulden falsely accused him of opposing the Restoration. [4]

The Rev. Charles Davison, who took part in the Doncaster Raid and who had been a tutor to Sir George Savile, died in a shipwreck off Flanders in 1658; John Cooper became a carver in the Royal household; and Gregory Paulden was granted the place of Master of the Excise Office for Yorkshire, but he had to be satisfied with a composition from the person in possession, who had paid a great price for it. [5] He did, however, obtain the value of a warrant for the making of Mr. Henry Graham a baronet. [6]

That Thomas Paulden was still engaged in the secret service and that not all the country was in favour of the King, as his majesty had declared, we learn from a letter to Thomas at Wallingford House, in The Strand, London (which belonged to the Duke of Buckingham) from Peter Crabb, dated 29 October 1662:

`There will be a disturbance in the night, for some desperate persons have sworn to shoot or stab the King. They are to wear plush jackets and plumes, in order not to be suspected. His Majesty must be cautioned to be aware of his company and his food. Alderman Tim Wade is active in the design, and prys into Court transactions; also Sir Thomas Alleyn, Thompson, a Parliamentary man in Spittlefield, Harrison of Harrow. Alleyn and Robert Walley, who are very active, should be secured, and Col. Kiffin interrogated.' [7]

The King 's arrival at Dover.

Thomas's name does appear in the long list of poor officers (some of whom were far from poor) claiming part of the £60,000 granted by his gracious Majesty to his most loyal sufferers in 1663.[8]

Also identified in the list are George Agehead, Thomas's ensign and Peter Kenner, who was quartermaster to Capt. William Paulden.

In his letter Thomas reveals that his financial situation `was made tolerable by the favour and bounty of the Duke of Buckingham', who used his services in several leases. The Duke, in the 1660's was also occupying himself with the installation of a large glass works at Lambeth, the first of its kind in England; and according to the Venetian ambassador, sometime later the glass trade in Venice had been completely ruined by the success of the Duke's factories in England.

The diarist John Evelyn, reports how he had inspected the `huge vases of clear ponderous and thick crystal, and mirrors that were better than those of the Venetians,' when he visited the Duke's glassworks. [9]

Perhaps Thomas was employed by the Duke in his business as is indicated by the issuing of a warrant on 4 August 1663 - `for a patent to Mr. Thomas Tilson, merchant of London, of the sole making of Crystal Glass & Looking Glass Plates, on the surrender of a grant made to Martin Clifford and Thomas Paulden, the inventors.' [10]

John Evelyn, founder member of the Royal Society, kept a diary from the age of eleven. It contains little about the man, but tells much of the age.

Glassworks, showing furnace, glass blowing and pack carriers setting out [11]

Martin Clifford was the Duke's secretary and he had been a friend of his at Cambridge, when he is described as `a buffoon, scholar and eccentric whose disregard for convention made him a conspicuous and entertaining figure whose influence on the Duke was less than desirable.' He wrote `A Treatise of Human Reason' and together with Abraham Cowley's `Guardian' was influential in the writing of the Duke's successful play `The Rehearsal'. [12]

Thomas Osborne, Earl of Danby / 1st Duke of Leeds 1631-1712. (See his letter p.84)

The inclusion of Thomas' name on the glass patent may have been a mere sinecure or in lieu of unpaid wages from the Duke of Buckingham but he could have had a real interest in glass making and it may not have been just coincidence that his 'cousin' William Gascoigne, of Thorpe-on-the-Hill, near Leeds, was the inventor of the wire micrometer, its application to the telescope and the quadrant, who wrote a treatise on optics. William was also a Royalist captain of cavalry under Marmaduke Langdale, who survived Marston Moor only to be killed in a skirmish at Melton Mowbray in December 1645. [13]

In January 1666 - Thomas wrote to Christopher Hatton, an ex-Royalist agent of means, thanking him for kindness done to him.

On 4 April 1668, the King requested the Treasury Commissioners to recommend Thomas to the office of Commissioner of Excise, on the first vacancy, with the usual salary but perhaps like his brother Gregory he had to be satisfied with a composition.[14]

I suspect that Thomas's poverty was somewhat relative. However, many years later, in February 1692, he was in great money difficulties and he wrote to Lord Hatton, begging to be taken into his household as a servant in order to be saved from a debtors' prison.[15]

A paragraph from *Sociability and Power in Late Stuart-England: The Cultural Worlds of the Verneys 1660-1720* by Susan E. Whyman, Oxford U.P. gives us some insight into the life style led by Thomas and Rebecca Paulden in London through their association with Sir Ralph Verney 1613-1696 of Middle Claydon, Buckinghamshire.

Sir Ralph often used venison from his own private deer park to reflect his power and esteem and send as gifts to re-enforce ties of patronage and friendship with those of his vast social network whom he wished to impress. However, the gift to the Pauldens, described as 'influential non-kin', came from another privileged source: Woodstock Park where his friend Edward Henry Lee, 1st Earl of Lichfield 1663-1716 Lee had been appointed ranger on his marriage to Charles II's illegitimate daughter Lady Charlotte Fitzroy in 1677. It gave him £3,000 a year and the right to dispense patronage and deer to others.

The other side of Lichfield's deer went to Captain and Rebecca Paulden. They were tenants of the house in Lincoln's Inn fields, where Sir Ralph lodged in London. Although he paid £30 rent 'for his share and part of the house', he had little privacy. Lodgers crowded in clusters like extended families and performed favours for each other. Mrs. Paulden, probably a relative of Grinling Gibbons [Britain's greatest decorative woodcarver employed by the Verneys and their Mason relatives on family monuments], *copied portraits for a living* [going to and from country houses] *and acted as Sir Ralph's landlady. She ordered food and found someone to lie in his bed before each of his arrivals. He, in turn, helped the Paulden family. In April 1696, when they borrowed his coach, its brass toppings were stolen. Even so, Sir Ralph sent them venison that July, as he had done the previous year.*

Despite being son and heir of Charles I's loyal standard bearer Sir Edmund Verney 1590-1642 who was killed at Edgehill, Sir Ralph held Parliamentary views but took no part in the war and fled to France in 1643 to escape the conflict. Returning at the Restoration he spent much of his time from about 1674 in London, lodging, perhaps from February 1684 when the previous occupier Lady Anne Hobart died, with the Pauldens at Holburn Row House and he was there for almost eight months, from October 1695 until July 1696, before returning home to die.

Like gifts of deer visiting was also considered very important to cultivate friendship and patronage in the best social circles; even Sir Ralph's landlady [Rebecca Paulden] being on the fringe of this social elite visited, perhaps in Sir Ralph's coach, the Verney relatives, the Palmer family in Chelsea.

Sir Ralph Verney 1st Bnt. 1613-1696.

Grinling Gibbons 1648-1721.

In London on 31 March, 1702, Thomas, in his seventy eighth year, wrote his account of how Pontefract castle was taken and how General Rainsborough was surprised in his quarters at Doncaster; at the request of an un-named friend who had been reminded of those exploits by the recent news from Europe of the surprising of Marshall Villeroy in his quarters at Cremona, by Prince Eugene.

Thoresby, the famous Leeds historian, visited the two aged virgins, mistresses Paulden at York in 1711 when they told him of their four famous brothers' adventures during the Civil War and the Interregnum.[16]

Perhaps he was motivated to visit them by the reported death of our hero, as Thomas's Account, first published in 1702, was reprinted in 1719 in aid of his widow.

It seems likely that Thomas's sisters were living in a house in St. Savour's Gate, York; a property belonging to their father William in 1649.[17]

I can't help comparing the life of ease led by the traitor Francis Corker, in his comfortable benefice at Bradford, with the struggles of the loyal Thomas Paulden and to this is added a touch of irony, in that Corker's ancestors sprang from my own home town of Ulverston in north Lancashire.

I am certain of one thing, however, that even given the opportunity, Thomas would not have considered changing places with his erstwhile friend.

Thomas Paulden's wonderful story, which as Richard Holmes says `reads like a romance' not only justifies the appellation I have given him `a true Cavalier' but it allows me to embrace personally Dr. Johnson's remark `I love Pontefract Castle - why, 'tis in all our histories' and even more than that it has fulfilled my wildest dream.

CHAPTER 8

Further Exciting Discoveries

When, years ago, I researched one of our maternal lines back through several yeomen families living in the hamlet of Thorpe in the parish of Burnsall in Craven, in the West Riding of Yorkshire, to the marriage of Thomas Rayner and Isabel Craven, which took place there on 1st July 1565: I certainly had no idea at the time, that this particular line would lead to a significant and exciting connection.

Having arrived at the beginning of the parish registers and found nothing in the local wills at York to help identify this Rayner man and this Craven woman from amongst the many others of their names in the locality I had abandoned research with the notion that I would most probably never discover which families they were part of.

There was, I have to admit one other reason, so familiar to many researchers, which made me less than enthusiastic about searching amongst 16th century manor court rolls and deeds in the unlikely hope of finding out more information on Thomas Rayner and Isabel Craven - We had a weak link in the pedigree!

Our ancestor Mary Sym, daughter of Robert Sym (see p.76) was baptised at Burnsall 14th October 1744, and yes there was a Robert Sym baptised 17th February 1679 who could, although aged 65, be her father - if he had not been buried four months later on 29th May.

There was no Robert Sym/Syme/Symm/Symme/Sim/Simm/Simme/Sime, (just to give some of the alternative spellings), baptised in Burnsall, or any other neighbouring parish in the Yorkshire dales, during the appropriate period, whom could be Mary's father.

The Burnsall parish register is, like many others, far from perfect and one of the particularly defective periods is that when Mary Sim's father Robert was born c1700. The bishop's transcripts at York have provided much missing information to add to the original register but alas there is a lot missing: besides Robert's baptism, his second marriage, his own burial and that of his 2nd wife, his father's marriage and burial and that of his wife, they are, together with many other entries, all lost.

When once again re-drafting my Thomas Paulden story an idea struck me that my relation James Knowles (c1550-1615) could not only be compared to the celebrated Dick Whittington but also to his immediate contemporary Sir William Craven (1548-1618), who had, like James, left his home in the Yorkshire dales, Appletreewick just ten miles from Long Preston, and become a successful merchant, and in 1610-11, Lord Mayor of London.

Having decided that this was a suitable inclusion I then realised that I must carry out some research on Sir William Craven to fill in my very sketchy knowledge of his background history.

The Dictionary of National Biography tells us that Sir William was, at the age of thirteen, sent to London by the common carrier to be bound apprentice to Robert Hulson, citizen and merchant tailor there. However, that William was not amongst strangers, we learn from the will of Robert Hulson, dated 18th July 1580 that Robert was himself born in Burnsall, to the poor of which parish he bequeathed the sum of five pounds in sterling, to be distributed by his executors within a year of his decease.

Whether he took his cat with him does not appear but William must have enjoyed good luck: certainly more than his friends who were executed for their part in the Northern Rebellion of 1569, for on 4th November of that year, having successfully learned the mysteries of his craft, he was admitted to the freedom of the Merchant Taylors' Company and soon afterwards became a partner in his master's business.

Robert Hulson, in his will, appears to be very fond of his ex-apprentice, who was apparently still a very junior partner at that time but he does not forget him:

I give and bequeath unto William Craven my Servant in Consideration of his faithful and diligent Service now and heretofore to me donne five pounds in Sterling in money and a mourninge gowne. And further my verie will and mind is that the said William Craven Ymmediately after my death shall have my Shoppe situate at Breadstreet Corner in Watling Street in London with the lytle Shoppe and Warehouse thereunto adjoyning for the tearme of three yeres yealdinge therefore yerely at the feaste of the birthe of our Lord god, one pepper corne, if that it be lawfully asked .[1]

A very successful business career, built upon that of his master Robert Hulson and culminating in his election to wardenship of his Company on 4th July 1593 was followed by further honours which reflected his many acts of public beneficence. On 2nd April 1600 he was elected Alderman and on 14th February 1601 he was chosen sheriff of London. He was knighted at Whitehall by James I on 26th July 1603 and in 1607, when the Merchant Taylors' Company decided to entertain the King and Prince Henry, he was, with others, deputed to carry the invitation to Norwich.

Sir William's success in business had not come about in the traditional manner of marrying the boss's daughter; he did, however, marry Elizabeth, daughter of William Whitmore, a rich alderman of London, but it was not until after he had been knighted and had reached the advanced age of 57 years.

When Sir William was elected lord mayor of London for 1610-11, the show, which had been suspended for some years, was revived with splendour. Christian, prince of Anhalt, was entertained with all his 'Germayne trayne' at the feast at the Guildhall afterwards: apparently presaging later events in our story.

An indication of Sir William's wealth at the time of his mayoralty can be gained from his name being connected with certain loans to the King; the lands to the value of £1,000 which he donated to Christ's Hospital and the many other 'public works' for which he was responsible.

He is described as 'One of the largest wholesale cloth dealers in London during the late sixteenth and early seventeenth century and probably the richest as well.' On another occasion he is said to be, 'a goldsmith [banker] in the strand.' The ill fated Earl of Essex was his debtor for £1,000.

In 1616 Lady Elizabeth Coke, wife of Sir Edward Coke, the famous lawyer, on occasion of a famous quarrel with her husband, was at his request handed over to the hospitality of Sir William, who entertained her at his house in Leadenhall Street. The King must have been grateful for this gracious act as he wrote a letter of thanks to Sir William. [2]

On 1st July 1618 Sir William attended the court of the Merchant Taylors' Company for the last time, his will being 'openly read in court' on the 29th after his burial at St Andrew Undershaft on 11th August.

It was only chance, or was it providence? That made it possible - I felt amazed and incredulous at the time - and still do, to be able to shout 'Eureka!!' for a second time.

It was the transcript of Sir William's will [3] encountered in an article on the Craven family in the Yorkshire Archaeological Society Journal by the Rector of Burnsall and chaplain to the Earl of Craven, (1893), W.J. Stavart, which first alerted me to the fact that he was my great uncle x 12! Amongst the many bequests to his brothers and sisters and their children of Appletreewick and Darley (a few miles away) there appears 'to Nicholas Rayner, son to my sister Elizabeth Rayner, £200.' Both mother and son, being our direct ancestors.

There is a discrepancy in the published Burnsall register, Isabel instead of Elizabeth Craven being given as the wife of Thomas Rayner at the marriage on 1st July 1565; which I attribute to the fault of the clerk or more probably owing to a mistake at the time of one of several copies from the original register being made. Fortunately the several other bequests by Sir William to his family leave no doubt that his nephew Nicholas Rayner (1576-1651) was son of his sister Elizabeth and Thomas Rayner (c1542-1621) married on 1st July 1565.

Despite his success in the metropolis Sir William, like James Knowles, did not forget the place of his birth and in 1602 he founded the grammar school in Burnsall, making his nephew Nicholas Rayner and several other of his relations its trustees. He later bequeathed money for its upkeep and he left money to build bridges, to beautify the church and to relieve the poor people in his native parish.

On 13 June 1616, Sir William had entered into an indenture of partnership with John and Robert Parker, both merchant tailors of London, for the formation of a stock to employ in 'the trade of buying selling and occupyeing of all manner and sortes and kyndes of woollen cloth & clothes whatever.' The initial stock of the business was £12,000 and the trade in partnership was to be carried on for a term of five years. Each of the partners had a one-third share of £4,000. The Parker brothers subscribed their shares in cash, while Craven's share consisted of £600 in money and £3,400 in cloth. The business was to be carried on at Craven's shop and warehouses in Watling Street.

Research revealed that Sir William had been in partnership with the Parkers before 1616. [4] In his will, written less than two months after the agreement with the Parkers, he refers to the account of the partnership as *that which we terme or call the new account.* The size of his bequests to the Parkers suggest that they had been in business together for a long time: £500 to John and £200 to Robert, increased by a codicil of 17 July 1618 to £700 and £300 respectively.'

In fact William Parker, a rich Merchant Taylor of London (probably father of John and Robert) who left £1,000 to beautify the old gates of London when he died in 1611, had accompanied William Craven on his journey to London in c1557 from their home in Appletreewick and had, like (and perhaps as partner with) Craven, become a successful merchant tailor.

With the outstanding success of at least three local boys from Burnsall; Robert Hulson, William Parker and William Craven, the country people of the Dales had just reason to believe *that the streets of London were paved with gold.*

To discover Sir William was exciting enough but this was just the first of even more exciting connections for a Civil War researcher.

Sir William's eldest son was another William Craven, born in 1606, who entered the service of the Prince of Orange when only seventeen years of age, before which he was said to have been a member of Trinity College, Oxford.

Under Maurice of Orange and his successor, Frederick Henry, he gained some military distinction and on returning to England was knighted by Charles I, 4 March 1627. Eight days later he was created Baron Craven of Hampstead Marshall, Berkshire, and not long afterwards was named a member of the permanent council of war.

In 1631 the Marquis of Hamilton was permitted by King Charles I to levy troops in England for Gustavus Adolphus. They were primarily intended to make the emperor, Ferdinand II, relinquish his hold of the Palatinate, which might thus be recovered for the deprived Elizabeth and her husband Frederick, electress and elector of Bohemia, sister and brother in law of Charles, now refugees at the Hague.

Lord Craven was named one of the commanders of the English forces in Germany, and early in 1632, he accompanied Frederick when the latter set forth from the Hague to strike a blow, if permitted to do so, in his own cause. This is the first occasion on which Craven is found in personal relations with the heroic Elizabeth Queen of Bohemia, the `Winter Queen' as she was known, and later `Queen of Hearts' because of her innumerable suitors, to whose service he was soon to wholly devote himself.

Frederick and Craven reached Hochst, where they had an interview with Gustavus Adolphus, the hero of European history, who allowed them to take part in the siege of Creuznach, which was taken on 22 February. Craven, though wounded, was the first to mount the breach and he had the honour of being one of the signatories of the capitulation.

The Swedish King, however, refused to allow Frederick to levy an independent force and only months later, it was the death of his hero Gustavus in his moment of victory at the Battle of Lutzen which was the final blow to Frederick, who suffering from fever and plague, died a broken man on 29th November, 1632 at the early age of 36.

Soon afterwards Lord Craven returned to England where he stayed until in 1637, when it had been decided that some of the king's ships should be lent to the young Charles Lewis, the eldest son of the Queen of Bohemia, and should put to sea under the flag of the Palatinate house. Several noblemen proffered voluntary contributions towards this enterprise, and foremost among them was Lord Craven, who declared his readiness to contribute as much as £30,000. In June the fleet commanded by Northumberland conveyed Charles Lewis and his brother Rupert to Holland and Lord Craven was in their company.

Disaster struck however, when at a place called Lemgo their force of 4,000 men was surprised and completely defeated by a much larger army under general Hatzfeld. Prince Rupert fought with obstinate valour in this his first action, and it is said that but for the interposition of Lord Craven he would have sacrificed his life rather that surrender his sword.

Both of them were taken prisoner and Craven, whilst in prison, continued his regular dispatches to Elizabeth, the Winter Queen, in which he had been sending her regular details of the military operations; in this originated their confidential correspondence, which was never afterwards suspended.

Craven, who had been wounded in the battle, remained for some time in captivity, refusing to ransom himself in order to be near the Prince but on being refused access to him purchased his own liberty for £20,000 in the autumn of 1639. Though still lame from his wound he paid a visit to the Queen at the Hague before returning home to England. Rupert, an even more valuable hostage, was not released until 1641.

Owing to the struggle between Charles I and his parliament, Elizabeth's English pension of £10,000 a year remained unpaid but Craven's munificence compensated her for the loss and it was he who re-drafted her claims when parliament annulled her pension after the execution of her brother Charles I.

By this time Craven had become a permanent member of the exiled Queen of Bohemia's court at the Hague and despite providing her youngest daughter Sophia (our present Queen's ancestor) with jewellery and arranging and financing her journey to Heidelberg in 1650, the graceless princess speaks of him as without esteem either for his wit or for his breeding, and unscrupulously makes fun of the family benefactor. However, as the princess had few good words to say about anyone, even her mother, we need not take her opinions seriously.

During the civil war Craven had repeatedly aided Charles I with money, and it is calculated that before his restoration Charles II received from the same loyal subject at the least £50,000 which tremendous support was particularly offensive to adherents of parliament as being furnished by the son of a citizen of London.

For this and other personal services to the King, plus the report of an agent provocateur, who said that Craven had described the parliamentary authorities as 'barbarous and inhuman rebels', his estates were confiscated and sequestered by the Commonwealth of England by an act dated 3 August 1652.

At the Restoration Craven followed Charles II back to England when he recovered most of his estates and he was loaded with honours and offices. He became lord-lieutenant of Middlesex and Southwark, colonel of several regiments, including the coldstream guards, and lieutenant-general; he was named master of the Trinity House, and high steward of the university of Cambridge; he was one of the commissioners for Tangiers, and of the lords proprietors for Carolina; he was sworn of the privy council; and in the peerage he was in March 1664 raised to the degrees of Viscount Craven of Uffingham and Earl of Craven.

In prosperity, however, as in adversity, he remained faithful to the service of the Queen of Bohemia, whose own return to England was delayed by her pecuniary embarrassments. When Charles II with undeniable indifference continued to leave her without the offer of any residence in England, Craven placed his own London mansion, Drury House, at her disposal, and thus enabled her to return to her native land on 26th May 1661.

During nearly all the remainder of Elizabeth's life she was his guest, and he generally attended her when she appeared in public. As to the precise nature of their private relations even in this period, we are naturally enough, without evidence.

William 1st Earl of Craven 1606-1697.

The office of Master of the Horse, which he had nominally held at her husband's court, he seems to have continued to fill at her's in his own house, and he is described as `proprietor of the house where the Queen lives, and principal director of her court'.

Not till 8th February 1662 did she remove from Drury House to Leicester House, hired as a residence for herself; and here a fortnight afterwards she died. At her funeral, when Prince Rupert was the chief mourner, the heralds who bore her royal crown were supported by Craven and his relative Sir Robert Craven. To the former she had bequeathed her papers, together with her unique collection of Stuart and Palatine family portraits. These, Craven placed at Combe Abbey, in Warwickshire, where they were preserved.

On the question of the well known popular belief, according to which Craven was privately married to the Queen of Bohemia, there is nothing in any of her published letters to him of more than friendliness or the most unembarrassed gaiety and neither family papers nor tradition support the notion. It is curious, however, that the Mar-gravine of Anspach, should refer to the report of the marriage without scepticism in her `Memoirs', and despite the Queen's conscious Royalty the mesalliance of her sister in law Henrietta Maria and Lord Jermyn prove it not to be beyond question.

Halliwell Sutcliffe speculates [5]:-

> `William Craven and Elizabeth stood in the fire glow one wintery evening, and she thanked him for his services.

> "What reward, my Knight? she asked. "Nothing is too much to claim."
> "Yes, one thing is," he said - and said no more till her two hands were on his shoul-ders.
> "You are so proud - proud of your humility. Have we not lived in camps together, you and I?"
> A wonder and a joy were showing now in Craven's face; but he told himself this thing could not be true. He had worshipped her from afar so long. This widowed Queen must always be remote from such as he.
> "Ah, dull and stubborn!" she said, with quiet raillery.
> "If I were a beggermaid and you the King, show me how you'd play the part."
> "If I were King," said he, with rough eagerness, "I'd build you golden steps right up to my throne. I'd take your hands in sight of all the world, and tell them you were mine. And I'd laugh with joy to know it true."
> " If I were Queen - who am one no longer, save in name - I'd marry where my heart was. And its yours."
> So Craven knew it true, and kissed her, not as royalty, but as a woman; and from that betrothal came a marriage, secret and guarded jealously, but happy as a song of old romance.'

After the Queen's death Craven continued to occupy a distinguished place among those who enjoyed the goodwill of her royal nephews. In the days of the plague and of the fire of London he actively exerted himself and it is a well know anecdote that his horse knew the smell of fire at a great distance, and was in the habit of immediately galloping off with him to the spot.

In March 1668 Pepys describes him as 'riding up and down to give orders like a madman to the troops assembled in Lincoln's Inn Fields on the occasion of a city tumult'.

To Elizabeth's son Prince Rupert their old comradeship in war and tribulation must have specially endeared him, they were lifelong friends sharing membership of the Royal Society and on Rupert's death, in 1682, Craven was by his will, made guardian of the Prince's illegitimate daughter Ruperta and sole trustee and executor of his estate in England and in Holland.

Elizabeth Queen of Bohemia.

William 1st Earl of Craven.

Frederick King of Bohemia.

Prince Rupert (1619-1682) Charles I's nephew whom he appointed General of the Horse at the outbreak of the war. Dobson's painting shows him when he was twenty-five.

Craven was the chief mourner at Rupert's funeral in Westminster Abbey, when the Prince was buried there in Henry VII's chapel. Among the treasures that the Earl discovered as executor was an iron chest containing 1,694 guineas and a `great pearl necklace' which was purchased by Nell Gwyne for £4,520. Perhaps the treasure was part of what his mother Elizabeth Queen of Bohemia left him in 1662 'To our son the Prince Rupert we give all monies owed to us as well as those already in our possession, all our most valuable rings and vessels and other pieces belonging to us.' [6]

At the accession of James II he was made a privy councillor and lieutenant-general of the forces, but soon afterwards, not surprisingly at the age of eighty two, he retired from public life. He died unmarried on 9th April 1697, and was buried at Pinley, near Coventry, his earldom and estates descending to a collateral line.

To discover our relation Captain Thomas Paulden and his story was as I have said `a dream come true' but then to discover another close relation, the Earl of Craven, to have been the lifelong friend and admirer of Elizabeth Queen of Bohemia, the `Winter Queen' and` Queen of Hearts', sister of Charles I; and her son Prince Rupert; prime actors in the English Civil War, I still find incredible.

Our Craven Family Connections

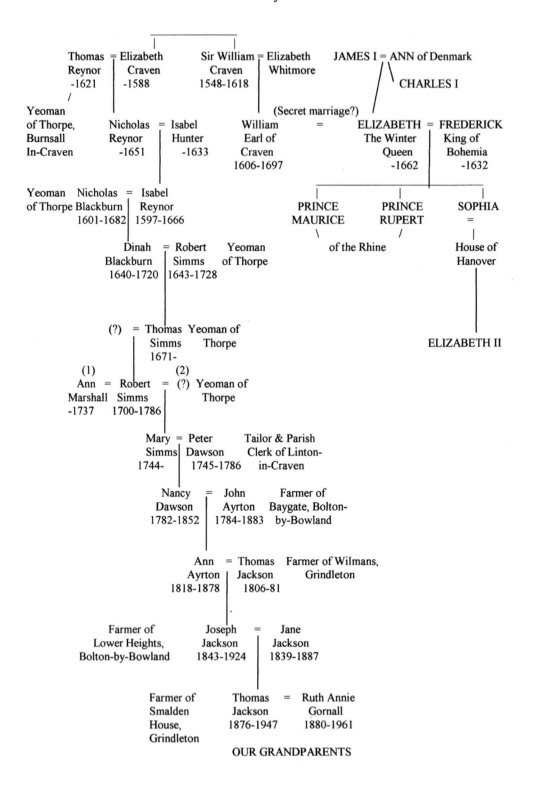

Prince Rupert was a legend in his own lifetime and has remained so ever since; he was handsome, impetuous and courageous, the epitome of the cavalier and cavalryman par excellence. Above all he was an honest and noble man - a man of honour. Arthur Bryant in his book on Samuel Pepys describes Prince Rupert, the gallant Earl of Ossory and the Earl of Craven as `the three paladins of seventeenth century chivalry.' Captain Thomas Paulden, the true Cavalier who fought in several battles, by the side of the Prince would, like myself, have been proud to be associated with him.

What modern day family historian, beginning from nothing but fascinated by the seventeenth century, could hope for more.

Besides fulfilling my every wish I know that my discoveries have thrilled my sister Sheila, who has hero-worshipped Prince Rupert since she first read about him in her teens, and my mother who is an authority on the Royal family, having read every book on them that has been available to her. It is my hope that my experience will give encouragement to all other family historians whose desire it is to feel personally, through the lives of their ancestors, part of our national history.

`Ah yes,' I can hear someone say, `but what about the missing link? Your family's possible connection with Sir William Craven and his family is all very interesting but not proven!'

This is quite true. I found no will for Thomas Sym (1671-?) or for his father Robert Sym(1643-1728), who lived to be 85 and outlived his son, and even though I am fortunate that there was only one Sym family living in the parish of Burnsall during the 16-18C, it appeared that I would have to be satisfied with a probable but not proven link with the Craven family.

That is until, as I mentioned earlier, I was able to shout eureka! For the second time! Which is something all researchers do, if they are fortunate enough, when they discover something unbelievable or something which they considered was irretrievable.

I had discovered something unbelievable which could be proved only if I could find something else which I believed to be irretrievable - the missing link!

It was in a library, not the most likely place, where I had to stifle my cry. I have long been grateful to Arthur Raistrick for his wonderful books and articles on the Yorkshire dales, and it was amongst his mss deposited at Skipton library that I discovered:

> *Assignment from Robert Syme of Thorpe, yeoman, grandson and heir of Robert Syme, elder, yeoman, deceased of the same, and Ann his wife, and James Syme of Thorpe, thother grandson of Robert Syme, deceased, and Henry Marshall of Grassington, gent. - to John Blakey for £36 -[property in Thorpe] - 24 Feb. 1728/9.* [7]

`Seek, and if you are lucky, you will find,' must be the motto of every family historian.

CHAPTER 9

Thomas' dream of becoming 'governor' of 'Holy Island'

Having completed the last word on my hero, which is what I fully expected it to be, I was quite amazed when further fortuitous research opened up a whole new chapter of his remarkable life story.

It was at Claremont, the headquarters of the Yorkshire Archaeological Society in Leeds, where the exciting event took place. I had finished checking through notes on Slaidburn parish register which my friend Chris Spencer and I were preparing for publication and I was almost idly and quite at random (whilst waiting for Chris to finish) making cursory glances through indexes of various publications that were at hand on a shelf behind me, in the vain hope of finding any reference to my Banastre family research, on which I was currently working, when the name PAULDEN, Thomas, suddenly appeared to jump out of the page at me.

I had to confirm even the title of the tome I'd been scanning and found it to be a Calendar of Treasury Papers. What a treasury of information I'd discovered. These large volumes had never before attracted my attention as I naively imagined them to contain nothing but pounds shillings and pence information on the financial matters of balancing the nation's books.

And there wasn't just one reference - there were many! It was some weeks later, after several visits to my nearest source, Manchester Central Reference Library and much hard work (owing to difficult and conflicting references), that I finally copied up seventeen A4 pages of notes relating to hundreds of entries, taken from seventy very large volumes covering the years 1660-1745 and published by HMSO, 1904-1962.

These entries, some small and brief others more extended, abstracted from the original documents: mainly reports from the Commissioners of Customs to the Lords of the Treasury, and some letters, recorded during the Restoration period and the reigns of James II, William & Mary, Queen Anne and the three Georges, recorded in the Treasury Books and Papers reveal at least the outline of Thomas' titanic struggle to achieve his dream and become (like Sancho Panza in Don Quixote) governor of an island. And it is almost exclusively from this source that the many quotations used in this chapter are taken.

I had greatly lamented the fact, but no more than he did himself, that Captain Thomas Paulden had apparently not received just reward at the Restoration for his heroic service and loyalty to the Crown, during the Civil Wars and the Interregnum.

It now appeared, however, I had been mistaken and Thomas had not had the grace to acknowledge the king's benevolence, as here was evidence that the Crown had, in 1661, granted him the lease of a massive estate in Northumberland: NINE MILES in circumference!

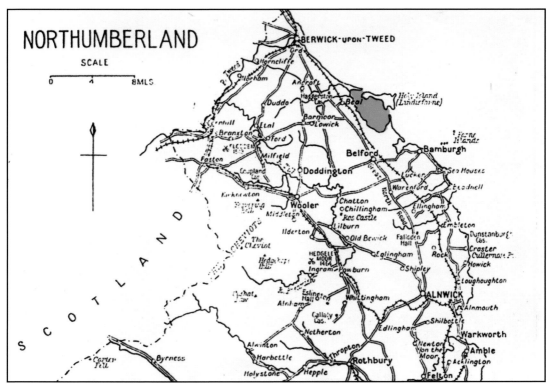

Holy Island showing the nine mile circular area 'left by the sea'.

But if Thomas had reaped the benefits from his 'just reward' for over forty years, what had become of his profits and how did he came to die in 'poverty'?

Could it be that his massive circular estate was just too good to be true? His 'estate', I was to discover, was not part of the normal rich fertile 'rolling' acres of Northumberland; in fact he could not husband his land with much confidence at the best of times, as it was not always available for cultivation! And he could not be sure that any labour and money invested in sowing crops such as barley and oats would, even with the most caring husbandry and best of weather, be rewarded with a profitable return.

The 'estate', so benevolently granted to our hero was, would you believe - under the sea! Not all the time you understand - just when the high-tide was in.

Having returned to England at the Restoration, Thomas told us in his own words 'with my old companion Loyalty and the usual companion of that Poverty' he was left to scramble for a living and decided one avenue open to him, was to search for any lands which could be claimed for the king, in the hope of obtaining a lease of the same for himself.

On 10 November, 1660, Captain Thomas Paulden petitioned the Crown for 'a grant of the overflowing oozy or sandy ground in or near to Holy Island, Co. Northumberland, estimated at 1,000 acres, at the fee farm rent of £20, per ann. 'in case he be able to effect the embaulkeing thereof'. 'I desire the Surveyor Generall to consider of this petition, and to advise what he conceives fitt to be done therein in respect of his Ma'ties service, and the petitioners undertakeing,' the Lord Treasurer, Southampton, recorded.

View of Holy Island from the castle showing the harbour and part of the sea covering Thomas' nine mile circular area of 'land'.

A view in the opposite direction showing the sandy oozy ground and Holy Island castle in the centre.

Even at this stage the Crown's surveyors were obviously very sceptical about the venture, but an enquiry was set up.

A Warrant from Treasurer Southampton was sent to the King's remembrancer for a commission of enquiry to be issued to Sir Robert Collingwood, Thomas Love, Richard Fincham, William Armories, John Wrenham, Bertram Orses, George Claverings and Marke Scott, to find out certain waste…lying by or near to Holy Island…to sort out the bounds…the acreage and yearly value…in what parish the same lies and what the charge of embanking same against the sea and the improvement thereof will be worth per ann.'

On 17 August, 1661, a 'Warrant was issued from Treasurer Southampton to the Surveyor General of Crown Lands for a constat and ratal, of the waste, oosy and sandy ground overflowed with the usual tides of the sea and lying in or near to Holy Island, containing by estimation 1,000 acres which yielding no benefit to the King, with a view to a lease thereof to Thomas Paulden for 31 years. Prefixing: (a) said Paulden's petition for same, as referred 1660, Oct 19, from the King. (b) Report dated July 25 thereon by the Surveyor General. By inquisition lately taken it is found that there are certain quantities of waste ground or sand lying between Holy Island called Sunck [Snook] and Tripping Chair east and northwards and a place called Lowford south and westwards, being between the high and low water mark of the sea, covered with salt water with the flowing of the sea and of so small value at present that the jurers could set no value thereon nor find in what parish same did lie; and they certify other parcels of waste and sandy ground there about 1,500 acres which cannot be enclosed from the sea nor valued by them at present. If the petitioner will undertake to embank the premises, giving the King a fourth part thereof, he will deserve the residue.'

It appears obvious from their report that the local landowners on the commission didn't consider reclaiming this area permanently from the sea a practical and therefore worthwhile proposition: their final poignant remark making this abundantly clear.

Holy Island castle by Susanne Postlethwaite.

Ten months later, however, on 21 September 1661, Treasurer Southampton issued a warrant to the Clerk of the Pipe, for a lease to Thomas Paulden of a piece of waste and sandy ground near Holy Island, Co. Northumberland, giving details of the 'premises'.

Having accepted the impractical (without massive investment and resources which he patently lacked) task of attempting to fortify his newly acquired estate against the sea, indeed in 1673 he claimed to have embanked 500 acres of it, he appears characteristically (like his hero Don Quixote) to have considered it a matter of honour to challenge the impossible.

Thomas's courageous but foolhardy (quixotic) character appears to be faithfully reflected in his vain actions regarding his forty three year unremitting yet hopeless battle of attrition to transform his 'reward' into a matter of pride, honour and success, worthy to enhance and reflect his previous heroic reputation for valour and loyalty to the Crown.

In January 1666, we have a letter written by Thomas from London to Sir Christopher Hatton (c1605-1670) of Kirby, Northamptonshire, in which he describes his wife as 'having given over all good fellowship and will scarce allow it in mee', and then both he and his wife **'But wee live together like Don Quixote & Sancho Panza the one still offending the other still pardoning...'.**

This makes it clear, not only that Thomas had read and was familiar with *Don Quixote* but also that he was, at least partly, aware of his own romantic delusions.

The high living of the Restoration period was beginning to fade for Thomas and his bride Rebecca; no doubt Thomas was spending money beyond his means like many in that era; a prime example being his master the Duke of Buckingham, and going further and further into debt to finance his dream of 'Holy Island' was perhaps the offence for which he was continually forced to crave his wife's pardon.

Despite the Crown Surveyor's pessimism, however, another soldier thought that Thomas' idea of reclamation from the sea might be worth pursuing and on 11 February, 1661/2, Col. Christopher Gardner petitioned for a grant 'of the fourth part of the same 1,500 acres. The colonel, however, failed in his petition and the fourth part of whatever land Thomas managed to reclaim from the sea (which the King had prematurely claimed) was granted elsewhere, as we shall see.

On 21 March, 1672/3, we read 'Treasurer Clifford's warrant to Sir C. Harbord, Surveyor General of Crown Lands, for a particular and ratal of certain salt marshes or sandy ground in or near to Holy Island in the Bishopric of Durham, containing about 1,500 acres, with a view to a fresh lease or surrender thereof to Thomas Paulden... granted to him 13 October, 1661, for 31 years, at [£10] 3s rent per ann...the embanking of the said land having further been prejudice or hindrance to the fishing of those parts.'

Despite the conflict of interests between keeping the sea out and fishing in the same large circular area; and fourteen years after his first petition, on 8 June, 1674, Treasurer Latimer issued a warrant to the Customs Commissioners for the Clerk of the Pipe to issue 'a new lease to Thomas Pauden [sic] of a parcel of waste between the mainland and Holy Island as leased to Thomas Paulden in 1661, one fourth part of what shall be recovered from the sea (which fourth part was by patent of 24 March 1662/3, granted to Martin Lister, gent. at £10 per ann. rent to the king, in trust for the said Thomas Paulden). The lessee to recover and embank the greater part thereof within seven years of the date of this lease.'

Not only was the Treasurer planning to get a return from 'profitless ground' he was laying down a time limit for improvements which would allow him to demand a higher rent!

Martin Lister may have been a relation of Christopher Lister, the previous owner of Holy Island and even a relative of Thomas Paulden himself, whose grandmother Alice nee' Firth, widow of Edward Bynnes, yeoman/gent. of Horbury (c1545-1599), had married in 1600, as her second husband, Mr Richard Lister, royalist vicar of Wakefield.

Without more detailed information we can only assume that Thomas's petition for an extension of his long lease, which was granted on 13 August, 1674, implies success or impending success, for his venture: at least to the satisfaction of the Treasury. This optimism appears to be confirmed when on 16 August, 1680, we find: 'Treasury Warrant to the Surveyor General of Crown Lands for a particular of certain waste and sandy grounds lying betwixt high and low water mark near Holy Island in the Bishopric of Durham, of which Capt. Thomas Paulden prays a fresh lease for 99 years on surrender of his present lease for 31 years granted 26 Charles I…Said former lease being on condition that petitioner should at his own cost embank and secure the same from the sea, he having by a commission of enquiry directed out of the Exchequer (14 May 1662) found the King's title thereof and the butts and bounds of the same, contain about 1,500 acres and having this last year embanked 500 acres thereof. Prays a grant for 99 years in view of his extensive charges and little liklihood of immediate profit (b) Reference dated 1679, Dec. 20. from the king to the Treasury Lords therein (c) Treasury Reference dated 1679/80 Feb 19, to the Surveyor General thereon (d) Report dated May 26 from William Harboard Surveyor General hereon.'

Twenty years of 'extensive charges'…'with little likelihood of immediate profit'! Yet operations going to plan - or so it would appear!

On 2 May 1681 'Treasury Warrant to the Clerk of the Pipe for a lease to Capt. Thomas Paulden of a parcel of waste…about 1,000 acres all for 99 years from Lady Day last at yearly rent of £10 3s 0d, all of the said present grant of the same to Thomas Paulden, gent. dated 1674, Aug. 17. And without fine in consideration of the loyalty and signal services of the said Thomas Paulden to the late King and of the great charge he has and must incur in enclosing, recovering, securing and preserving the premises from time to time. With memo. dated Jan 24, 1681, giving derails of the premises and stating that 'The lessee to covenant to do his best endeavour from time to time to embank, enclose, secure and defend the premises from the sea at his own cost and to preserve the walls, banks and fences thereof already made, and every seven years to deliver a Terrier or particular of the lands gained by such embankings.'

So, after twenty long years of work and investment and the successful re-grant of his lease for a further ninety nine years, Thomas must then, with this new security, have been well set to enjoy the benefits which his long-term vision deserved. He wouldn't have applied for this new long-term lease without achieving or having great hopes of achieving success; his dream of governing his own 'island', nine miles in circumference must have seemed within his grasp.

A further twenty two years on, however, on 24 June 1703, we find Captain Thomas Paulden in receipt of a pension of £50 per annum from the Crown for his eminent service in taking Pontefract Castle in 1648, (its seems likely that he had been receiving this since the Restoration) and at a meeting at St. James Palace on 16 July, 1703, when Her Majesty Queen Anne, Lord Treasurer and the Chancellor of the Exchequer heard Thomas' petition read, this annual sum was confirmed and they ordered his name to be added to Mr. Nicholas's list of the Queen's 'pentioners'.

Alas poor Thomas enjoyed his pension for but a very short period after this, as we learn from the Treasury minutes: 'June 10, 1706, Windsor Castle. Present: The Queen, Lord Treasurer, Chancellor of the Exchequer. The widow of Capt. Thomas Paulden prays the continuance of a pension of £50 per ann., which her husband enjoyed from the hands of Mr. Nicholas. Recommended by the Duke of Leeds. Half of it is to be continued.'

This was not as straight forward as it appears as we learn from the full text of the letter from Thomas Osborne, Duke of Leeds; dated May 21st 1706, endorsed:

D: Leeds in behalfe of Widdo[w] Paulden: and addressed to:

For The Rt. Hono'ble the L'd Godolphin Lord High=Treasurer of England.

My L'd

It is with some uneasiness that I trouble your Lord'p with anything of this kind, but the service of Capt. Paulden was so Emminent in the takeing of Pontefract Castle that he had a Constant Pension of £50 P. Annu. for his life, and his Widdow who is near eighty years of Age will starve without the continuance of Her Maj'ties Charity. The Arch=Bpp of Yorke,[1] did move Her Maj'tie for this bounty when Her Husband was Dyeing, and Her Maj'ties Answer was, that Her Husband was not dead and till then shee would give no answer to it, but Hee being now dead, it will be an high Act of Charity in yo'r Lord'p to remind her Maj'tie of it, and I have presumed to inclose Her Petition to yo'r Lord'p for w'ch I hope to have yo'r pardon, who am.

My L'd   Yo'r Lord'p' most obd't & most humble serv't.   LEEDS:

It must have been gratifying for Rebecca to know that both she and her husband had not been altogether forgotten by the high and mighty: at 48p a week she would be just a little better off than today's pensioners.

£25 a year, however, was very modest when compared with 'Lady Arlington, £1,000 a year' and 'Countess of Thanet £300 a year'. Indeed little more than the curious and incidental 'The Spaniard: give him £20 to go into Spain'; all who appear with the Earl of Abingdon, Countess of Anglesey, Earl of Westmorland, Duchess of Buccleugh, the poor ministers of the Isle of Man and many others in the lists of the Queen Anne's pensioners for the year 1706.

In an entry for 15 August 1712, we learn a little more about Rebecca's dire situation: 'Treasury reference to the Surveyor General on petition of Mr Paulden showing that in 1688 the Crown granted to Capt. Paulden a lease for 99 years of the Holy Island (now under water) [!!] situate in the county of Northumberland and joining to the borders of Scotland, 12 miles of this side of Berwick; between the island and the continent [mainland] is a piece of land about 2 miles in breadth towards the middle and about 5 miles in length, a rich soil and capable of rich improvements, especially for fishery[!!] in the Queen's dominions, Capt. Paulden is dead and Rebecca his widow now enjoys it and is willing to dispose of it: the Dutch would buy it, but she had much rather the Queen should have the refuse of it. Surveyor General to consider and report his opinion.'

Well! Do we respect Rebecca's generosity in considering her sovereign's welfare before her own? Or should we applaud her salesman like gambit?

Much as I would like to think it was the former: to continue to uphold the tradition of her husband's undoubted selfless loyalty to the Crown, I'm forced by the facts to accept the latter alternative as by far the more likely of the two.

The next entry reveals the sad truth and the unfortunate outcome of Captain Paulden's quixotic (courageous yet hopeless) endeavour to make his 'island' venture a success worthy to reflect his previous heroic exploits. What appeared obvious from the start to almost everyone else concerned, that it was a hopeless objective, must ultimately have been proved true to Thomas - but only after over forty years of struggle:

On December 19, 1716, ' …a petition of Rebecca, widow, showing that Charles II granted to her late husband, Thomas Paulden, for the Terme of 99 years parcel of a waste sandy ground containing 1,500 acres "known by the name of Holy Island, lying between the County of Northumberland and Durham under the rent of £10 per ann. to the Crown. That all the industry which has been used can't keep out the water from the said land and never any benefit having yet arisen to the petitioner or her said Husband from the said Grant, but on the Contrary, **they have been ruined, by the attempts to which they have made to drain the premises:** therefore praying that the rent may be remitted. Hugh Chomley his Ma'ts Surv'r General to Report a true state and value of the premises with his opinion.'

If Thomas Paulden had paid an average rent of £10 per ann. for his lease since it was first granted to him in 1661, which appears to be the case; then he had expended an absolute fortune of £550, without a penny in return from his 'investment'!

And further, the 'great costs and charges incurred' in labour and resources which must have been required to successfully embank 500 acres by 1674; and the costs of his constant attempts to reclaim and secure all the rest of the vast area during that long period of time would appear to be incredible. We cannot doubt that the failed venture had ruined them: what is much more difficult to comprehend is how, and why, he and then his widow, had managed to carry on their vain and frustrated attempts and hopes for so long without any apparent rewards whatever, during fifty five years of struggle!!

Thomas, having accepted the challenge of reclaiming his 'Holy Island' from the sea, could not voluntarily give up, as a matter of honour, his struggle to vindicate his dream; but one cannot help thinking how he must have longed for release from his 'slough of

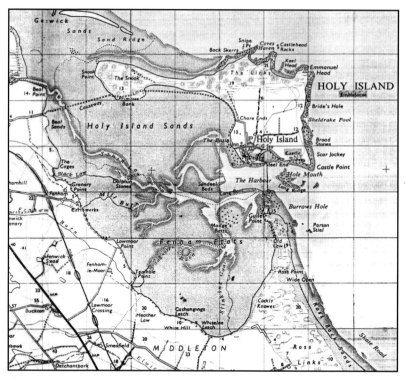

'A parcel of waste sandy and derelict land lying between the continent of Northumberland and Holy Island. Name of lessee, Thomas Paulden, Esq. Date of last lease, 1681. Term granted, ninety-nine years from Lady-day 1681. Expiation, 5 April 1780. Yearly value, per last survey, uncertain. Fine paid for last lease, —. Old rent, £10 3s. Increased rent, __.'

despond', which never ending battle must have driven him to despair and seemed far more arduous than defending Pontefract castle with sword and musket.

The last Paulden entry I have discovered in the Treasury Papers is dated 21 October 1718; when Rebecca, who would then be at least 92 years of age, was still attempting to sell the remainder of her lease (61 years remaining) of 'Holy Island' to the Crown

The harsh facts of the situation are revealed by an entry in Account of Crown Manors, &c published in 1787:

Despite all the efforts, time and money 'invested' by Thomas during forty-three years, in his 'reward for signal services to his sovereign' the end results were worthless! If the Dutch were interested in buying it, they never came forward with the cash and neither Queen Anne nor any of her successors considered Rebecca's 'generosity' nor the Dutch enthusiasm to buy, sufficient incentive to make the purchase themselves. Why should they? One might ask, when at the end of the lease 'the large piece of land of rich soil and capable of rich improvement' reverted to them for nothing.

If Thomas Paulden was with Sir Marmaduke Langdale, his royalist commander throughout most of the Civil War, when he unsuccessfully solicited Captain Batton, governor of the fort on Holy Island to surrender it to the King and later captured Berwick in May 1648, then Thomas must have seen Holy Island and the area surrounding, when they camped at nearby Haggerston House, which was to dominate the last two thirds of his life: indeed it may have been this visit to the Northumbrian coast and its beautiful environs which precipitated his later petition for the lease of the tidal waste, between Holy Island and the mainland.

As we know Thomas had travelled widely and often on the Continent when serving as a royalist secret agent during the Interregnum and he must have been greatly impressed by the schemes undertaken by the Dutch, which had enabled them to reclaim massive areas of land from the North Sea, and these successful polders (did Thomas think of them as pauldens!) had now realised thousands of acres of rich farm land for the speculators.

After the initial excitement of discovering Thomas' grant 'of land in or near to Holy Island' it was some time before I finally realised that no part of the island called Lindisfarne, (more commonly known as Holy Island owing to it being the home of St Aidan and St. Cuthbert and thus being the holiest place in England) was included in the area covered by Thomas's lease; his 'island' was the circular tidal area, nine miles in circumference, <u>between</u> Holy Island and the mainland of Northumberland.

I was also confused at first by the area being described as, in county Durham: surely that county was fifty miles away! And how could this be when Holy Island was patently in Northumberland - and it couldn't be in two counties at the same time could it?

But in fact it was. The answer lies in the fact that Lindisfarne, as the patrimony of St. Cuthbert, together with much of the adjacent mainland was originally completely owned by the Norman bishops of Durham: and the area became known as North Durham or Islandshire and was described as being in Northumberland and the Bishopric of Durham.

It was ten years after James I ascended the throne of England and created a crown lease of the royalties of Norham and Islandshire in 1613, (despite the existence of a bishop's lease), that the Bishop of Durham lost control of the Island.

In 1656 the lease of Holy Island proper was in the possession of Christopher Lister of Warcop, Cumberland, late of London, Esq.; but he was in dispute with Mr. William Currer, of the City of London, gent. who won a suit against him for debts of £1,000 and £400. (I can't help wondering if it just coincidence that both these men were descended from families long resident in the Craven district of W.R. Yorkshire).

Daniel Collingwood of Brunton, Northumberland, Esq. appears to have become one of Lister's creditors and in this way he gained an interest in Holy Island. Charles II was another of Lister's [he had been a farmer of the Excise for Cumberland and Westmorland during the Interregnum] creditors and on 12 July, 1662, we learn from an enquiry by Mr. Anthony Pearson on behalf of the Bishop of Durham 'it is reported his Maj'tie hath seized on Holly Island, for a debt owing by Mr. Christopher Lister.' And on 24 Dec.1664, Mr. Pearson reports again for the Bishop 'I fear all my Lord's right at Holy Island is conveyed away' ending with this prophetic remark: 'There is a marsh of severall thousand acres, overflowen att all spring tides, is possible to be preserved, but it will be att great charge if ever done.'

On 11 July, 1670, Mr Collingwood was called to a meeting of the Treasury Board to discuss the value and title of Holy Island 'his Majesty [Charles II] having signified his pleasure to my lords that he will buy the royalty of the island in regard to the harbour.'

On 7 November, 1670, Sir George Downing wrote to Sir C. Harbord 'to hasten his report about the business of Holy Island,' And on '10 February 1671/2, Sir George Downing wrote to the Attorney General: his Majesty having some intention of purchasing Holy Island for a fishery and a port, concerning which some propositions are made to his majesty by Mr Daniel Collingwood, my Lords desire you will enquire into the title of it and report thereon.'

On 10th February 1671, Col. Daniel Collingwood recommended to Charles II, 'the ideal suitability of the area, nine miles in circumference, between Holy Island and the mainland, to be exploited as a fishery.'

Can we believe that the king was persuaded by Col. Collingwood to join him in establishing a fishery and a port in the very same nine miles circular area, which Thomas Paulden had been granted and was endeavouring to embank from the sea? It certainly appears so: with obvious serious implications for our hero's drainage/embanking scheme.

On 8 February, 1671/2, Mr Christopher Lister was paid £1,050 'in satisfaction of the purchasing of his right and estate in Holy Island and for the purchase of the right and estate of other proprietors of the said island, according to certain conveyances thereof to the King, as lately prepared by the Attorney General.'

Soon afterwards on 13 April, 1672, appears:- 'Royal Sign Manual to the Attorney General a bill for the Great Seal for the demise to Daniel Collingwood of all that island commonly called Holy Island, in the County of Northumberland and Bishopric of Durham, and of all the tithes of corn and grain, hay, flax, hemp, lambswool and fish, and all other tithes, great and small in the said island, as also of all waters, fisheries, pools, liberties and privilages of fishing and all other rights, jurisdictions and priviliges to the said island belonging in as large and ample manner as the said island and premises were granted unto us by Christopher Lister Esq., all for 31 years from Lady Day last, at the yearly rent of £1 6s 8d: but with an exception to the King of the whole use and benefit of the port, haven and castle and power of enlarging and fortifying same, but with a grant nevertheless of keeping said castle for the King's use: and with a further exception of all lands deserted by the sea accruing and adjoining to the island.'

So Daniel Collingwood, Esq; became owner (leaseholder) and master of Holy Island, at a nominal rent, owing to the fact that he was at the same time granted, and expected to uphold, the office of Governor and keeper of the castle and its troop of soldiers; which he had to maintain against all enemies for the King.

Details of money being invested prove that Collingwood's command was certainly of consequence: Treasurer Danby, over a short period of just two years (1675-77), ordered several payments totalling '£649 14s, to be paid by the Customs Cashier of Newcastle to Major Daniel Collingwood, Governor of Holy Island, upon account for building the new fort there called Osborn's fort, and other fortifications in the said island.' And on 24th December, 1679, 'Daniel Collingwood, Esq., to be loaned £1,000 from Mr. Kent; by order of the King, (to be repaid in portions).'

Osborn's fort, named after the Earl of Danby, overlooked the harbour close to the castle, which haven for shipping the King obviously considered of great importance and one worthy of suitable protection. Ships of the Royal Navy had to be able to find safe anchorage there and Holy Island together with the north-east coast of England had to be guarded against attacks from Dutch privateers and ships of the French fleet, who were both active at that time.

The garrison did receive separate payments as we see from an entry dated Sept 9, 1672: 'to a company in Holy Island £88.'

The next entry, however, makes it clear that Col. Collingwood was not in sole command of Holy Island, being answerable to the governor of Berwick:

On July 28, 1675, we find:- 'Attorney General warrant to the Clerk of the Signet for £1,233 9s 9d to Lord Widderington without account being due to him as well as for several fees salaries and entertainments as captain of the two forts within Holy Island and Farne Islands Co. Durham as Governor of the said town and castle of Berwick from 1672, Sept. 29, to 1673-4 Mar 7, at the rate of £859 4s 2d per ann including £200 due to him from her Majesty's government for better appointment of his barony whilst Governor of the town and castle of Berwick.'

Governor Collingwood, when not mustering his garrison, must have had time to reflect on other matters besides defending the harbour of Holy Island. It will be remembered that his lease included 'all tithes - of fish - as also of all waters, fisheries, pools liberties and jurisdictions of fishing and all other rights, jurisdictions and privilages' **but with several exceptions including one which must have been of vital importance to Captain Thomas Paulden: 'all lands deserted by the sea accruing and adjoining to the island.'**

A vital question must have been, did Thomas Paulden's lease give him the right to keep the sea out 'permanently' from 'all those lands deserted (during normal low tide) by the sea'? So excluding and destroying the area and resource for Daniel Collingwood to create a fishery?

At the Restoration, Charles II and his ministers, considering all ways of raising revenue to support his administration, decided to establish The Royal Fishery Company of England and grant it a patent under the great seal, on 22 August, 1661, to help develop the industry. Several brief entries during the following twelve months indicate some of its plans:-

'July 29,1662, Royal Fishery Company to build 10 busses.' [type of fishing factory transport vessel]. And soon after: 'Estimate for building 10 busses, to be made.'

'Sept 2, 1662, Report on 10 busses of 10 tons each will cost £9,000 says the Masters of Trinity House - Committee of Fishing.'

Thirteen years later, after what we can only conjecture were years spent unsuccessfully attempting to build or buy suitable fishing vessels in England, we find:- 'Jan 3,1675/6. Warrant from Treasurer Danby to Customs Commissioners to register and enter as free ships the four vessels Holy Island, Experiment, Speedwell, and Success, bought in Holland by the undertakers for erecting a fishery in Holy Island, notwithstanding they may be sailed by foreigners and without the three fourths English mariners.

'9 June, 1676, Letters to [be written] to the Customs Commissioners concerning their report about the patent for the fishing [and requesting same] to be hastened. [in margin]: 'Done.'

The patent of 22 August 1661, had not, however, been put into execution and was revoked sixteen years later when, on 25 September, 1677, the Company was granted a Charter of Incorporation and we read:

'Considering the great plenty of fish in the waters of these kingdoms and the breeding of seamen, advancement of trade, manufactures and employment, etc., if the fishery trade were effectively prosecuted in this kingdom: and notwithstanding sundry designs and attempts have heretofore been made and set on foot and very great sums of money raised for the carrying on the said trade here in England, the same have hitherto failed and proved ineffectual until the Duke of York and others hereinafter named being willing to promote so good a work have for three years past maugre [overcome] all the difficulties and discouragements they have met with, undertaken and managed the said fishing trade with some effect: who finding by experience that if they were incorporated they should be thereby much better enabled and capable to prosecute the same, and have therefore prayed incorporation by the name of the Company of the Royal Fishery of England: these presents therefore incorporate said Duke of York (as Governor). Treasurer Danby, James Duke of Monmouth, James Earl of Suffolk, [and dozens of the nobility of England and officers of State then a score of knights and gentlemen who included: Daniel Collingwood, George Collingwood, Sir Antho. Deane, one of the Commissioners of the Navy and Samuel Pepys] to be one body politic and corporate, by the name of the Royal Fishery of England: with power to hold lands to the value of £1,000 per ann. - with a common seal - [&c &c &c] (Daniel Collingwood to be one of a committee of twelve) - with power to build, rig, and set out to sea so many doggers, busses and other fishing vessels as the General Court think fit, and to fish in all the coasts, etc. of England, Scotland, Ireland whereof the fishings are not already granted or appropriated, and in and upon the main, to carry their fish and fish oil to all ports of England and beyond the seas and sell same there: power to erect storehouses, graneries, warehouses, waterhouses and workhouses, wharves and docks on any Crown waste or common, or on any public rivers or seas in the King's dominions: the crews of their vessels, as well as foreigners as natives, not to be empanelled during their service: the King grants a yearly sum of £20 for each dogger, which they now have or possess or within seven years hereof shall build; viz., for and during so much of the said seven years as the said doggers shall be employed in the said fishing and no longer: same to be paid quarterly out of the Customs of London port: to enjoy all privilages in the City of London which any company of merchants do or may enjoy.'

Soon afterwards a Treasury warrant was sent to the Customs cashier to pay to the company of the Royal Fishery of England, £35 for last Lady day quarter, for what is due to them on the yearly sum of £20 for each of the doggers they were owners of in accordance with the patent of 1677, 25 Sept, certified by George Elton, Surveyor of the Navigation Act, that there are now seven doggers belonging to and employed by the said Company, viz., The King's Fishery, Success, Experiment, Frogg, Speedwell, Holy Island and Adventure, which certificate is sworn to by Robert Cragg, Husband of the said Company.

With four out of seven of these vessels being those bought by the undertakers of the 'Fishery of Holy Island' one cannot escape the impression that they formed a major part of the Royal Fishery of England.

Several entries giving details of payment show both fishing and subsidy to be in operation:

£60 was paid to the Company for the Spring and Christmas quarters of 1679, when six doggers were employed by them, and £60 was paid to the company 'for half a year' on 29 September, 1681, as appears by the certificate of George Elton, Surveyor of the Navigation Act and by the oath of Benjamin Watson, 'now husband of the said Company'.

Foreign fishing vessels, very much like today, must have been working the system and obtaining fraudulent passes to enable them to avoid paying excise duty on their catches. Stricter laws were therefore made governing the procurement of legal passes:-

'On 10 March, 1676, Entry of the King in Council dated Whitehall, approving and requiring the enforcement of regulations concerning the obtaining of sea passes: all as follows. In pursuance of an order [of Council] of the 8th inst. the Admiralty Lords did this day report to the King in Council the following rules prepared by the Committee on [the Privy] Council for trade for preventing the fraudulent procuring of passes: the said rules being as calendared S.P. Dom. 1676, pp. 9-10. Rule 6 has a marginal note as follows: Memorandum; that the four fisher boats [for Holy Island Fishery] lately made free are to be excepted. The rules are followed by the following forms in blank:

(1) Shipmaster's bond for the return of the pass.
(2) Oath of master of a foreign built ship that is made free, belongs to subjects of the King, has no other name and has no other pass, or if it has, what has become of it.
(3) Navigation Act officer's certificate (a) for London port, (b) for the outports, as to the navigation of said ship according to the Navigation Act and of its freedom.
(4) Oath of master of an English built ship that it belongs to the King's subjects, has no other name, and has no other pass &c.
(5) Navigation Act officer's certificate (a) and (b) ut supra [as above] in the case of such English built ship.
(6) Oath of master of a foreign built ship not made free (whether bought before or since 1 Jan., 1673/4) that it has been bought by and belongs wholly to subjects of the King, has no other name, and has no other pass &c. ut supra.
(7) Navigation Act officer's certificate (a) and (b) ut supra in the case of such foreign built unfree ships.
(8) Oath of proprietors of a foreign built ship bought since 1 Jan., 1673/4, and not made free, that none but the King's subjects have share therein.

Appending: A note dated Mar.11. In obedience to his Majesty's order in Council of the 10th inst. Sir George Downing and Sir Robert Southwell [?are requested by Treasurer Danby to] agree upon the size of parchment upon which the passes are to be printed. Memorandum: And the forms of the said passes are the same which are directed by the respective treaties with Spain and the United Provinces &c. Followed by: entry of a warrant for Treasurer Danby to the Customs Commissioners dated Newmarket, 1676, April 7, requiring them to observe and to cause to be observed the aforesaid rules and forms of certificates, oathes and bonds, as approved by the King in Council: all for the preventing fraudulent procuring of passes pursuant to the treaties with Spain, the United Provinces and all others (except those with Algiers, Tripoli and Tunis).'

The next entry gives us more details of one of the vessels:

'Jan 15, 1674/5. Treasurer Danby's subscription for the execution of a royal warrant, prefixed in detail, dated 1674 Dec 24, for naturalizing (for the encouragement of the fishing trade) the ship called "Speedwell", of Holy Island, 50 tons burden, Roger Newton master, purchased in Holland by Daniel Collingwood and others as proper for the fishing trade in Holy Island.'

And six months later on July 7, 1675, four more vessels, belonging to the Holy Island Fishery, are made free of customs:-

'Warrant from Treasurer Danby to Custom Commissioners. By Order of Council of Mar 31 last, the King has, on petition of the undertakers for erecting a fishery in Holy Island, therein ordered 4 dogger boats to be naturalized and made free, same having been bought lately in Holland by the said petitioners. You are to so register the said boats as free ships of this kingdom, taking care that they are not to be otherwise employed than in the trade of fishing aforesaid.'

All appears to be going well with the fishery; but just a few years later and we learn, after much interesting information about the history and the ownership of Holy Island, that success had turned to failure:-

'On 11 June, 1692, Treasury warrant was sent to Deputy Surveyor of Crown Lands for a particular of the island of Holy Island with a view to an extension of lease therein to Mistress Barbara Collingwood for 20 years at 26s 8d per ann. and fine of £150. Pre-fixing: report by William Taylor, Deputy Surveyor General, on said Collingwood's petition for same. The island was petitioned for in April, 1672, by Mr Daniel Collingwood and thereon Sir Charles Harbord, then Surveyor General of Crown Lands, reported that it was granted out of the Crown by James I to the Earl of Dunbar, from whom it descended to the late Earl of Suffolk (by his mother's right as daughter to the said Earl of Dunbar), who sold it long since to Sir John Brook, afterwards Lord Cobham, for about £600; and Charles II was induced to re-purchase it (at what price appears not) for a fish-ery, for which it was reported to be extraordinarily suited; that it had been certified in 1670 by Mr Daniel Collingwood and others to be almost circular, about nine miles in circumference, containing the best and safest port in the North, having a depth at low water of 2.5 fathoms or more and 5 at full water, the haven capable of receiving a hun-dred sail of ships, and with the expense of £200, might be enlarged to hold as many more, with an old town and castle situate on the south-west part, nigh the harbour, and consisting of a manor and about 50 or 60 freeholders, the revenue being then £50 per an. The lease to Collingwood is dated 1672, May 20, for 31 years at £1 6s 8d rent, and contains the whole island with all tithes, houses, mills etc. wreck etc. tolls, customs, anchorage etc. as amply as granted to the King by Christopher Lister, except the use of the port haven and castle, with power to enlarge and fortify same and all derelict and accressed lands: which exceptions aught to be continued in a new grant.'

'Daniel Collingwood is long since dead and did not assign in his lifetime. In 1685 Ralph Milburne petitioned for a reversion, alleging the consent of George Collingwood, brother and administrator to Daniel, and since dead. The present petitioner alleges that her said brother designed the premises for her and her sisters with whom she is agreed. No improvement was made of this island in Daniel Collingwood's time, "as he thought it capable of," nor was any fishery established. The Governor takes £4 per ann. out of the profits, which sum he claims for the anchorage. The chief profit arises out of the [rabbit] warren, which is lately destroyed by the soldiers, and the place very poor. A fine of £150 is therefore sufficient for the new lease.' A new lease was finalised 28 Nov 1692.

No fishery established! What had happened to the Holy Island Fishery and its vessels especially bought in Holland by the undertakers for that very purpose? They had been granted privileged freedom from customs and the law demanding four-fifths English crews, by King Charles II, for the trade's benefit. The King had also granted £20 per ann. per dogger subsidy, which was being paid regularly during 1677-1684, especially to encourage their fishing enterprise.

'No fishery established' appears to mean that the Holy Island Fishery failed to survive the end of the seven year subsidy period: perhaps it couldn't be made to pay on its own or maybe the death of its enthusiastic creator, Col. Daniel Collingwood in 1680, left it without a guiding light. Eight years later in 1692, when Mistress Barbara Collingwood was applying for an extension to her lease, it had almost been forgotten.

Charles II died in 1685 and his brother James, the Royal Fishery Company's governor, became king; his reign, however, was cut short by the glorious revolution of 1688, which was brought about mainly by his own ineptitude and his Catholic proclivities. The loss of its influential governor must have been a serious and perhaps fatal blow to the Company.

When Captain Thomas Paulden applied to extend the lease of his 'island' of 'land' nine miles in circumference between Holy Island and the mainland of Northumberland, on 21 March 1672/3, it was granted notwithstanding the highly significant remark that 'the embanking of the said land having further been prejudice or hindrance to the fishing of those parts'!

This is the only time that the apparently diametrically opposed objectives, of fishing, and embanking the same area against the sea, appears to have risen to the surface (forgive the pun). Did Thomas's rights through his lease take precedence over those of the Holy Island Fishery, as would appear to be the case with his extension of lease being granted, despite the said 'prejudice and hindrance to fishing of those parts' and was he partly or even wholly, responsible for the demise of their enterprise?

The Royal Fishery of England was nevertheless still fighting to maintain its rights as we see from the following entry:

On 2 November, 1687, the Custom Commissioners had received a petition from the Company of Fishermen, 'shewing that by his Majesty's charter they are empowered to seize all fish taken on the coasts of England which are exported and all prohibited fish imports: that they are informed that several fishmongers are endeavouring to obtain a licence to import prohibited fish beyond what is already granted, to the great damage to the English market: therefore pray "if such licence be though fit to be granted that the petitioner or some of them may be authorised to be the importers, [they] having vessels built for that purpose."

On '13 April, 1696, the Treasury ordered the Customs commissioners to observe that such ships and vessels as are designed for the [Holy] Island Fishery be permitted to proceed, notwithstanding embargo. Which 'embargo' appears to be against foreign fishing vessels and foreign crews:

'4 January, 1697, Duty as for foreign fish - foreign fishing prohibition by Act of 5 Eliz. [1563/4] - must be in English ship.' [with four fifths English crews]. Was it the Dutch ships and their foreign crews which, without having their special licence continually renewed, proved the fatal flaw in the make-up of the Holy Island Fishery?

Our next entry appears to confirm the submission that fishing without subsidy just wasn't economic - on this occasion they were endeavouring to evade salt duty to make the industry pay:

A petition from the Royal Fishery of England, was sent to the Treasury on 7 August, 1701, shewing that under the salt and re-export provisions of the Act of 5 & 6 Wm. & Mary, fishermen had their salt for several years free from duty, those that practised the cod fishery entered their salt at either for the North Seas, Iceland or for Dram or other port and spent [some] upon the fish and then the master of the fishing boat made oath that such salt was not re-landed: and that the petitioners "not forseeing another construction would be made of the said provision, fitted out three doggers in May 1700 for cod to the North Seas which loaded 33 tons of salt at Newcastle and gave securities in £220 for not re-importing the salt: which doggers brought home 93 hundred 16 couple of Cod to London, which only produced £286 10s 0d although the charge for fitting out and the prime cost of the salt came to £348" And now their affidavit of non-import is refused by the Excise officers: therefore shewing that they cannot prosecute their trade without loss if the Duty must be paid.

Another petition of 20 May 1702, from budding entrepreneur James Mackburny however, showed that being employed in the Royal Fishery of England he had discovered several fraudulent practices in the exportation of salt and fish at the time of the drawing up of the Bill for preventing frauds on Salt Duty and he prayed to be made Secretary of the Commission [if one is set up] for managing the Salt Revenue.

After this time references to both the Holy Island fishery and the Royal Fishery of England disappear altogether from the Treasury Papers, giving the distinct impression that they had both ceased to exist but the garrisons of Berwick and Holy Island, being paid £9 10d and 10s 6d a week, respectively, on 12 July 1699, shows that the island was still of military importance. On 8 February, 1714, there is a reference to 'Chaplain and Town Major of the garrison of Berwick, also gunners of the castle in Holy Island - gunns reduced upon the last establishment of 1713 as in A.D. 1700 after the peace of Ryswick.' (Peace treaty with France after years of continuous warfare).

Thomas, who was apparently still throwing good money after bad in his 'Holy Island' dream, must have been desperate for cash when on 24 October, 1685, he successfully petitioned for the 'office of a coal metre, London port', despite being in competition with Sir Hugh Middleton, who applied for the same post.

A few years later in February, 1691, Thomas was writing to Christopher Hatton, Esq. (son and heir of Sir Christopher) desperately asking to be taken into his service, not as a paid servant but to secure his patronage, which would enable him to escape his creditors and a debtors' prison; though he claims to be owed more than he owes and can gain employment at £100 a year, if he has his freedom, which will soon allow him to clear his debts.

Thomas obviously required a new patron to replace his late deceased master the Duke of Buckingham and perhaps it was the Customs & Excise service which he saw as his salvation regarding 'employment at £100 a year' when on 27 December, 1698, he was granted, either promotion or a further position: having apparently escaped imprisonment; when the Treasury directed the Customs Commissioners to employ Tho Pawlin, [sic] (formerly of the Coal Duty and later a deputy King's waiter London port) as a landwaiter, in place of Henry Keats deceased.

Col. Daniel Collingwood, died intestate in 1680, in possession of a 31 year lease of Holy Island which expired on 25 March, 1703 and on 23 December 1702, his son and heir Francis petitioned for a new lease, when he was a captain (on half pay) in Col. Edward Fox's Foot Regiment. George Collingwood, Daniel's brother, however, had inherited the lease, and he enjoyed it for thirty five years, along with his manors of Eslington, Whittington and Barton, before losing all his estates and his head, through deciding to support the Old Pretender and the rebels against George I. He was captured at Preston along with hundreds of other Jacobites and was one of five ordered to be executed at Liverpool.[2]

After George's death his sisters, Barbara, Elizabeth and Ann petitioned Surveyor of Crown Lands for a new lease on July 2, 1716, 'praying that in regard of the great long and faithful services of their father brother & nephew the said Barbara may have an additional term in the manner & royalties of Holy Island.'

Further petitions reveal more interesting details about several other claimants and their connections with Holy Island:-

On 16 July, 1716, the petition of Hayford Wainwright & Elizabeth his wife stated that Anne and in a later petition of Nov 20, 1716, Barbara Collingwood, had falsely obtained a renewal of the lease of Holy Island, whereas they, as mortgagees of Francis Collingwood, had the sole right of renewing same.

A further petition of April 5, 1717, by Francis, Jeremy & Phillip Peck, reveals several important aspects of the recent history, condition and situation of Holy Island at that point in time. It stated that a lease of Holy Island, was granted to Daniel Collingwood (under a small reserved rent to encourage improvement of the said island, instead of which the said Collingwood & his successors mortgaged the lease to Thomas Benloe, whose successor now enjoys it but never improved it; and the lease having expired Barbara Collingwood is endeavouring to get it renewed and is hawking about town for a purchaser to buy it, by which practice the said island will be ruined instead of improved if granted to the mortgagee of Collingwood. 'Therefore, petitioners pray a reversionary lease and they will undertake to improve the said island for his Majesty's service and the good of the inhabitants.'

On 20 July, 1717, The Treasury were considering granting a new lease of Holy Island to Barbara Collingwood, spinster, for 24 years from 1723 Lady Day at the old yearly rent of £1 6s 8d per ann. and a fine of £230. In 1692 the said Barbara had obtained a grant for 20 years from 1703 Lady Day at £1 6s 8d rent per ann. of the Holy Island with all appurtenances as above except the benefit of the port, haven and castle within the said castle and all land deserted by the sea. The said Barbara, the immediate tenant, mortgaged the premises for £250 to William Foster whose right to the mortgage is now vested in Hayford Wainwright and Elizabeth his wife with a proviso of redemption. The said Barbara about seven or eight years ago filed her bill in the exchequer against the mortgagee to compel a redemption and obtained an order for this. The Treasury agreed a new lease at £10 per an. for the reserved rent and other expenses, with a fine of £230. The petitioner is the immediate tenant, but the premises are also petitioned for by the said Hayford Wainwright and Elizabeth his wife, the present mortgagees.

The petition for the lease of Holy Island from another party, Henry Liddle Bart., on 26 March 1718, declared that Barbara Collingwood was about a year ago granted a further lease paying a fine of £230, but she cannot raise the money. The Surveyor proposes that if lease not completed in limited time, lease should pass to petitioner.

To complicate the issue further, on 14 Aril, 1718, we find General Macartney, Governor of Berwick, claiming that the Royalties and profits of Holy Island were formerly invested in the Governor of Berwick, but King Charles II granted the lease for a term to the widow and children of one Collingwood, who obtained a further grant. The term having near expired they are making application for another grant. The general prays on behalf of himself and subsequent governors to be heard thereon.

24 August, 1721, Order in Council on the petition of Barbara and Elizabeth Collingwood lease not renewed, and praying to be heard by Counsel "whereby they will discover a great scene of injustice done them". They state that the Surveyor General had put a new covenant into the proposed lease viz. that at their proper costs and charges, they were, " to erect and build a good and sufficient sea banks and sea walls in such convenient places as are necessary to preserve the said island, of any part being overflowed by the sea", and which they conceived was only designed to hinder them having a new lease. The Auditor certified that they had forfeited penalties of £29,838 15s[?] for non payment of rent, although they had duly paid the same (to Mr Douglas, the Crown Receiver, who had neglected to pay it into the Exchequer, 9 April 1718).

It was stated that all parties were to be heard after the surveyor made his report but strangely no interconnecting reference to Rebecca, who was, at the same time, 21 Oct 1718, still attempting to sell her lease of 'Holy Island', well 'all the lands left by the sea' there, to the Crown.

All the various merits of these contesting petitions were laid aside however, when on February 27, 1729/30, the new king, George II decided to grant a new lease of Holy Island to Col. George Middleton, and ten years later Middleton petitioned for an extension of his lease. 'with all tithes great and small, liberty of fishing, coney warren, and all other lands &c, rents, services, fines, profits of courts and other royalties to the said island belonging, except the benefit of port, Haven and castle, and excepting further all land left by the sea.

A Report of 1 October, 1715, from the Customs to the Treasury relates to seizure by their Riding officer of the ship "Mary", the master of which, Lancelot Errington, had surprised and taken possession of the castle of Holy Island. The riding officer apprehended that Errington (who had for several years been a common smuggler) might have brought stores for the Jacobite rebels then at Wooller; he (the surveyor) came to the island the next day, with about twenty soldiers, and retook the castle.

Capt. Phillips, no doubt one of the officers involved, alleged that the customs house officers had cleared that vessel, reporting her as containing nothing but salt bound for Norway, whereas on seizure a considerable quantity of brandy and other goods was found on board.

Thereafter a dispute arose over who, having made the first seizure, could claim the brandy, and on June 21, 1718, Treasury Minutes state that of the King's share of brandy, valued at £255 18s 9d, taken from the rebels' ship near Holy Island by William Hunter, officer of Customs, one third was to go to the Capt. Franks' officers and soldiers who took the castle, and two thirds were to go to the volunteers who assisted.

We find from several entries that Holy Island had its own Customs & Excise detachment under the control of Berwick:- In 1682, John Orde, waiter of Holy Island, was paid £6 [per ann.?]. On 27 November, 1704, Thomas Ord, customs officer with a boat at Holy Island, was paid £9. So was this 50% inflation over a period of twenty two years or extra expense for a boat ? However, just six years later again, on 7 September, 1710, Edward Bullman and Robert Jackson, waiters and searchers at Holy Island, were to keep a boat with pay of £27 10s each: a 300% increase in expenditure appears to indicate either a large increase in, or a determination to control, endemic smuggling.

Holy Island's garrison was almost defunct after the peace treaty between Britain, France and the Netherlands was signed at Ryswick on 20 September 1697 but with the Jacobite rebellion breaking out at home a report of 1 October, 1715 shows that once again it had to play its part in defending the north-east coast:-

General Charles Wills of the Town and Castle of Berwick-on-Tweed applied to the Paymaster General of H.M. Forces to allow master gunner and another gunner upon Holy Island their pay from 24 June 1713 to 25 Dec 1714 amounting to £82 7s. In 1715 the Garrison comprised of a Corporal, a Master gunner, a Gunner and seven soldiers. Stricter security, owing to the rebellion, brought to light smuggling in the area and corruption in the Customs & Excise service:-

A report of January 8, 1729/30, from the Customs to the Treasury concerns George and Jerrard Selby, and Robert Taylor of Holy Island, who are being prosecuting for smuggling by Mr. Kettleby at his own charge, and asking for the support of the Customs, despite a Letter from Sir William Middleton, and Ralph Jenison to the Lords of the Treasury, dated at Chillingham Castle, 1729, July 25, on behalf of Selby's and Taylor. The local gentry were either a party to the smuggling or just happy to turn a blind eye to it for the sake of their neighbours. Shortly afterwards, in 1732, John Miles, was appointed waiter and searcher, Holy Island, Berwick port, replacing Ralph Ord, who had been dismissed: which appears to indicate that Ord had either been involved with the smugglers or that he had refused to tolerate it.

Shortly after the last battle on English soil at Clifton near Penrith, we find perhaps the final reference to Holy Island's part in the military history of England:

'Nov 26, 1745. Petition from John Haxton, Master of the ship "Isabel & May" of Burntisland, now detained at Holy Island, prays release to go to Leith.' Haxton had been suspected of attempting to supply weapons and stores to the rebels.

After other minor incidents during the Rebellions of 1715 and 1745 Holy Island, its castle and harbour, was no longer of military importance and it disappears from the national records: smuggling and local disputes no doubt continued and Thomas Paulden's dream of turning the nine mile circle of 'land left by the sea' into a wealthy estate worthy of his honour was soon forgotten. Certainly when I made enquiries no modern local inhabitant nor the archivist at Berwick was aware of his quixotic attempts to reclaim 'Holy Island' from the sea.

In 1865 a Company formed to reclaim the same area submitted detailed plans to the Clerk of the Peace for Northumberland but the scheme was never implemented. [3]

Statues of Don Quixote and Sancho Panza with Cervantes behind them, in Madrid.
(Photo taken by my sister Mrs. Sheila Tomlinson)

I can't do better than quote directly Julian Evans' review of Edith Grossman's latest translation of *Don Quixote*.

The Daily Telegraph Books, Saturday 17, 2004

'Don Quixote' is the very air we breathe as writers and readers – and this new translation of the Spanish classic is a marvel.

Fresh wind in his sails

Julian Evans Reviews DON QUIXOTE by Miguel Cervantes translated by Edith Grossman.

Why do we so love Don Quixote? Why, though he rights no wrongs and rectifies no injuries, is our sympathy never strained? Because he is the outermost landmark of our own misguided idealism, the vessel of all our romanticism in a rotten, factual world. As Don Diego de Miranda, the gentleman of la Mancha met on the road in Part Two, says with only partial irony: "I can't convince myself that anyone in the world today favours widows, protects maidens, honours married women, and helps orphans, and I wouldn't believe it if I hadn't seen it in your grace with my own eyes." Sixteenth-century Spain, class ridden and greedy, was in decline. Today, in the 21st century, we also know that we know too much. As we read Don Quixote, we are heartened that in the embrace of an illusion people are capable of kind, funny, decent, unpredictable acts. But do we actually read him today? I don't think so. We do not read Quixote because of its vast length and difficult diction. We also don't read it because, in two senses, we don't need to. Harold Bloom, in his comparative introduction to this magnificent new translation, notes that "it so contains us that, as with Shakespeare, we cannot get out of it, in order to achieve perspectivism". And I once spoke to the Catalan novelist Eduardo Mendoza, who said he wasn't sure that Cervantes had influenced him, but he could still remember whole paragraphs of the Spanish translations of the William stories by Richmal Crompton. But who is William Brown but Quixote? Who Jumble but Rocinante? Who Violet Elizabeth Bott but Dulcinea del Toboso, "the empress of La Mancha"? We are impregnated by Cervantes's epic: by its lessons in systematic disenchantment, by its sombreness of loss and comedy of compassion, by the endless ambiguity of its relations between literary artifice and life. The American critic Lionel Trilling justly observed that: "All prose fiction is a variation of the theme of Don Quixote...the problem of appearance and reality." If you read The Pickwick Papers, or Madame Bovary, you read Cervantes without knowing you're reading him. Don Quixote is the very air we breathe, as writers and readers. This year, though, we have a new chance to breathe that air at source. I say, without hesitation, take it. Edith Grossman's new version is a marvel. why? Because her text seems to restore Cervantes's readability and tone, the vitality of his dialogue and characterisation; because, above all, it restores Quixote to a madness we can identify with. Her version of the Knight of the Sorrowful Face is no fool of an exhausted story but the ingenious, complex and kind architect of his own nostalgia for "that happiest of times". the thought patterns of his obsession 'whose involution in the poet was often made abstruse by over-loyalty to the courtly Spanish original) are rendered here as logical and alive (if mad), and thus progressively funnier and sadder. Take the watermill episode in Part Two: having hijacked a boat in the belief that it has been sent by an enchanter - as a sort of celestial cab - Quixote and Sancho argue their way downstream. Hurling curses - one at his servant's cowardice, the other at his master's madness – their comic exchange climaxes, as they enter the dangerous millrace, in a nerveless discourse by the knight on how enchantment actually works. "'Be quiet, Sancho,' said Don Quixote, 'for although they seem to be watermills, they are not; have already told you that enchantments change and alter all things from their natural state. I do not mean to say that they are really altered from one state to another, but that they seem to be, as experience has shown in the transformation of Dulcinea, sole refuge of my hopes.'" I have never so acutely felt the comic timing of which Cervantes was capable, or his sense of Quixote's pathos. Tobias Smollett's translation, most famous of the English translations, is a great novelist's version but now a little archaic; the most recent translation, by JM Cohen (1950), is mellifluous but respectful. Grossman's work is also respectful, but she delivers a fizzing idiom, and a contemporaneity that manages to be both of the 16th century and the 21st. I found her Quixote convincingly great. The contextualisation is excellent and even her footnotes add to its pleasure -except perhaps for the very first, where she implies that Cervantes began the novel in prison in Seville in 1597 or 1602. I'm inclined to think both dates are wrong, and that Cervantes started work after the painful incident in Argamasilla when he was locked up for several months in 1603 on a false charge of making a pass at a female relation of a local aristocrat. (In the novel, the "Academicians of Argamasilla" are depicted as ignoramuses, fawners, mockers and liars.) It doesn't matter. It is impossible not to approve of this book in every respect: as translation, as re-translation, as restitution of a novel that had slipped, almost beyond help, into the dusty stacks of scholarly commentary. I find it impossible to imagine that a better novel will be published this year. It is time for La Mancha's greatest knight errant to ask us, once again to believe in him. And time for us to acquiesce.

CHAPTER 10

The Royal Fishery Companies

Although it remains unclear what damaging effect Thomas Paulden's embanking of the 'lands left by the sea' did have on Daniel Collingwood's plans for a fishery at Holy Island, extracts mainly from *The Royal Fishery Companies* by John R.Elder, (1912) supplemented by relevant details from *Pepys: a Biography* by Richard Ollard, (1988), and *The Diary of Samuel Pepys*, Editors Robert Latham and William Mathews, (1971-83), explain the reasons behind the failure of The Royal Fishery Company and with it therefore, any hope of success for the Holy Island fishery.

Elder begins: 'The history of the Royal Fishery Companies of England is the history of a series of attempts made during the seventeenth century by the sovereigns of Britain to unite English and Scotch noblemen, gentlemen of private means, merchants and fishermen in an enterprise which had its ultimate object the ousting of the Dutch from the position of pre-eminence in the North Sea which the Hollander enjoyed as a result of centuries of strenuous toil and untiring enterprise.'

The British jealousy of the Dutch which is such a factor in the foreign policy of Britain during the seventeenth century, sprang in no small part from the growing knowledge of the wealth derived by the men of the Low Countries from the fisheries conducted, to a considerable extent, on the very coasts of Britain

The Dutch had been curing herring from the North Sea by pickling them with salt in barrels since the 14C, and by the 17C their quality was recognised in the principal countries of Northern Europe, by which time Holland had become engaged in a lucrative export trade.

Holland attained her utmost greatness as a maritime nation and the first sea power in Europe during the mid 17C, when the wealth created by the domination of her massive fishing fleet enabled her to finance a large and successful navy.

During the 1620s an armed peace prevailed in the North Sea where the fishermen of Britain and Holland were in competition. Men-of-war accompanied the fishing fleets of both nations and prevented open warfare, but frequent disputes, cutting of nets and violence, led to diplomatic missions and treaties which for one thing, although not always kept, required the Dutch to fish out of sight of the British coastline and the demand by Charles I that all Dutch vessels fishing off the coast of Britain should buy a licence granted by him at the rate of 12d a ton, in the early years of his reign at Scarborough Castle, was similarly often ignored.

The Dutch authorities themselves had no intention of submitting to Charles' demands and it was only their desire to enlist English help in their war against Spain which led them to suppress an edict already published against accepting his licences.

Elizabeth, Queen of Bohemia, daughter of James I, had also thrown herself on the side of peace, asking her brother as a favour to herself, to lay aside for the present, all controversial matters with the Dutch, since her kingdom had so much need of the aid of the United Provinces against Spain.

Having no intention of going to war, Charles now essayed the subtle paths of diplomacy, and when the Dutch Vessels were fishing without license under the protection of strong convoys, he gave orders to the Earl of Northumberland to send not a war vessel but a merchant ship with the licenses to the Dutch fishing fleet; but when they refused to accept them the King allowed the matter to fall into the background rather than have his diplomatic affairs adversely affected.

In the 1630's from 1st April Scotch fishermen fished for cod off the east coast of Scotland and continued down the English coast as far as the Wash. On 24th August (Bartholomew Tide) the foreign fishing fleet (mainly Dutch) of 1,100 vessels taking the same course, was joined by about 300 English ships in gathering the herring harvest; following the shoals until Martinmass (11th November), after which both fleets returned home.

Secretary Coke gives an interesting account of the Dutch fishermen and the great benefits which accrued to the traders of the East Coast from their visits:-

"Whilst the fishing continues, the Dutch, with about 1000 sail of busses, beside their jaggers and other ships, victual themselves from our shore with bread, beer, flesh and butter, and dry their nets upon the land, specially in a field near Yarmouth, which is two miles in length, and they come ashore sometimes about ten thousand persons, which, besides the victualling of their ships, carry from hence to supply their country both corn, beer and beans in a very great proportion."

What was to be gained by English fishermen in supplanting the Dutch was, to some extent at least, to be lost by Lincolnshire's farmers and brewers.

By 1632 Charles, despite great differences with the Scotch Burghs and the 'inland' (salmon) fishermen regarding their private privileges, had established an Association for the Fishing and a commission was addressed to the Lord Treasurer Weston, the Earl of Arundel and Surrey and many others constituting them the Society of Great Britain and Ireland, of which Charles himself was to be 'perpetual protector'.

Each member of the Association was to 'adventure' a certain sum; the Lord Treasurer agreed to pay £1000; the Lord Chamberlain and the Earl of Rutland £500 each; Katherine, Duchess of Buckingham £3000 and all others smaller sums, amounting to a total of £11,750.

Captain John Mason was appointed 'Receiver and Expeditor,' being authorised to provide fishermen, shipping and nets, while Edward Nicholas and James Philp were appointed Clerks of the Society.

The chief centre of operations for the enterprise was to be based on Lewis in the Western Isles; and it was the lack of knowledge of the area by Captain Mason; and locals who, not unnaturally resented outside interference in their fishing customs and interests which they put before those of the Association; plus the Dutch, who totally disregarded royal proclamations against them fishing and trading within that area and the North Sea, which created problems for the Association from the outset.

The Dutch fishing fleet was always accompanied by a convoy of men of war in order to protect it from the attacks of the Dunkirk and Ostend pirates who, at this period, were particularly active in the North Sea and English Channel. The English fishing vessels of the Association needing protection not only against the pirates but also against their Dutch rivals, carried an armament of 'Half Pikes and Muskets,' 'Physic and Surgery Helps' being also supplied:

Weapons: Half pikes, ten at 2s each	£1 - 0 - 0
Muskets with Bandaleers, rests and moulds,6 (at £1 each)	£6 - 0 - 0
Gunpowder, 6 lbs. at 10d	5 - 0
Leaden Bullets, 6 lbs. at 3d	1 - 6
	£7 - 6 - 6
Physic and Surgery Helps:	
Spermaceti, and a box for it	£0 - 3 - 4
Stone pitch, and a box for it	0 - 1 - 4
Aquavitae, 16 quarts are 4 gallons at 3s	0 -12 - 0
Zante oil, 16 pints are 2 gallons at 6s	0 -12 - 0
Honey, 16 pints are 2 gallons 5s	0 -10 - 0
Sugar, 4 pounds at 1s	0 - 4 - 0
Nutmegs, a quarter of a pound	0 - 1 - 0
Ginger, half a pound	0 - 0 - 6
Pepper, 16 ozs., i.e. a pound	0 - 2 - 0
Balsam and other salves and old linen	0 -10 - 0
Syzers (a pair)	0 - 0 - 6
A Steel Pleget, to spread plaisters	0 - 1 - 4
A Chest with Partitions, for these things	0 -12 - 0
	£3 -10 - 0

Equipped therefore, both for fishing and their own protection, the fishing vessels put to sea. It was not long before the expected trouble came; during the months of August and September, 1632, the Society lost no fewer than three busses - The Experience, of Yarmouth, taken by the Flying Horse of Groningen; The Flower of Yarmouth, seized by a man of war of Enckhuysen named Garrat Johnson Scummer, and The Concord of Yarmouth, seized by a Dunkirk privateer called Jan Peere. A fourth ship was lost towards the end of the same year. The managers of the Fishing Association had purchased a fishing vessel at Ostend, and in December sent a shipmaster, Benjamin Bowden, with a crew of three to bring it home to London. On 15th December, while on their way home, these men were attacked by a man of war of Enckhuysen, belonging to the United Provinces; the vessel was seized as a prize, the men were made prisoners, stripped of their clothes, thrown into irons, and carried to Flushing. Such outrages naturally made it increasingly difficult to get men to invest their money in a venture liable to such serious losses and lack of capital became a major problem for the Association.

In 1635 alone, damage received by the Association at the hands of the Dunkirkers was estimated at £2,000, though the pirates were a source of annoyance to all North Sea fishermen it was the wealth derived from the magnitude of the Dutch fishing fleet, with a total of 6,400 ships, busses, &c employed in the herring trade alone plus 1,600 doggers, pinks, well boats &c; maintaining 152,000 fishers and mariners plus double or treble that number of tradesmen, women and children, all operating within his coastal waters, which Charles felt to be a lasting reproach to Britain, with just 300 ships.

Sir John Burroughs, in his *Sovereignty of the British Seas*, written in 1633, estimated the yearly profit of the Dutch North Sea fishermen to be no less than ten million pounds (an incredible sum at that time).

In 1636, when Charles reviewed the situation, the subscriptions promised to the Association were £22,682 10s, but less than half had been received and £3,550 had been borrowed. The stock consisted of six busses - a strange contrast to the mighty fleet of the Dutch.

On October 21st, 1639, the Dutch Republic, by De Tromp's signal victory over the Spaniards at the battle of the Downs, showed all Europe how great its sea-power had become.

The Dutch were now masters of the sea and British fishers and mariners for many years to come were compelled to submit meekly to acts of outrage at their hands, from which Charles, engaged with troubles in Scotland and rebellion in England, could not protect them. The Dutch fishermen were able to exploit the resources of the North Sea without further let or hindrance from England.

Simon Smith, agent for the Royal Fishery, writing in 1641, gives a detailed account of their fishing season: at the beginning of June the fishers resort to the coast of Shetland to find the herring and then after harvesting on them for about seven weeks, as the shoals gradually swim southwards, they arrive to enjoy fishing 'for fourteen days more in the Fishing under Cheviot Hills and Cheviot Chase.' Thence the fishers followed the herring to the Doggar Bank, where they stayed sometimes a month, sometimes six weeks and about the beginning of September the herring were followed further southwards.

Charles readily saw the benefits which Holland derived from its fishing fleet and set himself the task of establishing the British fisheries as a national industry, whilst at the same time strengthening his navy with a view to the conflict which he knew must inevitably follow. In fact it was only the outbreak of the Great Civil War which prevented Charles's navy from engaging in war against the Dutch, and on its conclusion in favour of Cromwell, it was the sailors of the Commonwealth who gained everlasting glory against the Hollanders.

The Fishing Association did see some success during its existence but poor administration, corruption amongst its officers, outright opposition by the Scots fishermen and Dutch domination of the North Sea had brought it low before the outbreak of Civil War in 1642 crippled trade altogether.

During the Interregnum the naval war in the North Sea caused an almost complete suspension of fishing operations and even before the final declaration of war with Holland in 1652 there had been numerous instances of seizures of herring busses by both English and Dutch vessels which together with attacks from the Dunkirk pirates and from the portion of the English fleet loyal to the king under the command of Prince Rupert fishing became impossible.

In 1653 the Dutch owners, seeing the impossibility of securing their vessels from the attacks of the English fleet, kept their fishing fleet at home and the war did no less damage to the English fishing industry, and such towns as Yarmouth, who in December, 1652, made complaint to General Monk, stating that they had already lost £200,000, 'to the utter undoing of many families' and 'Not three boats are now prepared to go forth fishing where 150 sail used to be making ready at this season.'

During the Commonwealth, Oliver Cromwell was to bring deliverance and establish England as a sea-power; the naval wars of his day were the precursors of that series of naval wars which were the first cause of the ultimate decline of the Dutch fisheries. The treaty of Westminster, April 1654, ended the Dutch war but 'dog fights' still took place between English and Dutch fishermen and both were still under constant threat from the Dunkirkers. Trouble with Spain led to their seizure of all English ships and privateers, ironically sent out with commissions from the exiled Charles II, meant English merchant and fishing vessels were captured daily. In such times of trouble there was little to tempt either companies or individuals to risk capital in an attempt to revive the fishing industry of Britain and except for spasmodic efforts round the coast, therefore, the fishing industry was in a state of extreme depression when Charles II returned to Britain at the Restoration.

At the Restoration Charles II, so far as the scheme for a national fishery was concerned, was now in the identical position to that in which his father had found himself in 1630, when the British fishing industry, in contrast to that of their hereditary rivals the Dutch, remained small and insignificant, and the continuance of such a state of affairs amounted to a national disgrace.

Charles realised that the future of Britain lay in her sea-power and he perceived that a reserve of seamen could be created by the development of a national fishery, so necessary to his design. He therefore resolved to revive the Association for the fishing and on August 22nd, 1661, appointed James, Duke of York, along with numerous noblemen and officers of state, as the Council of the Royal Fishing of Great Britain and Ireland, with powers and priviliges identical with those held by the Council of the Royal Fishery of the time of Charles I.

The new company, however, was granted some further privileges. For seven years its fishing vessels were to pay no duty to the customs, while, to ensure that there would be a demand for its fish, all victuallers were to be compelled to buy yearly from one to four barrels of herring, at the fixed price of 30s per barrel. Those who invested money in the company were assured that the risk of loss was slight, since special attention was to be given by the authorities to the provision of an adequate convoy for the fishing vessels.

In response, moreover, to a special request by the Council for the Fishery, a lottery of the Royal Oak was granted them for three years, while, as a public recognition of the fact that the Council was about to enter upon the performance of a national service, orders were given which were supported by a special appeal and commendation from

Prosperous fishermen were the basis of sea-power. This is a model of the kind of ship in which they fished the North Sea a 'herring buss' of 56 tons. She was 58 ft. long and 15 ft. wide She carried a crew of about twelve.

the King, that a collection should be made in the churches throughout his kingdom to provide funds for the erection of wharfs, docks, storehouses and buildings necessary for the work of the company.

Despite a lack of enthusiasm followed by a disappointing result when, after expenses, only £274 16s was given to the company, Charles and the promoters of the Royal Fishery were not to be dissuaded from their enterprise and in September, 1662, it was resolved to order the building of ten fishing vessels of about 50 foot and 60 tons. These were to be built at Harwich and Deptford at a cost of £9,000.

The king, moreover, still anxious to foster the work of the company, and desirous of seeing its fleet increased as much and as quickly as possible, announced in November, 1662, his intention of giving £200 to every man who should, by the middle of the following June, build a fishing buss and equip it with all the necessary gear. Samuel Pepys tells how this announcement was first made public by Lord Sandwich, in the presence of a large number of naval officers and private gentlemen who had gathered at the funeral of Sir Richard Stayner.

As a mark of special favour the members and employees were freed from service on juries and from various other forms of public duty, and were given a monopoly of the export trade in herring.

To further encourage these companies, the king on 6th February, 1662, issued a proclamation enjoining the observance of Lent, (a custom which had been in obeyance since 1640); Wednesday, Friday, and Saturday were also to be observed as the three fish days, on which it was forbidden to eat flesh, butchers being warned not to kill or sell meat on those days; this for the benefit of the whole country and encouragement of many poor families who live by fishing. This proclamation was again made on 12th February, 1663 and on 2nd February 1664.

In accordance with the act establishing them, various fishing companies were formed throughout the country, but it was soon found that the old difficulties of individual interests and local customs still existed.

The Dutch, though still regarded as the experts in all things pertaining to fishing, were still feared and hated and in 1660, as in 1630, jealousy of their success was the moving factor in the attempts to develop the British fishing industry. Charles hoped to reduce the national wealth of the Dutch by taking over some considerable part of their fishing trade which would, at the same time, benefit the wealth of Britain.

Anxious to have as reliable information as possible concerning the Dutch fisheries, Charles sent Dr. Benjamin Worsley, Secretary of State for the Department of Trade and Plantations, into Holland, who, on his return, gave the value of the Dutch herring fishery, at the lowest estimate, as three million pounds sterling per year, a sum exceeding the value of the goods produced by the manufacturers of England or of France. This made Holland with her home manufacturers and East Indian trade, the richest state in Europe and Dr. Worsley deprecated the relinquishing of such a source of wealth to the Dutch, since to do so was to abandon for ever the supremacy of the seas.

Worsley was, however, convinced that owing to the great sums of money already lost in the fishing industry it would be impossible to get people to invest funds to encourage it, without the king giving 'his signall and expesse Countenance, with the Publick authority of the Parliament.'

About the same time as Dr. Worsley made his report, two public spirited men named Smith and Simon Watson, inspired by the same desire to see their fellow countrymen enter upon the business of fishery, set forth in great detail, 'The Charge and Profitt of one Busse of 70 Tunes imployed one year in the fishery, by wch may be computed the charge of a fleet,' showing that the fishery industry was far more profitable than men imagined and that it was folly to continue to pay Dutch fishermen to catch fish for English consumption.

Not only were the English dependent upon the Dutch their enemies for their supplies of fresh fish of all kinds but their 'slothfulness and improvidence,' allowed thousands of persons to be idle at home, while strangers were coming hundreds of miles to their very coasts, and were there reaping this rich harvest 'Which God and Nature had sent to us.'

The whole nation was aware that in spite of their heavy losses sustained during the naval war of the Commonwealth period, the Dutch still maintained, and reaped the benefits of, their powerful fishing fleet in the North Sea.

Finally, they drew up a formal proposal for the founding of a national fishery with full details of resulting benefits to be obtained.

Meanwhile an attempt had been made to raise money from many counties which had not responded to the king's appeal on behalf of the company in 1662 and a second collection was completed in 1664 when Samuel Pepys, along with George Duke, secretary to the Royal Fishery, was deputed to make a report on the result. It is in connection with this enquiry that Pepys writes in his Diary under date October 10th, 1664: 'To the office, and there late, and so home to supper and to bed, having at up till past twelve at night to look over the accounts of the collection for the fishery, and the loose and base manner that monies so collected are disposed of in, would have a man never part with a penny so disposed of, and above all the inconvenience of having a great man, though never so seeming pious as my Lord Pembroke is. He is too great to be called to account, and is abused by his servants, and yet obliged to defend them for his owne sake.'

Of the £1,076 collected the Earl of Pembroke, Treasurer of the company had a considerable amount of this still in his own hands; while Mr King, who had been engaged in the collection for the Earl, still retained £429. Statements had also been made as to £412 already gathered but not yet placed to the credit of the society. Pepys was indignant at the conduct of Mr King, who, instead of handing over the £412 entrusted to him, 'insinuated in his accounts' that he had assigned to the Fishing Company the lease of a house in Harwich worth £700.'It may be fitt.' Wrote Pepys, sarcastically, 'to inquire whether this house was not long agoe otherwise disposed of by him.'

Pepys also drew attention to another point in which Mr King was defrauding the company, since upon the collection of a certain sum of £115, he was awarding himself the disproportionate amount £47, 'which' he remarks, 'is after the rate of 8s in the pound and more.' Finally, so that the whole business of the collection might be placed on a business footing he suggests that both the Earl of Pembroke and Mr King should be compelled to give in an exact return of all the money received by them; particularly with regard to London, for which no account had been rendered by them.

In his Diary for 16th October, 1664, he writes, 'To the Committee of the Fishery, and there did make my report of the late public collections for the Fishery, much to the satisfaction of the Committee, and I think much to my reputation, for good notice was taken of it and much it was commended.' Again on November 1st of the same year his entry reads, 'My report in the business of the collections is mightily commended and will get me some reputation, and indeed is the only thing looks like a thing done since we sat.'

The final steps towards establishing the society were taken by the King on March 12th, 1664, when the Duke of York was appointed its Governor, and on April 8th, 1664 when a charter under the seal of England was granted to the Corporation for the Royal Fishery. Of this Corporation the Duke of York was Governor, Lord Craven, Deputy Governor, the Lord Mayor and the Chamberlain of London, Treasurers. 'Several other very great persons, to the number of thirty-two' are said by Pepys to have constituted the council of the governors of the association, appointed 'for their lives.' Pepys himself being one of these 'very great persons.'

From the very beginning, however, Pepys had no very favourable impression concerning those sitting with him among the governors, and feared the worst for the enterprise. On July 7th, 1664, for instance, he writes, 'To Whitehall and there found the Duke and twenty more reading their commission (of which I am, and was also sent to, to come) for the Royal Fishery, which is very large, and a very serious charter it is; but the company generally so ill-fitted for so serious a worke that I do much fear it will come to little.'

Two days afterwards, on July 9th, the members of the council were required to take an oath to be true to the interests of the company. Their conduct on this occasion confirmed in the mind of Pepys that opinion which he had already formed concerning them and the prospects of the society. Two motions were laid before them, the one that they should swear to be true to the company to the best of their power, the other, to the best of their understanding. The latter motion was carried, a fact which Pepys considered ominous for the success of the new society, since thus the governors would be, as he puts it 'least able to serve the company, because we would not be obliged to attend the business when we can, but when we list. This consideration did displease me, but it was voted and so went.'

It was not long before the fears of Pepys that the management of the company had not been entrusted to a body of men sufficiently interested in the enterprise were confirmed. A meeting of the council of the fishery had been called for September 3rd, and this Pepys attended, to find that so little interest was being taken in the affairs of the company that there were not more than four persons present. His thoughts on this occasion he records thus 'After dinner to Whitehall, to the Fishing Committee, but not above four of us went, which could do nothing, and a sad thing it is to se so great a work so ill followed, for at this pas, it can come to nothing but disgrace us all.'

With so slight interest on the part of those at the head of affairs, it is not surprising to find that the society was so unfortunate in its undertakings that, in a short time, various methods of subsidising it had to be adopted. The first proposal was that money should be raised for its support by giving it the monopoly of coining farthings. To this proposal Pepys consented readily enough. A second proposal, however, that the funds of the company should be increased by the establishment of lotteries to be administered on its behalf, was viewed by him with indignation; 'I was ashamed to see it' he writes, 'that a thing so low and base should have anything to do with so noble an undertaking.'

In spite of his opposition, however, proclamation was made on June 21st, 1665, forbidding any persons to use or exercise lotteries in Great Britain or Ireland, except Sir Anthony Desmarces, Joseph Williamson and three others, to whom the sole right of managing them was granted in order that they might raise a stock for the Royal Fishery Company.

On 20 July 1664, Pepys describes a lottery: '...by coach to White-hall to the Committee for Fishing; but nothing done, it being a great day today there, upon drawing at the Lottery of Sir Arth. Slingsby. I got in and stood by the two Queens and the Duchesse of York, and just behind my Lady Castlemayne, whom I do heartily adore; and good sport it was to see how most that did give ten pounds did go away with a pair of gloves only for their lot, and one gentlewoman, one Mrs. Fish, with only a blanke. And I stayed to see drew a suit of hangings valued at £430; and they say are worth the money, or near it. One other suit there is better then that- but very many lots of three and four score pounds. I observed the King and Queens did get but as poor lots as any else. But the wisest man I met with was Mr. Cholmly, who insured as many as would from drawing of the one blank for 12d - in which case there was the whole number of persons to one, which I think was 3 or 400. And so insured about 200 for 200 shillings, so that he could not have lost if one of them had drawn it - for there was enough to pay the £10; but it happened another drew it, and so he got all the money he took.

Another lottery took place at 2 p.m. in the Banqueting Hall, by the King's permission. The goods consisted of a coach, plate, jewels and a variety of furnishings (tapestry, gilt-leather hangings, chairs, cabinets and marble tables): Evelyn's view (19 July) was the same as Pepys's; 'the sale was thought to be contriv'd very unhandsomely by the master of it, who was in truth a meer shark'. Lotteries, as well as being commonly used for raising public funds in all countries of W. Europe, were also granted as favours to private individuals, though in England they were supposed to number no more than eight a year at this time.

Greatly disappointed with the low income to date Pepys suggests that the Earl of Pembroke, Treasurer and George King, Secretary, to the Royal Fishery, both of whom were defrauding the company out of money collected for it in 1662 and 1664 following the King's appeal, should be compelled to give in an exact return of all the money received by them; particularly with regard to London, for which no account had been rendered.

He was therefore deputed to make a report and in his diary for October 10th, 1664 he writes: 'To the office, and there late, and so home to supper and to bed, having at up till past twelve at night to look over the accounts of the collection for the fishery, and the loose and base manner that monies so collected are disposed of in, would have a man never part with a penny so disposed of…'

On November 1st of the same year his entry reads, 'My report in the business of the collections is mightily commended and will get me some reputation, and indeed is the only thing looks like a thing done since we sat.'

The Society, however, had become too much perturbed by the outbreak of war with Holland to inquire into the way its affairs had been conducted. The outlook for English merchants was gloomy and particularly for the fishing industry, which must lie in practical suspension until peace was proclaimed.

Pepys, in his Diary under the date 22nd December, 1664, thus voices the general feeling of foreboding when he wrote: 'To the Change, and there, among the merchants, I hear fully the news of our being beaten to dirt at Ginny by De Ruyter with his fleet. The particulars, as much as by Sir G. Carteret afterwards I heard, I have said in a letter to my Lord Sandwich this day at Portsmouth; it being almost wholly to the utter ruine of our Royal Company, the reproach and shame to the whole nation.'

The sequel brought a state of affairs more desperate than even the most pessimistic could have deemed possible. London, ravaged by the Great Plague, devastated by the Great Fire, heard in 1667 the guns of the Dutch as they destroyed the English fleet in the Medway, and witnessed the Dutch fleet supreme in the Channel. Overwhelmed by the troubles of the time, the Governors of the Royal Fishery Company, in the same year that saw the fortunes of England at their lowest ebb, represented to the King, the desperate condition of their affairs, and asked that a grant of the whole power of coining and issuing farthings should be given them, their intention being to give twenty one shillings' worth of farthings for one pound in silver. The same proposal was made in 1668, it being declared then that this seemed to be the only practical method of supporting the work of the society.

Charles, however, deeply involved in the world of intrigue, had no longer the will or energy to devote towards the revival of the Royal Fishery. Moreover, he knew that though peace had been declared with Holland in 1667, the result of his own understanding with Louis of France must be to render inevitable a renewed outbreak of the struggle, and that it was futile to attempt to raise up the national fishery until that struggle had passed and there was safety for fishing vessels in the North Sea.

Meanwhile, Charles' desire to establish Roman Catholicism in England weighed far more heavily with him than the wish for the prosperity of his country; the Royal Fishery, along with every other branch of English commerce and industry, was sacrificed for the sake of his schemes, which included an alliance with France and demanded for their success the downfall of Holland. The renewed outbreak of war which the king sought came in 1672; not till 1674 did Charles find it politic to yield to the wishes of his subjects and make peace with the Dutch.

During these ten years of trouble from 1664 to 1674 - for during the period, whether England and Holland were technically at peace or war, there was no cessation of hostilities between the rival fishing fleets - fishing in the North Sea was very much at a standstill. The fact that fishing boats and their fishing gear deteriorate rapidly when left idle impelled some of the more hardy fishermen to set out for the fishing grounds, in defiance of all dangers, but the number of these was comparatively small. Even in 1669, when peace was supposed to reign, only twenty-three vessels set out from Yarmouth for the fishing grounds and in 1672, while the war was still raging, the North Sea was almost deserted by both merchant and fishing vessels for fear of the Dutch.

A state of affairs which drove English commerce from the seas for such a considerable period must have ruined many English ship-owners and done incalculable harm to the fishing industry. When the war with the Dutch ended, the Royal Fishery Company had ceased to exist: its business had been brought to a standstill and the enterprise had been abandoned, its vessels being left to deteriorate into useless hulks.

Even when the Royal Fishery Company was thus sinking to oblivion, however, there were not wanting pamphleteers to represent the folly of allowing the fishing industry to fail completely. In 1670, a pamphlet appeared, entitled, *The Royal Fishing Revised* which contains many interesting particulars concerning the state of the fishing trade in England at this time.

The writer acknowledges that the Dutch have possession of the fishing trade. The reasons for this he summarises thus: They have multitudes of men, cheapness and convenience for building ships, advantages in barter and exchange, and an admitted excellence in packing and curing all kinds of fish, with the one exception of red herring. They give facilities for trade to all nations and have low customs duties. England, on the other hand, suffers from lack of population. This he ascribes to the peopling of the American plantations, the re-peopling of Ireland after the great massacre, the Great Plague of 1665, the law against naturalisation, and finally, to the corporations, which restrict trade to those who are freemen of them.

English ships, he affirms further, are dearer than Dutch ships, a Dutch ship being built for half the price of an English one of equal dimensions. This he attributes first to the dearness and scarcity of timber in England, and, secondly, to the Act of Navigation, 'which not only restrains the importation of Timber, Pitch, Tar, Hemp, and Iron, to those dear built ships, and the ships of the natives of the places from whence they are had, whether they have ships or not, but also it gives freedom to the Dutch to import all sort of Manufacturers made of these Growths, which they acquire for half the price the English can; whereby the English have wholly lost the Trade for fitting up ships for this or any other trade.'

The English ship, moreover, the writer says, is not of convenient size, a Dutch ship of equal size being manned effectively by half the number of hands. This he ascribes to the fact that the building is confined to Englishmen, 'Who are very few and know no other way.' The English also suffer from a 'want of sale of commodities,' due to the greatness of Customs, since these are twenty times more than in the Netherlands.' to the dearness of the English ships and their want of suitability for foreign trade, and finally to the high rate of interest in England, this being 'about one-third more than in the Netherlands.'

Lastly, the writer refers to the negligent and corrupt curing of fish by the English, which 'proceeds from lack of council of trade to inspect.' and sets forth several ingenious ideas with regard to reviving the fishing industry. He wished this branch of trade to be open to all sorts of foreigners, and 'restraint by Corporations' to be abolished. Beggars and all other poor people, provided they were not sick or impotent, were to be employed in the fishery. All persons who had been condemned for any less crime than that of murder, were to be 'compelled to redeem their crimes, and in some measure to make some compensation, by extraordinary labour in this trade.'

All persons who had been imprisoned for debt were to be sent to the Fishing. He proposed that the Act of Navigation should be repealed and foreigners encouraged, and that a Council of Trade should be established in England. Finally he suggested that 'all houses built upon new foundations within the City and suburbs of London, since 1657 (except such as have been consumed by fire), pay a fine to the value of one year's rent, to be employed towards the carrying on of the Royal Fishery.'

Fear inspired by the Dutch was such that it was but rarely that owners allowed their ships to leave port and the North Sea was almost deserted by both merchant and fishing vessels. Thus, in 1672, while the war was still raging, the crew of a solitary fishing vessel belonging to Yarmouth who had braved the dangers reported on their return that 'sailing all along the coast they saw not one sail since they came out of their fishing grounds till they came here.'

In a letter written in 1674, by a certain Mr Roger L'Estrange, who was already seeking to promote a new fishery Company, to Mr Secretary Williamson, he writes, 'His Majesty has several vessels that lie rotting for want of care and employment, many of which were built for the fishing.'

Since they came contemporaneously with Charles' second declaration of war on Holland, it was not to be expected that this pamphlet and those of a like nature that accompanied it could do much towards reviving the waning fortunes of the Royal Fishery. The war, however, had scarcely ended when some of those many Englishmen who were still of opinion that the fishing was an industry worthy of national support, where endeavouring to rouse public interest.

A clear understanding of the measures necessary to overcome its failings did not, unfortunately, lead to their implementation and the Royal Fishery Company continued to suffer from the same problems here outlined.

As we have appreciated from his diary, Samuel Pepys was ideally placed to explain in detail the problems faced by the Royal Fishery Company and for this and other closely related matters I think a brief biographical sketch taken mainly from *Pepys: a Biography* by Richard Ollard, (1988), is worthy of inclusion.

CHAPTER 11

Samuel Pepys

Samuel Pepys (1633-1703), famous for his diary, was the son of a London tailor and a contemporary of Thomas Paulden, who rose to the top of his profession by dint of hard work and great administrative ability. The opportunity to use his talents may never have come about however, had he not attaching himself as a servant to the rising star of his cousin, Cromwellian colonel Edward Mountague, who as a Commissioner of the Admiralty, member of the Council of State and General-at-Sea, was charged to escort Charles II back from Holland at the Restoration: being created Earl of Sandwich and granted the signal honour of the Order of the Garter for his services.

Samuel Pepys

Pepys may have begun as Mountagu's servant but he soon rose by application to become his much valued secretary and at the Restoration he was allowed to share his master's good fortune by being appointed Clerk of the Acts to the Navy Board; other appointments swiftly followed including appointment to the Tangier Committee in 1662 and in 1665, the lucrative Treasurership of the same Committee.

A significant sign of Samuel's swift rise in society was seen when, in January 1669, he saw fit to give a dinner party in honour of his patron 'my Lord' the Earl of Sandwich, who came accompanied by his brother Sidney Mountagu, Lord Peterborough (late governor of Tangier), Sir Charles Harbord and Sir William Godolphin.

Pepys had reached such dizzy heights that he saw (revealed in his secret diary) Sandwich and Sir William Coventry, Sir William Penn, Sir William Batten, Surveyor of the Navy; Monck and Prince Rupert, the King and the Duke of York, patrons, colleagues, politicians, admirals, princes, as forces constantly in a rich state of flux and acting on each other, to be collectively held in equilibrium to promote his own career.

In 1677 when the Royal Fishery Company was incorporated, with James Duke of York as its Governor, Treasurer Danby, Sir Anthony Deane, Daniel & George Collingwood, Henry Norwood, Esq. (late deputy governor of Tangier), James Pierce, Surgeon-General of the Navy and William Hewers, gent. Two of Samuel's life-long friends were, with Samuel Pepys and many other leading figures in the government, appointed to that body.

The Earl of Sandwich, who had been replaced by the Duke of York as Samuel's patron, was killed in action at sea, fighting against the great Dutch admiral De Ruyter at the battle of Solebay. Treasurer Danby had been Joint Treasurer of the Navy from 1668, subsequently holding the office alone from 1671 till his elevation to the Treasurership in 1673. Pepys respected him as a colleague, both men disdaining easy popularity and both were struck down in the Popish Plot: Shaftsbury taking Danby's place at the Council table. Later in 1695, when the Commons pursued Danby, now Duke of Leeds, on corruption charges, Pepys was unable to save his old ministerial colleague from impeachment.

The study of naval architecture led to one of the longest and most fruitful of Pepys's long and fruitful professional relationships, Anthony Deane, assistant shipwright at Woolwich, taught Pepys enough to hold his own against the experienced sea officers on the board and supplied him with drawings, still preserved in his library, that were much admired by John Evelyn, one of the greatest connoisseurs of the century. In return Pepys was a zealous promoter of Deane's career. In October 1664 when war was imminent he secured his appointment as Master Shipwright at Harwich. The ships he built won him a European reputation. Louis XIV and Colbert courted him: at the end of the century his son went to Russia to superintend the shipyards of Peter the Great. But eminent as he might become, he was the protégé, Pepys the patron. Strong paternal admonition characterised such a relationship.

'...I will not dissemble with you because I love you. I am wholly dissatisfied in your proceeding about Mr Browne and Mr Wheeler... Mr Deane, I do bear you still good respect, and (though it may be you do not now think that worth keeping) I should be

glad to have reason to continue it to you. But, upon my word, I have not spared to tell the Board my opinion about this business, as you will shortly see by letter we have wrote to Commissioner Taylor. Wherein I have been very free concerning you, and shall be more so if ever I meet with the like occasion.

The letter was written after Deane had established himself at Harwich and was within a few years of a knighthood and a large fortune. Perhaps the vehemence and openness of Pepys's communications with his subordinates, so very different from Sandwich's well-bred reserve, made friendship easy. Certainly Deane's attachment never weakened in fair weather or foul.

The same is true of the closest of all Pepys's associations, that with Will Hewer who lived with him for a time, becoming his right hand man in the Navy Office, closest friend and the son her never had. He succeeded Pepys as Tangier Treasurer. In his old age Pepys lived with Will at Clapham as his guest. After leaving the Admiralty Hewer joined the East India Company, becoming Deputy Governor in 1704.

Harbord, Admiral Russell's brother-in-law and Major John Wildman were two of those who reappeared with William III and had tried to have him executed.

Sir Jeremy (Jerome) Smith, a tarpaulin admiral, (a seaman master mariner) favourite and protégé of the Duke of Albemarle who had a notable fighting record, was given his flag in 1666. He fought in the Dutch wars, was a close personal friend of the poet and secret agent Andrew Marvell and exerted considerable local influence in the borough that returned Marvell to Parliament and paid his wages. Marvell acted as his executor.

James Pierce another life long friend and colleague of Pepy's becoming Surgeon-General of the Fleet and Surgeon to the Duke of York; he reformed the Navy's whole approach to its medical services, bringing in hospital ships and raising surgeons pay but died in poverty in 1696.

Sir William Penn, was General-at-sea under Blake when he had earned his highest praise at the battle of Kentish Knock and rescued the great Admiral from a very tight corner at Portland. Vice-admiral to Lord Sandwich and greatly respected for his unrivalled abilities at sea but no friend of Pepy's.

Pepys, who enjoyed rapid promotion to the Secretaryship of the Admiralty, was, however, one of those accused of Roman Catholicism in 1673 and treason in 1679, owing to his having married a Catholic wife and for his regular intimacy and friendship with James, Duke of York, in his capacity as Lord High Admiral. Pepys was seen, by the Earl of Shaftsbury and the Duke of Buckingham (leaders of the faction opposed to the Lord High Admiral) as one close enough to the Duke of York whose destruction could lead to the fall of their rival. The King's brother, as heir to the throne, had enraged Protestant feelings at that time by publically avowing his conversion to Catholicism.

The popular conviction that the Great Fire of London had been a piece of Catholic sabotage, the smouldering resentment over the alliance with Catholic French and the Declaration of Indulgence, which was seen as suspending penal laws against Catholics, all aroused the pent-up hatreds and fears of a society that had known revolution and who were only too ready to believe the ridiculous lies put forward against Pepys, firstly by Colonel John Scott, in his charge of treason and then Titus Oates in his anti-Catholic Popish Plot of 1679.

The witch-hunt initiated by Col. Scott (backed by Shaftsbury and Buckingham) and carried forward by Titus Oates planned to bring down The Duke of York, sent Samuel Pepys and his close friend Sir Anthony Deane to the Tower on 22 May 1679. Danby, the King's first minister, was only saved from impeachment by the Lords; the Duke of York escaped exclusion from the succession by a hair's breadth and the banishment of his Catholic Queen Catherine was avoided only by Charles proroguing Parliament on December 30 and dissolving it by proclamation in February 1679.

Wild and reckless charges of Catholicism had been made by John James, an ex-butler of Pepys, at the instigation of William Harboard M.P. for Thetford, Shaftsbury's spokesman, who was to become Surveyor General of Crown Lands and was Pepys' most vicious enemy. The charges, which as well as corruption and negligence during the Dutch war also included treason, could not be substantiated and Pepys' stout defence soon brought about his release. He was fortunate to escape the scaffold but he had lost his position and was to remain out of employment for nearly three years.

The Duke of York, as heir, had been recalled from his ignominious exile in the Low Countries when the King fell dangerously ill in August 1679 but he was sent abroad again on his brother's recovery. Soon after this, however, James was appointed High Commissioner in Edinburgh.

Pepys, having failed to secure several appointments including that of Provost of King's College, Cambridge, spent his time at the Royal Society and in the company of his great friend and fellow diarist John Evelyn. In May 1682, however, his master the Duke of York was rehabilitated and invited Samuel to accompany him on a visit to Edinburgh.

The voyage was unfortunately marred by disgrace and disaster. The Duke's ship the Gloucester was wrecked off Yarmouth in calm clear weather close inshore through the carelessness of the pilot. Nearly all the ship's company of about two hundred souls, including many noblemen and great persons were drowned, though the Duke escaped in a boat with the future victor of Blenheim at his side. Public horror was increased by the private loss of Pepys, who was assumed to have accepted the Duke's pressing invitation to join him on the Gloucester. Happily he had preferred an ampler berth in one of the escorting yachts the Catherine shared only by Sir Christopher Musgrave Lieutenant-General of the Ordnance.

Unfortunately for us, the shame and upset over the accident overshadowed his normal excitement in travel and his letters tell us very little about his observations on his only visit to Scotland and the north of England.

Although taken with the beauty of Glasgow, he says nothing about Edinburgh. He did not return to England with the Duke but took the opportunity to travel with Col. George Legge, (one of the survivors from the Gloucester picked up by Pepys' yacht the Catherine) who as Master of the Ordnance had business at several northern towns, having a yacht for the purpose. They were at Berwick on May 17th from where they made an expedition to Holy Island, arriving at Newcastle on the 23rd to receive the freedom of that city and then to Durham 'Where the Bishop seems to live more like a prince of this than a preacher of the other world'. On Friday 26th they were back at Seaton Delaval near Newcastle, where they dined with a local magnet, the great iron master, Sir Ralph Delaval.

Back in London Pepys was rapturously received by his friends and twelve months later in June 1683 he was asked to accompany his erstwhile fellow traveller George Legge, now ennobled as Earl of Dartmouth, on another voyage, this time to Tangier, where the enormous cost of maintaining the garrison after the vast capital which had been required to construct the mole (harbour wall) was proving much beyond England's resources.

The decision had been taken to liquidate the commitment by slighting the fortifications, blowing up the mole (England's greatest engineering feet at that date) and evacuating the population of Tangier. Pepys had been sent as secretary to the Earl to assess and advise on the proper amount of compensation required to settle accounts with private property owners.

On his return to England in June 1684 Pepys was re-appointed Secretary to the Admiralty and in November elected President of the Royal Society. Charles II died in February 1685 and Samuel walked in James II's coronation procession as Baron of the Cinque Ports. In April 1685 he was elected M.P. for Huntingdonshire and in July Master of Trinity House.

James II's attempts to return England to Catholicism were short lived and he fled to France in 1688. Pepys lost his seat in Parliament was forced to resign his Secretaryship of the Admiralty and was once again imprisoned on 4th May 1698, along with his friends and colleagues William Hewer and Sir Anthony Deane, as 'suspected of dangerous and treasonable practices against his Majesty's Government'. He was released in July but arrested again almost a year later in June 1690 but allowed bail after just five days and proceedings against him were dropped in October.

Pepys was a rich man having led a successful business career and he kept busy in retirement being still involved with a wide stimulating circle of friends including those in the Royal Society. In April 1697 he was seriously ill but recovered to enjoy a few more happy years surrounded by his family and friends until his death at Clapham, where he had been living with his life-long friend and executor William Hewer, on 26th May 1703, at the age of 70.

Other abstracts from Pepys' Diary referring to the Royal Fishery Company:
19 October 1661, *Mr. Coventry, Sir G. Carteret, Sir W. Penn and myself by coach to Captain Marshes at Lime-house...where close-by they have a design to get the King to hire a docke for the herring-busses (which is now the great design on foot) to lie up in.*

The establishment of the Royal Fishery Council on 22 August 1661 had been followed shortly afterwards by the issue of letters patent inviting subscribers to a central fund by means of which a fleet of herring boats would be set out: The scheme failed, like others before it. Pepys became a member of the Fishery Committee of 1664.

28 November 1662,.To Ironmongers Hall to the funeral of Sir Richard Stayner, there we were, all the officers of the Navy and my Lord Sandwich, who did discourse with us about the Fishery, telling us of his Majesty's resolution to give £200 to every man that will set out a Busse and advising about the effects of this encouragement, which will be a very great matter certainly.

In September 1662 a scheme similar to those of 1580, 1615 and 1661 - for building her-ring busses had been inaugurated by the Council of Royal Fishery, the King himself undertaking to provide 10. The Council had been established in August 1661: Pepys became a member of the commission appointed to succeed it in 1664.

29 November 1662,...To my Lord's where my Lord and Mr. Coventry - Sir Wm. Darcy - one Parham (a very knowing and well spoken man in business), with several others, did meet about stating the business of the Fishery (1) and the manner of the King's giving of his £200 to every man that shall set out a new-made English Busse by the middle of June next. In which business we had many fine pretty discourses...Having come to some issue, wherein a motion of mine was well received, about sending these invitations from the King to all the fishing ports in general, with limiting so many Busses to this and that port, before we know the readiness of subscribers - we parted…

Of the persons mentioned, only Sandwich was a member of the Royal Fishery Council. Richard Parham was a freeman of the Fishmongers' Company; D'Arcy a courtier with Northumbrian interests.

3 December 1662, [with Mr. Peter Pett, Navy Commissioner]...we did also call at Lime-house to view two Busses that are building - that being a thing we are now very hot upon. Our call was to see what dimensions they are of, being 50 foot by the Keels and about 60 tons.

1663, 6 November. After dinner came in Captain Grove, and he and I alone to talk of many things; and among many other, of the Fishery, in which he gives me such hopes, that being at this time full of projects how to get a little money honestly, of which some of them I trust in God will take, I resolved this afternoon to go and consult my Lord Sandwich about it and so...thither and sent for Creed and discoursed with him about it; he and I to White-hall...~I took my Lord aside, who doth give me the best advice he can; and telling me how there are some projectors, by name Sir Edwd. Ford, who would have the making of Farthings, and out of that give so much to the King for maintenance of the Fishery; but my Lord doth not like that, but would have it go as they offered the last year; and so upon my desire, he promises me when it is seasonable to bring me into the commission with others, if any of them take. And I perceive he and Mr. Coventry are resolved to fallow it hard.

Sir Edward Ford(e), soldier and inventor, published his proposals in Experimented proposals how the King may have money to pay his fleets with ease to his people (1666). Ford proposed to make farthings from Swedish copper, claiming that this method made counterfeits impossible. The Fishery Company, led by the Duke of York, supported the project: so too, did the Queen Mother. A meeting in December 1664 (attended by Pepys) once more approved it. But there was some dispute about the payments to the King (Ford offered 6s 8d in the pound), and the officials of the Mint were from the beginning hostile. The plan was revived in 1667-68, again without effect: Ford was allowed to issue Irish farthings, but died before the scheme could take effect.

4 March,1664,....my mind in great ease to think of our coming to so good a respect with my Lord again and his Lady,...as also my being put into the commission of the Fishery for which I must give my Lord thanks; and so home to bed...

10 March, ...I to White-hall; and at the Privy Seale office enquired and found the Bill (2) come for the Corporation of the Royal Fishery; whereof the Duke of Yorke is made present Governor and several other very great persons, to the number of 32, made his assistants for their lives: whereof, by my Lord Sandwich's favour, I am one and take it not only as a matter of honour but that that may come to be of profit to me.(3) And so with great content went and called my wife; and so home and to the office, where busy late; and so home to supper and to bed.

(2). The royal warrant authorising the issue of a charter.

(3).The Royal Fishery Council of 1661 was now replaced by a corporation on the Dutch model by a charter (8 April). '32' should be 36.

14 March, (after meeting with the Duke of York) ...Being broke up, I followed my Lord Sandwich and thanked him for his putting me into the Fishery; which I perceive he expected, and cried "Oh!" "in the Fishery you mean. I told you I would remember you in it" - but offered no more discourse...[Not being on very good terms].

13 July 1664, [after talk on navy matters at his office]...Thence to White-hall to the Fishery, and there did little. So by water home.

24 August 1664, ...to White-hall to a Committee of the Fishery, where my Lord Craven and Mr. Gray mightily against Mr. Creeds being joined in the warrant for Secretary with Mr. Duke. However, I did get it put off till the Duke of Yorke was there - and so broke up, doing nothing.

5 September 1664, ..By and by to the Fishery, the Duke of Yorke there - where after Duke was made Secretary, we fell to name a committee; whereof I was willing to be one because I would have my hand in that business, to understand it and be known in doing something in it. And so after cutting out work for that committee, we rise...'

13 September 1664, Up and so to the office, where we sat busy all morning. Dined at home; and after dinner to Fishmongers hall, where we met the first time upon the Fishery committee - and many good things discoursed of concerning making Farthings, which was proposed as a way of raising money for this business; and then that of Lotterys, but with great confusion. (2) But I hope we shall fall into greater order.

(2). Three methods of raising funds were now proposed - voluntary collections; the grant of monopolies for coining farthings; and the grant of licences authorising public lotteries. The coinage scheme was never tried. For the use of lotteries for raising public money, They had been used in 1639 for the benefit of the Fishery Association of 1632.

> 20 September 1664,...At noon to the Change and there met by appointment with Captain Poyntz, who hath some place, or title to a place, belonging to gameing;(1) and so I discoursed with him about the business of our improving of the Lotterys for the King's benefit, and that of the Fishery; and had some light from him in that business - and shall, he says, have more in writing from him. So home to dinner and then abroad to the Fishing committee at Fishmongers hall, and there sat and did some business considerably...

(1). John Poyntz was Clerk Comptroller of the office of the Master of the Revels, which licensed lotteries and entertainments of all sorts.

> 24 September 1664, ...after dinner comes one Phillips, who is concerned in the lottery,(1) and from whom I collected much concerning that business. I carried him in my way to White-hall and set him down at Somerset-house. Among other things, he told me that Monsier du Puis, that is so great a man at the Duke of Yorkes, and this mans great opponent, is a knave and by quality but a tailor.(2)

(2). Lawrence Dupuy was Yeoman of the Robes to the Duke of York. Courtiers obtained a stranglehold on lotteries, though the licences were intended at the Restoration to be granted for the benefit of and indigent officers. Dupuy had with others been licenced in December 1663 to set up a lottery for the benefit of the Fishery: There is a complaint of his dishonesty.

> 26 September 1664,..my mind a little troubled that I have not of late kept up myself so briske in business, but minded my ease a little too much and my family,...so that I have not kept company, nor appeared very active with Mr. Coventry; but now I resolve to settle it again. Not that I have idled all my time; but as to my ease, something; so I have looked a little too much after Tangier and the Fishery - and that in the sight of Mr. Coventry. But I have good reason to love myself for serving Tangier, for it is one of the best flowers in my garden.

> 27 September 1664, ...to the Fishing committee and had there very many fine things argued - and I hope some good will come of it.

11 October 1664, [talk of a bawdy play - acted by nothing but women!] *Thence to the Fishery in Thames-street - and there several good discourses about the letting of the Lotterys; and among others, one Sir Tho. Clifford* (d.1673 became Secretary of State (1672) and Lord Treasurer (1672-3)., *whom yet I know not, doth speak very well and neatly.*

18 October 1664, ...In the afternoon to the Fishery, where very confused and very ridiculous my Lord Cravens proceedings, especially his finding fault with Sir J. Collidon and Collonell Griffin's report in the accounts of the Lottery-men). Thence I met with Mr. Gray (member of the Fishery Corporation) *in his coach to White-hall; but the King and Duke being abroad, we returned to Somersett-house. In discourse, I find him a very worthy and studious gentleman in the business of Trade...*

25 October 1664,...and to the committee of the Fishery, and there did make my report of the late public Collections for the Fishery). much to the satisfaction of the Committee, and I think much to my reputation, for good notice was taken of it and much it was commended.

1 November 1664, Thence I to the committee of the Fishery and there we sat, with several good discourses and some bad and simple ones and with great disorder, and yet by the men of businesss of the town. But my report in the business of the collections is mightily commended and will get me some reputation; and endeed is the only thing looks like a thing well done since we sat. Thence with Mr. Parham to the tavern but I drank no wine, ... And he brought one Mr. Greene, an able fishmonger, and good discourse to my information.

4 November 1664,...So home to dinner, and Mr. Duke our Secretary for the Fishery, dined with me. After dinner, to discourse of our business - much to my content.

7 November 1664,...By and by a meeting of the Fishery, where the Duke was; but in such haste, and things looked so superficially over, that I had not a fit opportunity to propose my paper that I wrote yesterday; but I showed it to Mr. Gray and Wren(2) before, who did like it most highly as they said, and I think they would not dissemble in that manner in a business of this nature. But I see the greatest businesses are done so superficially, that I wonder anything succeeds at all among us that is public.

(2). Thomas Grey and Mathew Wren, both members of the Fishery Corporation.
18 November 1664, Up, and to the office and thence to the committee of the Fishery at White-hall; where so poor simple doings about the business of the Lottery, that I was ashamed to see it - that a thing so low and base should have anything to do with so noble an undertaking. But I had the advantage this day to hear Mr. Williamson discourse, who came to be a contractor with others for the Lotterys; and endeed, I find he is a very logical man and a good speaker.(2) But it was pleasant to see my Lord Craven the Chaireman, before many persons of worth and grave - use this comparison, in saying that certainly those that would contract for all the lotteries would not suffer us to set up the Virginia Lottery for plate before them. "For" says he "if I occupy a wench first, you may occupy her again your heart out; you can never have her maiden-head after I have once had it," which he did [say] more loosely, and yet as if he had fetched a most grave and worthy instance. They made mirth, but I and others were ashamed of it.

(2). With four others, Joseph Williamson (secretary to Arlington) was in June 1665 appointed to manage the Fishery Corporation's monopoly of lotteries.

3 December 1664,..and thence Sir W. Rider and I by coach to White-hall to a committee of the Fishery - there only to hear Sir Edwd. Ford's proposal about Farthing's (1)...At last,[after hot dispute between Arthur Annesley, 1st Earl of Anglesey and Lord Berkley] *though without much satisfaction to me, it was voted that it should be requested of the King, and that Sir Edwd. Fords proposal is the best yet made.*

10 December 1664,....After dinner to White-hall to the Fishery, where the Duke was with us. So home and late at my office writing many letters...

17 December 1664,...so abroad by coach to White-hall; and there to the Committee of Tangier, and then the Fishing.

10 March 1665,.Home to dinner, and thence to the Committee of Tangier at White-hall where my Lord Berkley and Craven and others, but Lord to see how superficially things are done in that business of the Lottery; which will be the disgrace of the Fishery, and without profit.

CHAPTER 12

'I Despise Wealth but not Honour' says Don Quixote

"Don Quixote" by Miguel de Cervantes: part 1 first appeared in January 1605, and part 2 in late 1615. The first translation from Spanish into English, was by Thomas Shelton in 1612 and part 2 followed in 1620. Nothing quite like it had appeared before and it would, in every sense, be 'a modern classic', which Thomas Paulden read, when he was receiving his education either at Wakefield Grammar School or perhaps more likely when he went up to Cambridge in the early 1640s.

'Don Quixote' - by far the most famous book in Spanish literature - was originally intended by Cervantes as a skit on traditional popular ballads, but he also parodied the romances of chivalry. As a result he produced one of the most entertaining adventure stories of all time and created, in Don Quixote and his faithful squire, Sancho Panza, two of the greatest characters in fiction. By 1615, when he died 'old, a soldier, a gentleman and poor', his book was already famous in both French and English.

Don Quixote del a Mancha, a poor Spanish gentleman and his peasant neighbour, Sancho Panza, are the principle characters. Cervantes has written a parody (at one remove, as Don Quixote himself is the inadvertent parodist) on chivalry, where we see confrontation is between two kinds of fiction, one highly romantic and the other relatively realistic, about a man who tries to turn his life into a romance of chivalry by becoming the most valiant and virtuous knight-errant; (a medieval knight who gives up his life to adventures where he may rescue damsels in distress, right the wrongs done to poor widows and orphans, redress grievances, relieve the oppressed and the enchanted, punish insolences, conquer giants and trample down fiends).

'I journey along the narrow path of knight-errantry, in which exercise I despise wealth, but not honour' says Don Quixote.

Through his passion for reading all the books ever written on romantic chivalry Don Quixote has become obsessed with the idea of becoming a knight-errant and he is inspired to set off in search of adventure. To his fevered imagination, everyday objects seem to pose irresistible heroic challenges: Whenever anything related to the subject is mentioned, he falls under its spell and becomes quite mad. The result is an extended and comic series of absurd exploits, which raise questions about reality and illusion, fact and fiction.

His actions, such as tilting at windmills, which he imagines to be giants, have become mythical and memorable and capture the essence of what has become known as "Quixotic" - misdirected chivalry or heroism, the admirable and the futile combined.

Sancho Panza is a foolish simpleton, but nevertheless likeable and loyal; who, when striving to show his scholarship, which he does with great regularity, misquotes inappropriate proverbs by the score and the humour derived and understood by Shakespeare's contemporaries is, just like the Bard's, still fully appreciated today.

After describing Sancho as an idiot whose words should not be heeded Don Quixote remarks:

'On the other hand I would have your Lordships understand that Sancho Panza is one of the drollest squires that ever served knight errant. Sometimes his simplicities are so shrewd that it gives me no small pleasure to consider whether it is simplicity or shrewdness that prevails. Some rogueries in him convict him of knavery, and his indiscretions confirm him as a fool. He doubts everything and believes everything. When I think he is going to tumble into folly he comes out with clever sayings which exalt him to the sky. In fact I would not exchange him for any other squire, even if I were to receive a city to boot; and therefore I am in doubt whether it would be right to send him to that governorship which your Highness has favoured him.'

As a jest, the Duke of Trifaldi, to humour his fantasy, has promised to make Sancho governor of an island.

At the beginning of the story, Don Quixote persuades Sancho Panza to accompany him on his adventures as his squire, by promising him great rewards and riches: even to make him governor of an island. Which promise Sancho, is forever anticipating throughout the story, until it comes about after they have experienced many setbacks and disasters.

On one of their adventures, a beautiful and fabulously rich heiress, Princess Dorothea Miconicona, begs Don Quixote to redress a grievance done to her, by killing a giant; and in return she is willing to shower him with lands and riches and also offers herself to him in marriage.

Don Quixote is only too pleased to have the opportunity to enhance his reputation as a knight-errant; but as he is (on becoming a knight), already enamoured and pledged to the peerless Dulcinia del Toboso, (his imagined betrothed) he has therefore, to reluctantly inform the princess that he cannot consider marriage with her as he is already bound in love with another.

When Don Quixote declined to accept Princess Micomicona's marriage offer, it so displeased Sancho that in a great fury he said, raising his voice:

'I vow and swear, Senor Don Quixote, your worship cannot be in your right senses; how else is it possible you should scrouple to marry so high a princess as this lady is? think you, fortune is to offer you at every turn such luck as she now offers? is my lady Dulcinia more beautiful? no indeed, not by half? nay, I could almost say, she is not worthy to tie this lady's shoe-string. I am like, indeed, to get the earldom I expect, if your worship stands fishing for mushrooms in the bottom of the sea. Marry, marry out of hand, in the devil's name, and take this kingdom that is ready to drop into your mouth; and, when you are king, make me a marquess, or a lord-lieutenant, and then the devil take all the rest if he will.'

Don Quixote, hearing such blasphemies against his lady Dulcinia, could not bear it, and lifting up his voice, without speaking a word to Sancho, or giving him the least warning, gave him two such blows, that he laid him flat on the ground; and, had not Dorothia called out to him to hold his hand, doubtless he had killed him thereupon the spot.

'Thinkest thou,' said he to him, after some pause, 'pitifull scoundrel, that I am *always to stand with my hands in my pockets, and that there is nothing to be done but transgressing on thy side, and forgiving on mine? Never think it, excommunicated varlet; for so doubtless thou art, since thou hast dared to speak ill of the peerless Dulcinia. Knowest thou not, rustic, slave, beggar, that, were it not for the force she infuses in my arm, I should not have enough to kill a flea? Tell me, envenomed scoffer, who thinkest thou hast gained this kingdom, and cut off the head of this giant, and made thee a marquess (for all this I look upon as already done) but the valour of Dulcinia, employing my arms as the instruments of her exploits? She fights in me, and overcomes in me; and in her I live and breathe, and of her I hold my life and being. O whoreson villain! what ingratitude, when thou seest thyself exalted from the dust of the earth to the title of a lord, to make so base a return for so great a benefit, as to speak contemptuously of the hand that raised thee!'*

On another occasion Sancho insults Princess Dorothea, whom Don Quixote greatly admires, by slandering her and being more interested in filling his belly than in her good name.

He remarks: '*I am sure and perfectly certain, that this lady, who calls herself queen of the great kingdom of Micomicon, is no more a queen than my mother.*'

Followed by: '* - - let every drab mind her spinning, and let us to dinner.*'

Good God! how great was the indignation of Don Quixote at hearing his squire speak thus disrespectfully! I say it was so great, that, with speech stammering, tongue faltering, and living fire darting from his eyes, he said:

"*Scoundrel! designing, unmannerly, ignorant, ill-spoken, foul-mouthed, impudent, mumering, and back-biting villain! darest thou utter such words in my presence, and in the presence of these illustrious ladies? and hast thou dared to entertain such rude and insolent thoughts in thy confused imagination? Avoid my presence, monster of nature, treasury of lies, magazine of deceits, storehouse of rogueries, inventor of mischiefs, publisher of absurdities, and enemy of the respect due to royal personages! Begone! appear not before me on pain of indignation!*"

And on saying this, he arched his brows, puffed his cheeks, stared round about him, and gave a violent stamp with his foot on the floor: all manifest tokens of the rage locked up in his breast. At whose words and furious gestures Sancho was so frightened, that he would have been glad had the earth opened that instant, and swallowed him up. And he knew not what to do but turn his back, and get out of the enraged presence of his master.

But the discreet Dorothea, who so perfectly understood Don Quixote's humour, to pacify his wrath, said: *'Be not offended, good Sir Knight - - '* , explaining that Sancho must have been under enchantment to say what he had.

'By the omnipotent God I swear,' quoth Don Quixote, *'your grandour has hit the mark, and some wicked apparition must have, [enchanted him] for I am perfectly assured of the simplicity and innocence of this unhappy wretch, and that he knows not how to invent a slander on anybody.'*

'So it is, and so it shall be,' said Don Fernando: *'wherefore, Senor Don Quixote, you ought to pardon him, and restore him to the bosom of your favour.'*

Don Quixote answered, that he had pardoned him; and the priest went to Sancho, who came in very humble, and, falling down on his knees, begged his master's hand in forgiveness, who gave it him; and, after he had let him kiss it he gave him his blessing.

On another occasion, Sancho attempts to take advantage of his master's good nature (and assumed madness), by asking to be paid daily for his services as his squire, and pretending it is *"twenty years and three days more or less"* since they set out on their adventures.

Don Quixote gave himself a good clap on the forehead with the palm of his hand, and began to laugh very heartily, and said:

'Why, my rambling up and down the Sierra Morena, with the whole series of our sallies, scarce take up two months, and say you Sancho, it is twenty years since I promised you the island? Well, I perceive you have a mind your wages shall swallow up all the money you have of mine; if it be so, and such is your desire, from henceforward I give it to you, and much good it will do you; for so I may get rid of so worthless a squire, I shall be glad to be left poor and penniless. But tell me perverter of squirely ordinances of knight-errantry, where have you seen or read, that any squire to a knight-errant, ever presumed to article to his master? and say, so much and so much per month, you must give me to serve you? Launch, launch out, cut-throat scoundrel, and hobgoblin (for thou art all these) launch, I say, into the mere Magnum of their histories, and, if you can find, any squire has said or thought, what you have now said, I will give you leave to nail it to my forehead, and over and over to write fool upon my face in capitals. Turn about and bridle, or halter, poor Dapple, (Sancho's ass) and begone home; for one single step further you may go not with me. O bread ill-bestowed O promises ill-placed! O man that has more of the beast than of the human creature! Now when I thought of settling you in such a way, that, in spite of your wife, you should have been styled Your lordship, do you now leave me? now you are for going, when I have taken a firm and effectual resolution to make you lord of the best island in the world? But, as you yourself have often said, honey is not for an ass's mouth. An ass you are, an ass you will die; for I verily believe, your life will reach its final period before you will perceive or be convinced that you are a beast.'

Sancho looked very wistfully at Don Quixote all the while he was thus rating him: and so great was the compunction he felt, that the tears stood in his eyes, and, with a doleful and weak voice, he said:

'Dear Sir, I confess, that to be a complete ass, I want nothing but a tail: if your lordship will be pleased to put me one on, I shall deem it well placed, and will serve your worship in the quality of an ass, all the remaining days of my life. Pardon me, sir, have pity on my ignorance, and, consider that, if I talk much, it proceeds more from infirmity than malice: but, he who errs and mends, himself to God commends.'

'I should wonder, Sancho,' quoth Don Quixote, ' if you did not mingle some little proverb with your talk. Well, I forgive you, upon condition of your amendment, and that henceforth you show not yourself so fond of your interest, but that you endeavour to enlarge your heart, take courage, and strengthen your mind to expect the accomplishment of my promises, which, though they are deferred, are not therefore desperate.'

Sancho answered, he would, though he should draw force from his weakness.

They meet up with the Duke and Duchess of Trifaldi who find great amusement in listening to their fantastic adventures and take great delight in encouraging them to describe and take part in even greater fantasies, which the Duke and Duchess help to contrive.

It is the mixture of foolishness and good sense of both Don Quixote and Sancho which so entrances their new hosts; the more they are made fun of, the more their good sense prevails.

The Duke's priest who is jealous of their success with his master says sarcastically *'Are you perhaps, brother, that Sancho Panza they speak of, to whom your master has promised an isle?'*

The Duchess was dying with laughter at Sancho's remarks concerning the priest, considering him madder and more entertaining than his master.

'I am,' answered Sancho, 'and I deserve it as much as anyone on earth. I'm one of your - keep company with good men and you'll be one of them - yes, and of your - not with whom your bred, but with whom you're fed.' I've leant on my good master, and I've been going about in his company for many months and, God willing, I shall come to be like him. And if he lives and I live he'll have no lack of empires to rule, nor I of isles to govern!'

'No, of course not, Sancho my friend,' interposed the Duke, who could not restrain himself from, (as a practical joke) further encouraging Sancho's fantasy *'for in Don Quixote's name I can offer you the government of an odd one of mine, and no poor one either.' 'An isle round and well proportioned, exceedingly fertile and fruitful; and there, if you know how to manage things, from the riches of the earth you can gain the riches of heaven.'*

'Well now,' replied Sancho, *'let the isle come. For I'll try to be such a governor that I'll get to heaven, despite all rogues. And its not out of greed that I want to leave my poor huts and rise to greater things, but from the desire to find out what it tastes like to be a governor.'*

'So be it', said Don Quixote *'If you govern badly the fault will be yours, and the shame mine. But it consoles me that I have done my duty in advising you as truly and*

wisely as I can. God govern you in your government, and deliver me from my suspicion that you will turn your whole isle upside down, a thing which I could prevent by informing the Duke of your character, and telling him that all that fat little body of yours is nothing but a sackful of proverbs and mischief.'

'Sir,' answered Sancho, *'if I don't seem to your worship worthy of this gover-norship, I give it up from this moment. For I love a single black nail's breadth of my soul more than my whole body, and plain Sancho can live just as well on bread and onions as Governor Sancho on partridges and capons. What's more we're all equal while we're asleep, great and small, poor and rich alike; and if your worship reflects, you'll see it was only you who put this business of governing into my head, for I know no more of governing isles than a vulture; and if anyone thinks that the Devil will get me for being a governor, I had rather go to heaven plain Sancho than to Hell as a gov-ernor.'*

'By God, Sancho.' said Don Quixote, *'if only for those last words of yours, I con-sider you worthy to be governor of a thousand isles.'*

Don Quixote wrote down, for Sancho, comprehensive advice on good governorship and handed him a copy, so that he might get someone to read it to him. But no sooner had he given them to Sancho than they fell into the hands of the Duke, who showed them to the Duchess, and the pair of them were again surprised at Don Quixote's mad-ness and good sense. So, to continue with their jest, they sent Sancho that evening with a great escort to the village, which was to serve as his isle.

Now the man who had charge of the matter happened to be a steward of the Duke's, a very shrewd and humorous fellow - for there can be no humour without shrewdness - and carefully coached by his master and mistress as to his conduct towards Sancho, he was miraculously successful in his design.

At length Sancho set out, accompanied by a great number of people, dressed as a lawyer in a very broad overcoat of tawney watered camlet and a hunting-cap of the same material. On taking leave of the Duke and Duchess he kissed their hands and begged his master for his blessing, which Don Quixote gave him with tears and Sancho received with blubberings.

Sancho's dream had come true, but Don Quixote misses him so much that he imme-diately falls into a melancholy state, withdrawing into his own quarters, willing to see no one.

Sancho, for his part, revels in his governorship, making laws and dispensing justice as did Solomon. However, after just seven days of sitting in judgement, deciding causes, and making statutes and proclamations; he is called upon to lead his subjects in defend-ing his 'island' against a pretended attack, for which he finds himself manifestly unfit-ted; and after being trampled, battered and humiliated, he craves release from his responsibilities.

His dream of becoming governor of an island has been shattered and he protests:
'Good God, I will no more continue in this governorship, nor accept of any other, though it were served up to me in a covered dish, than I will fly to heaven without wings. Every

sheep with its like; and, Stretch not your feet beyond your sheet: and so let me be gone, for it is late.'

So ends Sancho Panza's fantasy of becoming governor of an island and the salutary experience of Don Quixote's squire must have struck deep into Thomas Paulden's thoughts when he reflected on his own dream of governing 'Holy Island': the circular area of 'land' nine miles in circumference between Holy Island and the mainland of Northumberland which proved to be almost as fanciful and fantastic as the make-believe 'island' provided by the Duke and Duchess of Trifaldi for Sancho
to govern.

At the very end of the story when Don Quixote, just before his death, recovers his sanity and makes his will; the author Cervantes tells us that :

'For me alone Don Quixote was born and I for him. His was the power of action, mine of writing. Only we two are at one —. For my sole object has been to arouse men's contempt for all fabulous and absurd stories of knight errantry, whose credit this tale of my genuine Don Quixote has already shaken, and which will, without doubt, soon tumble to the ground. Farewell.'

Here again in his later years Thomas Paulden can't have failed to see himself as Don Quixote and even so as Cervantes the author *'old, a soldier, a gentleman and poor.'* Yet contented, we hope, as a man of honour, having striven to succeed and sharing Shakespeare's and Cervantes' precept, *'to thine own self be true.'*

Sometime before Thomas was fleeing from his creditors and a debtors' prison, when he wrote his desperate letter desiring Lord Christopher Hatton to be his patron, we find this intriguing entry in the Calendar of Treasury Papers:

'5 June, 1691. Royal Warrant under the Queen's sign manual to Auditor Bridges to allow the earl of Ranelagh [paymaster of the forces] in his Army account ending 1689, April 30, the sum of £1,732. - Appending a particular of sums [inter alia] to the steward of Bethlehem Hospital for curing Tho: Palden and James Walker of their lunacy who were sent out of the Earl of Lichfield's Regiment and the Royal Regiment of Foot, £14.17.3.'

If Thomas Paulden, at the age of 63, was still attached (possibly in an honorary capacity or even on half pay) to the Earl of Lichfield's Regiment in 1689, then here we have proof that his ideas of knight errantry - enhancing his heroic reputation like Don Quixote – or becoming governor of an island like Sancho Panza - had led him, in attempting to emulate his heroes in those respects, at least to follow Don Quixote's example in another - being driven mad by his delusions!

Or is it possible that Thomas devised this idea of pleading insanity in order to escape his creditors and a debtors' prison'?

Shame on us for questioning his honesty when we have already accepted his 'madness' as a consequence of his quixotic obsession, owing to his belief and passion in real, as well as romantic, chivalry.

The great drawing room at Kirkby Hall as it may have been in the late 17C.

Additional Mss 29551

[Envelope addressed to]: For the Honourable Christopher
                         Hatton Esq. at Kirkby
                         To bee Left at the Postmasters
                         at Stamford
         post pd 2d   Lincolnshire. ,

Feb. ye 4th (91) [1691] 136

My 'Lord
The long acquaintance and many favours I have received from
your Lordship gives mee the Courage and Confidence to begg one
more which to mee will bee of great importance, and I hope of
no inconvenience to your Lordshipp whom I know too well to aske
any thing of which may bee either dishonest or dishonourable. My
Lord my request is that your Lordshipp would bee pleased to bee
my patron and master & protect mee as your servant, tho I shall
not expect any wages And my Lord this I doe assure you will bee
as much to the Advantage of my Creditors as my owne, for if I
have my liberty I shall bee able in a short time to pay my debts

(having more owing to mee in good debts than I owe) which a
prison would make mee incapable of, if I have my liberty can
have an employment worth £100 a yeare & doe not doubt but in
that time I shall bee able to pay all my debts and to make your
Lordshipp such a gratefull acknowledgement of this singular favour
as you will thinke mee not an unprofitable servant; I hope your
Lordshipp knowes mee so well that you will believe mee when I
tell you that this is the true state of my Condition, and that
I act with all the Sincerity an honest man ought to doe, and if
your Lordshipp pleases to employ mee in anything wherein I may
serve you I shall obey your Commands with all diligence & fidelity
as

I shall waite upon your Lordshipp for an answer in two or 3 dayes

My Lord

your Lordshipps most humble
& most obedient servant

THOM. PAULDEN

Additional Mss 29565 137

My Lord
I was to waite upon your Lordship the day before you
left the towne & your servant told mee you was indisposed so
that I did not come to recieve your Lordshipps Commands till
the day after your Ldshipps departure which is the cause I give,
you the trouble of this paper to renew my humble Request to you
for your Lordshipps Patronage which you was pleased to have the
goodness to take into your consideration to advise how it might
be conveniently bee done; but the suddennesse of you leaving
the towne has deprived mee of the knowledge of your Lordshipps
pleasure therein which if you please to lett any of your servants
signifie to mee by two or three lines directed for Captaine
Paulden at Toms Coffee house in Princes Street Covent Garden,
you will add to your many former favours, this singular one
of preserving

My Lord your Lordshipps most humble
& most obedient servant

THO. PAULDEN

British Library - Hatton Mss.
Additional Mss 29551 (155)

[Capt. Thomas Paulden to Sir Christopher Hatton, Jan.1665/6]

Sir
I had not beene so late before I returned you my humble
thanks for your Civilities but that I thought I should
have had the honour to have kissed your hands in the
Country before this. But my Lord Duke of Buck [ingham] his
incertainty of remoove to oxford and the approach of the
tearme has disappointed my journey for the present. But
I hope I shall have the happinesse to see you here as soone
as the Court comes uppe which wee persuade ourselves here will
bee within a fortnight In the meanetime I can onely acknowledge
a debt which I am not able to satisfye, and send this paper to
testifie that you have infinately obliged one who will
eternally confess it, which I doe and drinke your health with
My Queene as often as I see her and shee as often as shee
drinkes but that is not very often for shee has given over
good fellowship and will scarce allow it in mee. But wee live
together like Don Quixote & Sancho Panca the one still offending
the other still pardoning but in one thing I am sure wee never
differ that is in wishing you all the happiness in the world I
should end my letter like an oxford Gazette (viz) The
Quarterly Bill runs thus. But they are not yet come in so that
design is lost, But that I may recompense it wth a little news
though not very good take it as wee have it Ruyter is gone out
a fortnight agoe wth 30 saile of men of warre his designe
security but is imagined to follow Sir Jerome Smith into the
Straites because no Body can guess anything else pray give
service to Nuncle[1] & to the Doctor & all at Yelverloft if
you have opportunity

I am Sir,

Lond[on]. Jan. ye [?]th   your humble & most
[16](65)   obedient servant

                                  THO. PAULDEN.

The great court of Kirkby Hall, Northamptonshire, home of Sir Christopher Hatton.
From Cassell's History of England Vol. 2.

CHAPTER 13

PAULDEN and its Origins

Quite soon after discovering my connection with Captain Thomas Paulden and reading about his exciting exploits during the English civil war, I unexpectedly, while browsing through an accession calendar at Lancashire Record Office, Preston, came across a collection of papers relating to an estate called Paulden in Oldham, S.E.Lancashire, dated 1884-1902.[1] I had found the surname Paulden to be quite rare but a place by that name in Oldham in the late nineteenth early twentieth century immediately brought to mind an image of cotton mills and industry presaging no connection with a 16th century Yorkshire family - nevertheless, a seed had been planted and I did jot down the reference which a number of years later was to prove most fruitful.

When I had exhausted most available research sources for the 17th century history of Thomas Paulden and his family, I became inquisitive about his earlier ancestry and found that his family had resided in Halifax from the beginning of the parish registers. I was then delighted to discover through wills, deeds and rentals that they had been in the area from at least the late 15th century and probably earlier; which I felt at the time was probably as much as I could reasonably hope or expect to find, about the origins of a yeoman family.

When enjoying studying local maps and reflecting on the derivation of place-names some years ago, which I often love to do, it occurred to me on the spur of the moment to see, if by a long-shot, I could find the name Paulden on the 2.5" O.S. map of Oldham and district; but as I'd expected, it did not appear. Several years later, however, when researching other families in Rochdale library, I did discover Paulden's whereabouts; finding it on the 1848, 6" O.S. map, to be on the north-eastern outskirts of Oldham.

Having no instinctive feelings that the 19-20C Paulden estate bore any real relevance to Captain Thomas Paulden, I did not follow up this discovery, being fully convinced anyway, that an estate existing on the outskirts of Oldham at that time would almost certainly have been swallowed up by the immense growth of industry and population experienced by that town famous for its vast cotton manufacturing production in the late nineteenth and early twentieth century.

However, about three years ago when coming to an impasse in other research avenues when on another visit to the Lancashire Record Office, I decided to fill in the time by taking a cursory glance through the Paulden estate papers of 1884. A large account book full of details revealed that the owners at that time were Elkanah and Thomas Moss, cotton manufactures with the farm tenant Mr. Thomas Winterbottom paying £140 per annum. The 1871 census tells us that Thomas was aged 56, farming 60acres and employing 2 men. His rent was reduced in 1884 to £133 and in 1889 to £70 p.a. after Mrs Winterbottom took over. Many details of repairs and costs and tithe of £2.10s.2d still claimed by the Rector of Prestwich in 1888; Property Tax and Land Tax £3.2s.7d. and Income Tax £2.10s.7d in 1904.

Of great interest was a large scale map of the estate showing the individual fields and various farm buildings plus two stone quarries, new dwelling houses and land sold to Oldham Corporation in connection with the waterworks, which no doubt accounts for the reduced farm rent. What would have been even more interesting (had they been included) were the original title deeds: unfortunately in their place was a brief tantalising note from the solicitors to say that the deeds had been 'examined and attested' - but were not included with the deposited estate papers. Attempts to trace the solicitors - and the deeds - proved fruitless.

One Sunday in June last year (1993), after a long rainy spell had kept us indoors for what seemed weeks, and quite unanticipated, a warm sunny cloudless day with a pleasant breeze presented itself out of the blue. 'Where can we go to make the most of such wonderful unexpected weather?' asked my wife Jennie, testing my initiative. With unusual immediate inspiration I rose to the occasion and responded, without having had any previous conscious thoughts on the matter 'I know - we'll go and see if we can find Paulden!' Perhaps my subconscious organiser had been anticipating just such a question.

I can readily admit now, having studied modern maps of Oldham and district before then, that I fully expected to find little else but serried rows of 19th century terraced houses and neighbourhood cotton factories, or perhaps more likely their demolished remains; covering the site any Paulden estate that may have managed to survive until 1884.

After travelling east from Oldham town centre, through Greenacres and then getting lost through Lees, to somewhere near where I thought Paulden to have been, and after receiving several negative answers to my enquiries, one of these being to a local policeman, I felt that my previous suspicions regarding Paulden's demise were proving to be only too accurate.

But, not to be denied, and feeling that some local old aged person might at least have heard of the name, I parked the car with Jennie left inside listening to the radio, and ventured on foot to investigate more thoroughly. Once again, however, my enquiries were proving to be depressingly fruitless and having got to the point of being forced to accept inevitable defeat (having hoped all the time that I might be proved wrong) I was attempting to find interest in the unfamiliar surroundings for their own sake.

The positive answer I received from a woman tending her garden, to what I'm sure I felt in my own mind was by that time but a rhetorical question, was exhilarating. Not only had she heard of Paulden, she was directing me to it 'If you go to the end of this street, turn right up Howard Street and go up the hill past Locking Gate, you will come to the farm.' A farm!! In the centre of a housing development? I dashed back to the car and jumping in hardly having breath to tell Jennie 'There's a farm, come on!' It felt like having discovered a chest full of gold after following the vague directions of, what I half suspected all-along to be, a fake treasure map.

We drove up through a neat new housing estate to find the last house built with its garden extending, literally, up against the farm-yard gate. Parking on a bit of spare land and imploring my camera-woman to get our newly acquired video camera into action, I walked quickly into the farmyard, trying not to run, with my wife Jennie left struggling along behind gathering the equipment, and, overtaken by my enthusiasm at the sight of a very old and interesting farm building with 'arched' windows; I found myself uninvited in the very centre of a typical farm-yard scene.

'Paulden's farm [front view] at Waterhead. The single story building was once a church [no authority given] and is now used as a shippon. News Cutting 1968-69.'

Paulden's Farm shippon, rear view.

Paulden's Farm barn, rear view.

Above left:*Shippon doorway.*
Above: *Nearby houses.*

Farm-yard gateway.

White and brown hens and cockerels fluttered about in their noisy efforts to escape the flying hooves of a young black and white pony, which was being cantered up and down the yard by its owner, who was keen to impress and then close a sale with the scrutinising red-faced farmer looking on.

Normal reserve was unconsciously cast aside as, overcome by excitement, I managed to get close enough to the farmer, without interrupting the pony which was still showing its paces, to ask him: 'Would it be all right to look around and take a photograph of the buildings?' 'Aye - go where you want and take what photo's you want' was his most friendly reply as he self consciously tucked in his shirt and pulled up his trousers at the sight of Jennie, who, without waiting for permission and apparently oblivious of being trampled on, was advancing on the pair of us with her camera rolling. Thinking about it later, kindness was perhaps not Mr. Clarke's uppermost priority at the time; he no doubt wanted us out of the way as quickly as possible, so that he could continue with his horse trading.

Nevertheless we took him at his word and for the next hour and more, I must have become unbearable - continually instructing Jennie to 'get those hens! - And that cock!' 'Have you got the mother lying over there? Take that cow on the hill!' Have you got this angle of the barn? Make sure you get a good shot of the arched windows, etc, etc. Three playful friendly goat kids were gambolling about plucking at leaves here and buds there; jumping along and on top of a broken down wall to reach some other tasty tree shoots. It was a delight, the farm may have looked broken down and unkempt but the poultry, the horses, the cattle and yes even a large pig, made my day. Discovering the fascinating ancient building and finding the old farmstead so unexpectedly was marvellous, but to see it still being run as a working farm was like a dream come true.

After videoing all the buildings and the horses, goats and poultry around them, we climbed further up the hillside to enjoy a picnic close to the cows, who were chewing their cud peacefully in a field overlooking Paulden Farm. It was one of those few perfect summer days, with a deep blue sky and a blazing sun accompanied by a pleasant breeze, which we wonder what we have done to deserve when they arrive. After satisfying our appetites we were able to take marvellous panoramic views of the scenery, looking down from an almost forty-five degree angle onto the farm-buildings below and then Middy (our brown and black Manchester terrier) being warned to keep away from its beautiful young calf, by a prancing Guernsey cow as it menacingly flicked its horns to show it meant business.

When we arrived back at the farm, after surveying the Paulden estate, Mr Clarke had gone home. We learned later that the farmer, a Mr Fred Ashworth, had died in the last couple of years or so and that was no doubt the cause of the rather derelict and dilapidated state of the two terrace type houses in which he had lived as well as the rest of the farm. Mr. Clarke lived some distance away in Lees and only rented the farm fields from the new absent owners, Mr. Ashworth's relations, who are estate agents! Prospects don't look good for Paulden and we felt very grateful to have seen the old buildings and fields and very conscious of the fact that providence had sent us there, perhaps in the nick of time.

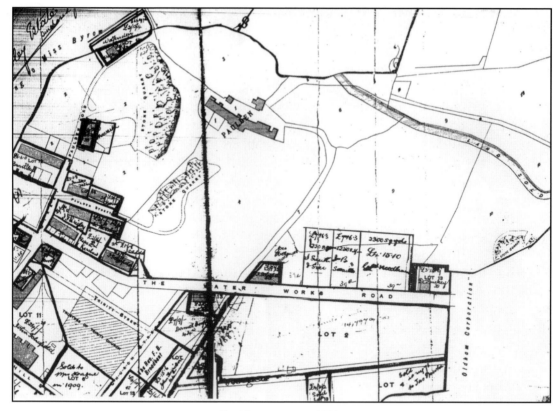

Paulden estate map 1881.

One day a few weeks later I took the opportunity to visit Oldham Local Studies Library and, with the help of the staff, discovered some old newspaper photographs of Paulden [2] and a few brief references to previous residents, when they had taken their turn as church warden, police commissioner &c.[3] The librarian kindly provided me with details of local historical organisations and I wrote to them when I got home. A good while later, owing to summer holidays &c. I received a helpful letter from Mr. Duncan Gurr, Chairman of the Oldham Historical Society, including some useful local maps and advice to contact the vicar of Holy Trinity church, Waterhead, as he was a long term resident well known for his local historical knowledge.

As it turned out Rev. C.E.Shaw wasn't a local historian at all but an international authority on weeds &c, often referred to on that famous radio programme Gardeners' Question Time. The vicar however, kindly passed my letter of enquiry on to an appropriate member of his flock, Mr. Fred Lees, local resident and historian who has written a history 'Home in Waterhead' in a series of most interesting monthly instalments, in the Holy Trinity parish magazine, (1990-1993) and who has, over the past months, become a valued friend; generously putting all his great local knowledge at my disposal and giving me kind help and encouragement in my efforts to research the history of Paulden.

The present Paulden Farm, consisting of a mere 13 acres, lies high on the hillside, completely overlooking the industrial town of Oldham nearby, and now in the ecclesiastical district of Waterhead, which was created out of the parish of Oldham, S.E.Lancashire in 1844. Although operating as a parish for many years, Oldham was long before this time, and still is technically, attached to the mother parish church of Prestwich, which in earlier times was always styled the parish of Prestwich-cum-Oldham.

Owing mainly to the dramatic growth of its industry and its population from hundreds to over a hundred thousand during the past two hundred years, Oldham has greatly outgrown its parent parish and because of this several administrative and ecclesiastical boundary changes have occurred in the area. From the earliest times too, there were many boundary changes owing to the ownership of great estates being divided by inheritance, grants, marriage settlements, and of course the Dissolution of the Monasteries, when new owners bought the requisitioned lands from the King's Commissioners, so creating new estate boundaries which led to further parochial and manorial complexities. Other changes which took place so long ago now that through the mists of time and lack of documentation, precise details can only be guessed at.

A medieval Custumal and Rental of 'Assheton Subtus Limam' was in the possession of Joseph Pickford Esq. of Royton [and of Lower Alt Hill, Ashton-under-Lyne] in 1795 but the original document has disappeared. John Harrop of Bardsley House, Ashton-under-Lyne, possessed a (not strictly accurate) copy of this document taken c1749 and his descendant Dr. Hibbert-Ware used this in his private publication, which was reproduced with his 'dissertation' of 1822, for the Chetham Society.[4]

Winifred M.Bowman, on whom I have relied heavily in this chapter, gives us a fully detailed and fascinating re-appraisal of the 'Rental' with all its ramifications, in her splendid publication 'England in Ashton-under-Lyne' 1960. Also in Mrs. Bowman's book opposite to p.8 is a map of Ashton-under-Lyne in relation to the surrounding south Pennine area. Paulden is shown just outside the northern tip of the present parish of Ashton-under-Lyne next to Strines Dale and close to 'Street', the Roman Road running from Chester to York and passing close to Halifax on its way.[5] I was excited to see a medieval route way running from Besom Hill near Paulden to Elland Hall near Halifax and an even earlier route way actually running from Paulden to Halifax. If I was in any doubt before, this new information (plus the fact that I had been unable to discover any other place called Paulden) convinced me that this was the place where Thomas Paulden's ancestor lived before moving to Halifax and from where his family had acquired their surname.

Lees village, now a suburb of Oldham but previously in the northern part of the parish of Ashton-under-Lyne, has evolved from a field of the name Lees, existing in the 13th century. However, whereas today we might think of a large field as containing perhaps ten to fifteen acres, that would be very small indeed compared with the vast open-fields existing for centuries before and long after the Norman Conquest in the north of England. Many were several hundred acres in extent as must have been Lees Field in the lordship of Ashton-under-Lyne, (which from early times included the manor of Alt); it once stretched well to the north of its present bounds and in the Middle Ages included part of Strinesdale, with Paulden Ley and Paulden Wood [6] and probably most if not all of the present district of Waterhead.

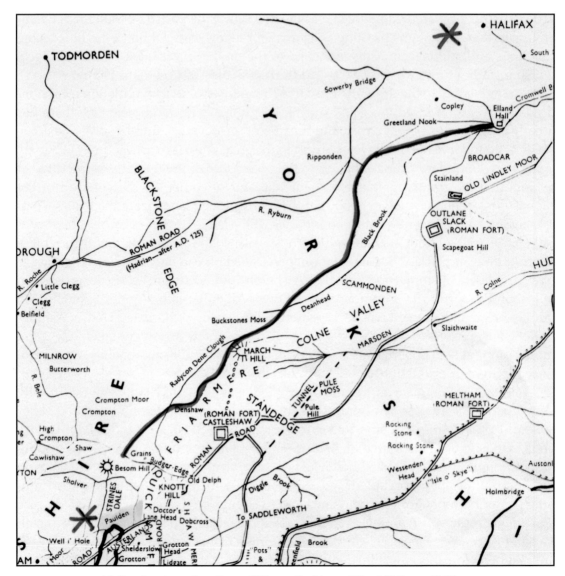

Medieval rout way from Besom Hill near Paulden to Elland Hall near Halifax.

At least as early as 1190-1212, Paulden Ley seems to have been part of this great field when, in an undated deed computed by W. Farrer to be of that date, Albon de Alt granted to the monks of Kersal [in Salford near Manchester] of the moiety of Palden Ley, in the parish of Ashton-under-Lyne. The land must have lain in what is described in 1422 as 'old Alt'. The whole of Alt was once part of Adam Fitz Swain's estate of Kaskenmoor, which covered much of the area between what is now Ashton-under-Lyne and Rochdale, and passed to his son-in-law William de Neville. A few years later just before 1227, Albin de Alt, sub-tenant of an estate in the northern part of the manor of Ashton, granted to 'God, and the blessed St. Leonard of Kersall and the monks who minister to God there the whole half part of Paldenley', a long narrow strip of land which once must have extended from the banks of the river Medlock at Nether Lees almost to Besom Hill [covering the whole of the present districts of Lees, Greenacres and Waterhead] beyond Cross Bank. Portions of the great Common-field, from which the hamlet of Lees took its name, were included in the grant, and were recognised long afterwards as 'part and parcel' of the property of Kersal.[7] After the Suppression of the Monasteries this land produced a free rent of 14s 4d. per annum, which was shared by those whose forefathers had been the original lessees from Kersal, or who had obtained it by purchase from the King.[8]

In 1276 Thomas son of William de Alt claimed a messuage and 12 acres in Paldenley against Richard son of Robert de Tounton [the Poll-tax returns show the wife of Richard resident here] and Margery de Hache, but failed in his claim, it being stated that Palden Ley was 'not a town nor a borough, but only a place in the fields of Ashton'.[9] The title to this deed names William de Alt as 'William de Alche'. In the semi-phonetic dialect spelling employed to describe people of Alt in pleas of 1276 and 1293, i.e. 'Alche' and Hache' (Margery de Hache was daughter of Robert de Alte). Alt, which the Survey of Manchester, 1320, shows that John de Asheton held of the Lord of Manchester by an annual rent of 2s.[10]

What remained of this medieval common field retained its name as 'Lees Field' and is recorded in the will of Ottiwell Andrew of Lees, yeoman, in 1592.[11] It had by then, however, been reduced to thirteen Lancashire acres (20 statute acres) but was still divided into strips of varying size and shape. By the 16th century, it seems that free-holders had obtained almost the entire ownership of land in this former 'common field' and Ottiwell Andrew's thirteen Lancashire acres were finally enclosed by a very late award of 1841.

Referring back now to the medieval rental:- 'Of this record that part relating to Sir John Assheton's covenant with his tenants regarding their swine (1379-80) is the earliest. The agreement re the Cornmill was made in (1399). Finally comes the record of tenure, existing or newly taken out, as they stood recorded on Wednesday November 11th 1422, when following the death of his master and military leader, Henry V, Sir John Assheton III had returned from France to inspect his manor.

The list of Free-Tenants, under the Days when Their Rents were Due. [All, or in part recorded in or before 1397], when Sir Richard de Byron - named here as a free tenant - died, and during the period when Thomas de Staveley was still living.'

[Abstract only relating to Palden Ley, Palden Wood and Paulden or their tenants; being less than one tenth of the whole rental.]
'Libi tenent de Termo Pentecost

Petrus de Trafford p Alston Londes and Palden Wood	10d
Idem Petrus de terra in Sherewinde	3d
Heres Ada de Mosley p Alston Londes and Palden	5d
Heres Roberti le [Dane?] p Palden Wood and Alston Londes	6d

[Alston Londs is now the village of Austerlands close to Waterhead but over the border in Yorkshire].

Libi tenant de Termo Scti Johis Bapt.

Johes del Knolles p Rhodes ffield	3s & 5d
The same John for an intake in Palden Wood	2s & 3d
Ricus de Hollingworth for an intake in Palden Wood	2s & 3d
Johes de Aspinhalgh for an intake in Palden Wood	2s & 3d

Libi tenant de termino Scti. Micht. Archi

Adm de Leghes for an intake in Palden legh	3s & 4s
Thomas de Leghes for an intake in Palden legh	3s & 4d
John del Knolles, p redy Legh	3s & 5d
Idem Johes, for an intake in Palden wood	2s & 4d
Ricus del Hollinworth for an intake in Palden	2s & 3d
johs de Aspinhalgh, for an intake in Palden	2s & 9d

Libi tenant de termino Sancti Martini.

Petrus de Trafford, p terra in Sherewinde	3d
Idem Petrus, p Alston Londs and Palden wood	10d
Heres dde de Mosley, p Alston londs and Palden wood	5d
Heres Robti Dane, p Palden wood and Alston londs	6d

This is the Rental of Thomas of Assheton, son and Heir to Sir John Assheton, of the lands and tenements, the which the said John gave him at his marriage, within the lordship of Assheton, and to his wife, as their Deed makes mention. [Thomas de Assheton was married in 1415 (aged 12 years), to Elizabeth de Byron. His father was Sir John de Assheton III, who inherited the manor c1402.]

Thomas of the Leghes, Richard of Hollinworth, for their lands in Palden Legh, the farm XXIIs VIId.

The Rent-roll of John de Assheton, Tempus. 1st of Henry the 6th A.D. 1422.

At the ffeast of Martyn in winter, the year of King Henry (the sixth after the conquest) the first. All the Tenants of the Lordship of Assheton-under-Lyme, taking their tenements to ffarm for twenty winter term, at John of Assheton, Knight, the which came out of Normandy. At the same ffeast, with all the services, customs, and usages, as after this is, in this same Book written and rehearsed and as it has been used and customed of old time, and every man to pay his ffarm at two tymes in the year, as the Rental of this said Book makes mention.

The service of the said Tenants is this, that they shall give their presents at Yole [i.e. Christmas] every present to such a value, as it is written and sett in the Rental, and the Lord shall ffeed all his said Tenants and their wives, upon Yole day at the dinner, if them like for to come, but the said Tenants and their wives, though it be for their ease not for to come, they shall send neither man nor woman in their name, but if he be their son, other their daughter dwelling with them unto the dinner, ffor the Lord is not bounden to ffeed all save only the good man and the good wife. Also every Tenant that plow has shall plow two days, and he that half plow has, shall plow a day, whether the

Lord beleiver in wheat seeding, other in Lenten seeding; and every Tenant harrow a day with their harrow in seeding time, when they bin charged, and they shall cart, every Tenant ten cart full of turve, fro Done a Mosse, to Assheton; and shear ffour days in harvest, and cart a day corne, and they shall pay a principal at their death, that is to wit, the best beast they have, which other deed next after Holy Kirk.'

This is the whole Rental of the Tenants-at-Will of the said Lordship of Assheton, and the value of their presents at Yole, the year and a day aforesaid, the which Rent shall be payd at two terms of the year, that is to wit: the ton half at the ffeast of St. John Baptist, and tother half at the ffeast of St. Martyn, 'ith' winter.

Rentale Tenent ad voluntarem de doma de Assheton Anno Regni Regis Henri Sexti primo [i.e. Tenants-at-will or 'Copyholders'].

Alys, that was Pole wife, the same service for a cottage, [less than 4 days shearing, which was 'a whole sevice'] and shall pay 12d., and a present at the value of 4d.

Thomas of the Leghes, and Syssot that was the wife of Dycon of Hollinworth, for the tone half of the intake in Palden Wood, 13s 4d. The same Thomas of the Leghes for an intake besyde Alt hey 10s.

Rental Liber tenent de Dome. de Asheton sub Lima, Anno Suprado solvend ad six Terminos annl. &c.

The Heir of Thomas de Staveley, for the Bastal and Hurst.	
[Thos. de Staveley was living when earlier list was compiled]	2s 1d
The same Heir for the Three Houses	0s 6d
The same Heir of Staveley, and the Heir of Thomas de Trafford	
[the younger Thos.de Trafford] and others, for Ashton [Corry gives	
Alston] (History of Lancs.) Londs and Palden Wood	4s 0d
Richard of Hollinworth for his part of an intack in Palden Wood	[4s 6d
from Hibbert-Ware].(Chetham Soc.)	
Thomas of the Leghes, John of the Knolles, Richard of Hollinworth,	
John of the Aspenhalgh for their tenements in the Leghes	0s 6d
The Heir of Adam of the Leghes, for his tenement in Leghes	0s 10d
The same Heir of Adam of the Leghes [? Thomas], for an intake	
in Palden Wood	3s 4d
John of the Knolles, for the Rhodes ffield	6s 10d
The same John, for his part of an intake in Palden Wood	4s 6d
John of the Aspinhalgh and his wife, for their part of an	
intake in Palden Wood	4s 6d'

The tenants could, if they so wished, give up their tenements at Martinmas after giving twelve months notice. An important part of their agreement being to leave their lands, houses and closes in as good a condition as when they entered them.

The free tenants did not have to perform the onerous and menial boon services previously listed but they, together with the tenants-at-will, were obliged to grind their corn at the Lord's mill and could be fined up to the large sum of 40s for failing to do so, and they had also to pay tolls at the Lord's fairs and attend his manor court and abide by its injunctions.

Tenants who had lands in the fields were allowed to have two swine, to range in the demesnes of the town from the latter end of August until sowing time, provided they were properly ringed and did no harm; and cottagers with no land were allowed one.

Although many of the free tenants and the tenants-at-will appear to have surnames in the forgoing rental the custom was not firmly established by this period and the heir of Dycon Robinson could well become Robert Dickenson; William the Walker's son could well become William the Arrowsmith, if he took up that occupation; and Adam of the Leghes might well become Adam of the Knolles if he took up residence in that place.

Of the many lands, tenements strips &c appropriated, over the last 700 years, from the original common field of Lees, I believe the following to be the first reference to the buildings and land still know today as Paulden Farm.

Polden/Palden, described as 'in Sholver part of the township of Oldham', is mentioned in February 1300-01 when the Bishop granted Matthew de Sholver, Rector of Prestwich, leave to take part in the obsequies of Roger de Pilkington, lord of Sholver, until the following Pentecost.[12] Long afterwards it was alleged that he had without licence appropriated to the church of Prestwich a messuage called Palden in Oldham. Inquisition had been made in 1371 and account had been demanded from the executors of Robert de Donington, John de Radcliffe and Richard de Pilkington.[13] In 1397 & 1404 the Rector of Prestwich's successors were called upon to account for 10s rent which should have accrued to the Crown for the same.[14]

The Prestwich family, were lords of Prestwich in the 12th & 13th centuries and when the male line failed the manor descended through the female line to the Langleys of Agecroft. The patronage of Prestwich church was vested in the lords of Prestwich, who appear also to have inherited the messuage called Palden in Oldham.

In an indenture dated 7 February 17 Henry VIII [1526], 'Richard Brerele' is named as a trustee, along with Ralph Prestwich, Esq., (who held the wardship of Edward Hobkyn), Robert Langley, jun., Esq., and Edmund Langley, gent., for a marriage settlement and wardship of lands in Oldham, to go to Edward Hobkyn on his marriage to Margaret daughter of Seth Walker. The Brearley family probably originated from a settlement of that name in Rochdale [15] land called Brerylees in Hollinworth, 1303; and this Richard Brearley was probably a member of the family which was to be leaseholders of Paulden for the next one hundred and fifty years.[16]

In 1556/7 Sir William Langley, parson of Prestwich, brought an action in the court of the Duchy of Lancaster against three of his tenants in Oldham. Sir William complained 'that whereas he and his predecessors, parsons of the said Church, from time immemorial have always been seized in their demesne as of fee of 13 messuages, two barns, and 160 acres of meadow and pasture lying in Prestwhiche and Oldam and whereas three messuages with the appurtenances are in the several tenures of Rauffe Jackson (the parish clerk), James Brereley and Sir Thomas Sharokes, clerk (the last parish priest of Oldham)...that in the holding of James Brereley of the yearly rent of 10s.' Since the death of his predecessor Sir William Langley, late parson of Prestwich, about five years ago, Rauffe, James and Thomas have got the deeds into their own hands and now refuse to pay their rents and are attempting to disinherit him. A commission was to be set up to decide the issue but its findings are not extant. Apparently the patron of the living Sir Robert Langley, knight, was claiming priority over the parson and collecting the rents himself, and when Sir Robert died without a male heir in 1561, he must have been vindicated as his estates were divided between his four daughters and the advowson of Prestwich with other lands, which included Palden,[17] were in the portion inherited by Dorothy, wife of James Asheton of Chadderton.[18]

In a dispute over the certain lands in the manor of Quick in Saddleworth between James Brearley and George Whewell, we learn that waste lands in Strines being part of that manor were also claimed to be part of the common of pasture rights of Palden Farm. This appears to give credibility to the idea that 'Paulden' bestrode the Lancashire Yorkshire county boundary even at this late date but it just may be that James Brearley was taking advantage of common rights of pasture belonging to 20 messuages with lands in Quick and Saddleworth bought by the Ashton owners of Paulden in 1581.[19] James Brearely, who had his horses, young beasts, sheep and cattle driven off the said moor, claimed to hold the land under lease dated 24 Eliz [1582] from James Ashton of Chadderton and Dorothy his wife. Whewell claimed to hold it under Francis Tunstall, Esq., Lord of the manor of Quick and Strines.[20] No outcome of the suit has survived but in 1629 when Sir George Boothe of Dunham Massy Knt., lord of the manor sold 21 acres of Quick Moor in Saddleworth, to Robert Taylor of Walton-le-Dale for £20, Miles Andrew of Palden Lees, was one of the witnesses who named the boundaries.[21] and in a Chief Rent Roll of Saddleworth for 1712, we read 'Paid 7½ d. Palden Men.'[22]

Dorothy Asshton died without issue[23] and her husband James, although taking a second wife, also died childless in 1613. He appears to have had an absolute gift of the advowson of Prestwich, for in 1607, he stood 'lawfully seized of an estate of inheritance in fee simple or fee tail of and in the advowson,' In his will dated 5 May, 1612 and proved 8 October 1613, James Asseton of Chadderton Esq. declares, inter alia, that 'Robert Brearley of Pawden, his tenant, owes him £11 by a bond dated 20 October last.'[24]

The heir and successor of James Asheton, Esq., was his nephew Edmund Asheton of Chadderton and High Shuttleworth, only son of Richard Asheton, Gent. deceased.[25] Edmund married Dorothy, daughter of Richard Duckenfield of Duckenfield, Esq. and had five sons and six daughters.[26]

In an Indenture dated 11th February 1621/2 between Edmund Assheton of Chadderton Esq. and Robert Taylor of Horsedge, Oldham, gent. - [summary] on surrender of an old lease, a new one for the farm at Horsedge is granted by Edmund Asheton to Robert Taylor for the three lives of his children Edmund, John and Grace Taylor and the longest liver of them, at 20s per year annual rent, which Robert promises to pay on time, or suffer destraint for the same.

It includes some very apposite details: 'And the said Robert Taylor doth covenant promisse and grant to and with the said Edmund Asheton his heires and assignes that hee the said Robert Taylor or his assignes <u>shall finde a suffycient able man furnished</u> <u>with a Muskquet or such a furniture as the said Edmund Asheton his heires or assignes</u> <u>shall appoyt to serve in the Warres when and as often as hee the said Edmund Asheton</u> <u>his heires or assignes shall serve And yf the said Edmund Asheton or his assignes do</u> <u>make forth horsmen or footmen and do not go themselves then the said Robert Taylor</u> <u>or his assignes to be contributary as other tenants of the like having</u> And to paye unto the said Edmund Asheton his heires or assignes yearly for their boones fower dayes shearinge or reapinge of Corne in tyme of harvest fower dayes harrowing, fower hennes at Christmas, two capons at Easter, And a harryot or principall of their goodes at the death of every tenant of the premisses and do all such other sutes and services as hereto-fore have bine due or accustomed to be done And allso p'mitt and suffer the said Edmund Asheton his heires and assignes to digg delve and to gett Coal or stone in any part of the premisses And to make damme or dammes wheele or wheeles to convey or carye water from the said Coal or stone And to make house or houses to laye the Coales in And to have egress and regress to cary the said Coales or stone aweay by wayes most convenient and all other necessaryes Concerninge the same at the will and pleasure of the said Edmund Asheton his heires and assignes.' [27]

The wording of this lease sounds very much like a matter of form left over from feudal times, but tenants, and not just copyholders or tenants-at-will, but apparently, leaseholders, being yeomen and even gentry were, still expected to follow their over-lords to battle in the 17th century. So, were any 'Warres' afoot in February 1622; and was Robert Taylor likely to have to make good his agreement and join his landlord, (who we find, was himself, very well prepared with equipment) in fighting for any nec-essary military cause?

Just twelve months after signing this lease, Edmund Ashton (1601-1650) of Chad-derton Esq., a descendant of the Assheton family of Ashton-under-Lyne and the 1422 Rental, was very ill and in December 1623 he made his will, leaving a detailed list of goods to his son and heir James, which included 'Armes, Guns, Pykes, Halberts, and all other furniture standing and being in the Hall' apparently for the use of their retain-ers & 'In the Stearhead Chamber, two large Presses with all the Armour and Furniture for the Lord, for the Wars, in them' for his own use, or his heir James when he attained manhood. [28]

King James VI of Scotland and I of England had united the two crowns on his acces-sion in 1603, so uniting the two kingdoms - well almost; the official union did not take place until 1707. However, in 1618, peace reigned on the northern border but although he had contrived to avoid war in Ireland and the religious conflicts on the Continent for sixteen years, James was now thunderstruck by the news that his Calvinist Protes-tant son-in-law, Frederick the Elector of the Palatine, had been offered their Crown by the Bohemians, to prevent Ferdinand, the prince of bigots, the Catholic Emperor of Aus-tria from acquiring it, and had been imprudent enough to accept. All Europe stood in expectation of the bloody quarrel which was destined to spread over all Germany, draw into its vortex Sweden, Denmark, Holland, France, and England, to be for ever remem-bered in the world as the most terrible of contests, the 'Thirty Years' War.'

Frederick was a mere youth of twenty, with more ambition than ability; but he was spurred on by his wife, Elizabeth of England, who told him he had courage enough to aspire to the hand of a king's daughter, but not to grasp a crown when offered, and who, when reminded by him of the electoral province which they possessed in safety, exclaimed, 'Better a crown with a crust, than a petty electorate with abundance.' Frederick was crowned king of Bohemia in Prague on 25th of October, 1619; but reigned only until 8th of November of the following year, when, by displaying luxurious effeminacy inattention to government and impolitic treatment of the native nobles, he was forced ignominiously to flee the country, accompanied by Elizabeth his queen, now reduced to the crust, far advanced in pregnancy, and deeply pitied by all generous and chivalric minds.

James was distracted by the fear of his daughter and son-in-law being reduced to beggary. Yet if he attempted to prop up the king of Bohemia on his tottering throne, he should offend the Catholic King of Spain, the sworn ally of the Emperor, and with whom he was at this very time seeking an alliance of the Spanish princes and his own son the Prince of Wales.

Without being able to save his Protestant son-in-law, he should thus lose a Catholic daughter-in-law. If he lay still, all men would call him an un-natural father, all Protestants would declare him an apostate to his religion. Never was a man in such a straight. One moment he declared to the Spanish ambassador that the Elector was a fool and a villain, and that he would abandon him to his fate; at another he assured the Protestant envoys from Germany that he would support him to the utmost.

At length he hit upon the only rational course; which was, not to attempt an impossibility - the support of Frederick on the baseless throne of Bohemia - but to send a force to defend his patrimonial territories from the Spaniards. The first enterprise was, in fact, soon out of the question: Prague had fallen, his son-in-law and daughter were fugitives; but the second object was still possible, and more necessary than ever.

He sent an army of four thousand men under the Earls of Oxford and Essex to rescue the Palatinate, but the force was altogether inadequate to cope with the massive Spanish army under Spinola. Having exhausted all his means James was forced to summon a Parliament which assembled on 30th January, 1621, when, by confessing his faults, he attempted to wheedle money from them to carry on the war in the Palatine. After obtaining some small financial support James was put to further demands; increasing the rights and privileges of Parliament in return for sanctioning heavier taxes. Both sides stood upon their prerogatives and anger and disagreement ensued which led James to summarily dissolve Parliament on 6th January, 1622. The great contest of constitutional government, which was to lead to the Civil War, was now fully begun. [29]

Such was the agitated political situation when Robert Taylor of Horsedge, Oldham, gent. and Edmund Asheton, Esq., drew up and signed their new lease of Horsedge on 11th February 1622. The military obligation detailed in the lease, which they agreed to, may sound feudal to us but it must have been considered very real to the parties concerned.

In June 1625, twenty seven Lancashire men were sent to Liverpool for embarkation to Ireland.[30] Three hundred were conducted to Hull for embarkation to the Netherlands. On April 27th 1627, two hundred arrived in Hull and sailed for Stade in Hanover.[31] And in September of the same year a levy of one hundred was drafted to Plymouth to join the Duke of Buckingham's ill-fated expedition to the Isle of Rhe.[32]

In 'A Rowle or List of all such gents and ffreeholders [for beareing of the Armes of Rawffe Assheton of Midleton Esq.] as are under the conduction of Edward Rawsthorne gent sonne & heire apparent of Edward Rawsthorne of Newhall Esq. charged upon their Allegiance to bee ready upon 24 howers warning for his Ma'ties service shewed at Bury the sixth day of June 1639 & on the 27 June.' appears:

		Pikes	Musketts
Chatterton:	Edmond Assheton Esq	2	3
John Taylor & Edmond Schofield			
Isaac Ogden Richard Ogden & Mark Whitehead			
Oldham:	Robt Taylor		1 [33]

John son of Edmond Taylor of Horsedge Hall, gentleman, did fight in the Civil War and the Royalist Composition Papers tell us that he 'was killed on 13th September 1643 at the battle of Newburgh'. The first battle of Newbury, (twenty six miles south of Oxford) was fought between a large Royalist army of about 14,000 troops, commanded by King Charles I himself and a similar sized army under the command of the Earl of Essex, Lord-General for the Parliament. Prince Rupert commanded the Royalist cavalry with Sir John Byron as one of his five, brigade commanders.[34]

Initially, being of Horsedge, I thought John Taylor (killed at Newbury) was the son and heir of Robert Taylor of Horsedge, gentleman, referred to in the 1622 lease with Edmund Asshton, but other deeds made it clear that he was son and heir of Edmund Taylor of Horsedge Hall. Whether these two Taylor families were closely related (which seems likely) I have yet to discover. The Horsedge Hall Taylors were freeholders, having held their land there since at least 1540, when they paid 10½d a year to the Knights of St. John of Jerusalem. They did, however, also hold a lease on a tenement called Church Cross from Edmund Asshton of Chadderton Esq., and would therefore, no doubt, be obliged, (as was Robert Taylor and his successors) to support their master in times of war.

John Taylor may have fought under Captain Edmund Ashton of Chadderton Esq. in Sir John Byron's brigade, as Royalist leaders in Lancashire had been ordered south by the King to re-enforce his main army. This is why we find Edmund Ashton at Oxford when the royalists surrendered there in 1646.

Bateson tells us that John Taylor received a commission in Sir John Byron's Regiment of Horse.[35] The main battle took place at Newbury on 29 September when the Earl of Essex won a famous victory and the Royalists suffered heavy losses, so that John Taylor may have been killed in an earlier skirmish; but more probably he was killed

Sir John Byron, (c.1600-52), who fought at Powick Bridge and commanded a regiment at Edge hill.
Detail of a portrait by Dobson.

during the battle but the Composition Commissioners, widow Elizabeth Taylor or a clerk, confused their dates.

It is very likely that John Taylor was with Richard Brearly in Edmund Ashton's company at Warrington on the 5th April and no doubt at other conflicts in between and later. On 8 May 1649, his estate at Horsedge Hall was sequestered from May 1643 and his widow Elizabeth Taylor, on behalf of her three children, compounded for her husband's delinquency in assisting the King in the first war: his estate was valued at £100 and the fine was set at 1/10, which meant she had to pay a fine of £10.[36]

It was fascinating to discover (not least because of Thomas Paulden's Civil War exploits) that Edmund Asshton of Chadderton, Esq. the owner of Paulden, also fought for the King but then to find that Richard Brearley, yeoman (leaseholder) of Paulden, not only also fought in the Civil War but was making his will because he had been mortally wounded (probably on 5th April at the siege of Warrington) was almost too good to be true.

Will and Inventory of Richard Brearley of Palden (1643) [37]

In the name of God Amen the Nynth daie of Aprill in the Nynteenth yeare of
the raigne of our Sovereign Lord Charles by the grace of God of England, Scotland, ffrance & Ireland kyng defender of the faith &c I Richard Brearley of
Palden in the parishe of Oldham in the countie of Lancaster yeoman sick in
bodie by reason of a wound received but of good & p'fect memorie (praised be
God) knowing death certaine & the tyme thereof uncertayne & being mynded
to make my last will & testament d£ publish & declare the same in manner and
forme following ffirst and principallie I comitt my soule into the hands of
almightie God trusting through the meritts of Christ to have remission of my
sines & my bodie to the earth from whence it came to be buried at the discretion
of my executors hereafter named And as concerning my lands messuages lands
& tent's with thappurtenances situate lying & being in Crompton in the countie
of Lancaster I devise grant & sett the tearme unto my executor hereafter named
for Nynteen yeares & six monthes next ensuing the daie of the date hereof
uppon trust & confidence & to the ende that my said executors & the survyvor
of them his & their assignes shall & maie dispose of the rents yssues & proffitts
thereof equallie amongst my foure daughters Alice, Ann, Elizabeth & Susan &
their survyvors & survyvor of them & reserving alwaies nevertheless to Ann
now my wife one equall third pte. during her lief for her dower in the said messuages, tents, lands & pr'misses And whereas I owe ffiftie pounds to John
Shawe w'ch my lands stand charged with all my will & mynd is that ffiftie
pounds & what interest is thereuppon due & all other my debts whosever be
discharged out of my wholl goods And after my debts paid & funerall expenses
discharged I give & bequeath unto Ann my wife one third pte of my goods
debts & cattells & all the rest & residue thereof I give bequeath to James my
sonne & my said foure daughters Alice, Ann, Elizabeth & Susan equallie to be
divided amongst them Also I give unto James my sonne & his heires the reversion & inheritance of all my messuages, lands & tents after the expiracon of the
said tearme of Nynteen yeares & six monthes And whereas I stand seized or
possessed of two messuages, lands & tents with thappurtenances called Palden
situate lying & being in Oldham in the countie of Lancaster by the demise or
grant of Edmund Asheton, Esquire made unto James Brearley my father & by
him assigned unto me duringe the tearme of the lease paying unto my said
father Tenn pounds xiiis iiiid a yeare during his lief & after his decease to Jane
my sister Tenn pounds p' Anno during my lief, my will & mynd is the said
payments be made by my executors hereinafter named And I give devise &
bequeath unto Ann now my wife one third pte of the said messuages, tents,
lands & premisses unto Ann during the tearme of ffourescore yeares next ensuing if the said Ann my wife s£ long happen to live in pure widowhood & chaste
conversation & if that Jane my sister s£ happen to live also or anie tearme I have
in the said lands & premisses so long endure And as concerning the other two
parts of the said messuages, tents, lands & premisses my will & mynd is that

& I devise & bequeath the same to my executors hereafter named paying the said rents to my father & sister for the use of all my children for James, Alice, Ann, Elizabeth & Susan for their bringing up & preferment during the tearme of Nynteen yeares & six monthes next ensuing the date hereof If Jane my sister, soe long live, or anie tearme I have in the said messuages, tents, lands & premisses soever long endure And after the said tearme ended my will & mynd is that & I give & devise all my tearme & estate in the said messuages, tents, lands & premisses to James my sonne & the heires of his bodie & for default of such yssue to my eldest daughter & her heires And for want of such heires to the next daughter & her heires as they shalbe in prioritie of birth nevertheless it is my will & mynd as concerning my messuages, lands, & tente in Crompton that if James my sonne happen to depte this lief without anie yssue of his bodie begotten that then the said messuages & lands shall discend & tearne to my daughters & their heirs as whereas at the common law equallie amongst them Also I make executors of this my last will & testament Ann my wife & Edmund Fytton my brother in lawe And I desire ffrances Clegg & John wolfendon my neighbours to be Supervisors desiringe they will see the same p'formed as my trust is reposed in them & I doe hereby revoke all former willes legal legacies & bequestes in anie former will & have hereunto putt my hand & seale

Richard Brearley *
[good signature]

Signed published & delivered in pr'sence of William Walker, James X Dunkerley, Willm X Jackson.

xi die Aprilis 1643. And I the said Richard Brearley upon further consideracon & for the better pr'ferment of my foure daughters doe add this codicill & further declare my will & mynd & d£ hereby further give devise & sett unto my said executors all my said messuages, tents, lands & pr'misses in Crompton aforesaid for the tearme of foure yeares next ensuing t£ the tearme of Nynteen yeares & six monthes in my said will formerlie expressed in all for the tearme of Twentie three yeares & six monthes And after the expiration of the said xxiii yeares & six monthes the reversion & inheritance of the said messuages, lands & premisses I give & bequeath as in my said will is formerlie expressed And whereas John Shawe hath one absolute estate of the said messuages, lands & tents to him & his heires I desire the said John Shawe when he shalbe satisfied what is due unto him to grant his estate in the said lands to my executors & their heires for I am mynded to trust my executors also with the inheritance of the said lands & pr'misses the better to enable them to p'forme my will & to provyde for my children And I have hereunto also putt my hand & seale the daie & yeare first above written.

Richard Brearley *
[not as good signature]

Sealed & delivered in pr'sence of Willm Walker, Anne Walker, John X Jackson his marke.

The Oldham parish register is defective for this period, no doubt owing to the civil war disturbances, and Richard's burial is not recorded but the date of Richard's Inventory (28th April) tells us that he must have died just over two weeks after making the codicil to his will on 17th April 1643.

A true p'fect Inventory of all the goods Chattells Cattells and debts of Richard Brearley late of Pawden in the Parish of Oldham in the Countie of Lancaster yeoman late deceased praised the Twentie eight day of Aprill Anno Dmi. 1643, by ffrancis Clegg senior, Anthony Hallowes, Henry Mellor, William Jackson and ffreancis Clegg junior.

	£	s	d
Imprimis in nyne kyne and a little calfe	20	0	0
Item in Corne uppon the ground	24	0	0
Item two mares	5	10	0
Item Twelve Sheepe of a yeare old	2	0	0
Item in Arkes and cofers in the Chambers over the house and Parler below the house	2	10	0
Item two bedstids w:th their furniture in the same chamber and one Truckle bedd	3	10	0
Item one load of oat malt	0	8	0
Item Seaven hoopes of meale	1	2	0
Item one Th..ell and a board in the said chamber and one paire of weights	0	8	0
Item one standing bedd w:th the furniture in the Parlor below the house	2	10	0
Item three Cofers in the same p'lor togethr w:th one truncke and one Cofer in the house	1	0	0
Item one standing bed and one presse in the p'lor above	2	0	0
Item one great garner and one arke in ye chamber over ye kitchin	1	0	0
Item one payre of bedsteads with furniture in the Same Chamber	0	10	0
Item one table one forme and one Cupboard in the house	1	10	0
Item in pewter and brasse	4	0	0
Item one Arke and other things in the buttery and milkhouse, together w:th creeut ware	1	5	0
Item in chaires and stooles and Cushions	0	10	0
Item in Lynnens	1	10	0
Item in wooll and hemp	0	4	0
Item in sackes	0	5	0
Item in armo'r	**2**	**10**	**0**
Item in maner	1	0	0

	£	s	d
Item in husbandrie ware, Carts and			
wheeles saddles and horse geeres	4	2	0
Item in Bookes	0	12	0
Item in loose boards	0	2	4
Item in Iron ware	0	8	0
Item his apparell and money in his purse	3	0	0
Item in huslement	0	1	0

Suma totalis   £LXXXVI VIs IIIId

It would obviously be of great interest to know what 'arm'r' worth '£2 10s' constituted but we must be content in the knowledge that, be it perhaps some of these: sword, helmet, buff-coat, breast-plate, pike, halberd or musket; it was valued at the same cost as fifteen one year old sheep: and therefore quite substantial.

If the covenants in Richard Brearley's eighty year lease of Paulden, first agreed to by his father James Brearley with Edmond Asheton of Chadderton, Esq. in 1582, were similar to those of Robert Taylor's of Horsedge, in Oldham; who also held his lease from the same Edmund Ashton of Chadderton, Esq.; and the covenants in Joseph Twedall's lease, (Richard's successor at Paulden in 1666), then he too would be obliged to follow his landlord to do battle, or like Robert Taylor and Joseph Twedale:

'...finde a sufficient man to serve in the Warres with a Musket when and soe often as the said Edmund Ashton or his heires shall serve and if the said Edmund Ashton or his heires doe make forth a foot man or horseman and doe not goe in their owne person or persons then to be contributarie thereunto as other Tenants of the like tenements have beene and are used to doe.'[38]

The reason why Richard Brearley's widow Ann, does not appear in the Royalist Composition Papers, for his delinquency; is that they were just not wealthy enough to be worth sequestration. In the Oldham Assessment for 1641, Richard Brierley [of Paulden] was assessed at £5 per ann. and had to pay 1s and Ann his wife had to pay 6d. Substantial yeoman but not of gentry status.

Edmund Asheton of Chadderton, Esq., (1601-1650) was high sheriff of Lancashire in 1628, and in 1631 he was forced to pay £25 to the King when he declined to accept the honour of knighthood. He was however, loyal to his sovereign and, as we have noted, fought for the Royalist cause during the Civil War. His name appears in the Lancashire Royalist Composition Papers where we find he was fined £1414 for:

'Delinquency, deserting his dwelling, living in the enemy's quarters assisting those forces against the Parliament. He was in Oxford at the time of the surrender, and was to have the benefit of those articles as appeared by Sir Thomas Fairfax's certificate, dated 24 June, 1646.' In the Parliamentary re-arrangement of the magistracy, Edmund Asheton of Chadderton, Esq. was removed from the Commission of the Peace, on 24th Oct 1642.[39]

At the Manchester Quarter Sessions in 1632 Edmund had to adjudicate in a family dispute concerning his Brearly tenants when he bound over Edmond Brearley of Pawdin in Recognisance of £10 to keep the peace towards James Brearley and appear at the next Quarter Sessions, Samuel Brearley of same bound in £5; and John Brearley of same bound in £5. This man was bound by warrant of Mr. Hopwood. [40]

The composition papers also reveal divided loyalties in the Ashton household, when we read '22 Oct. 1646. Request from J. Bradshaw, sheriff, and Ralph Asheton, that, Edmund's son James may not be prejudiced as to a settlement made on him by his father on his marriage, because of his adhering to Parliament, the old man having called him a rebel, and threatened not to leave him a foot of land if he could help it.' James Ashton was appointed to the Lancashire Committee by the Parliamentarians on 29th August 1645,[41] Edmund either relented or he died before implementing his threat, as his son James inherited his father's estates.[42]

If Richard Brearley did follow his master, and fought for the King, which appears highly likely, then we must look at the conflicts which took place in Lancashire just before 9th April, when he tells us he was 'sick in bodie by reason of a wound received', to try and elicit where he may have received the fatal blow.

This short summary is taken from Chapter five of 'The Great Civil War in Lancashire 1642-51', by Ernest Broxup, which is entitled 'The Crisis. January to June, 1643', and he begins "The next six months was the really critical time in the Lancashire Civil War. In it the issue was finally decided, and by the end of the summer the royalist resistance was practically overcome.

In February the Parliamentarians captured Preston...and on February 16th a determined attack was made on Bolton by the royalist garrison from Wigan...Bolton was garrisoned by 500 men under the command of Colonel Asheton, drawn from various places. It included the companies of Captain James Buckley of [Lowerhouse, Whitefield], Oldham; Captain Schofield of Rochdale, Captain Holt of Bury, and Captain Ashhurst of Radcliffe Bridge. The royalists, consisting of 11 companies of foot and two of dragoons, together with two troops of horse, left Wigan, which is nine miles away by road, early in the morning, surprised the enemy scouts, and were within sight of Bolton before their movements were suspected...they surrounded Bolton on all sides before help could be summoned. They then advanced towards Bradshawgate, and overpowered the soldiers in the three outworks which were at a little distance from the walls. Captain Ashhurst with 24 men, was intercepted by 60 royalists as he retreated towards the town; but with some loss he cut his way through, and gained the shelter of the chain and mud walls at the end of the street. The royalists followed and set fire to a house outside the chain, while they occupied some others and from them fired on the Parliamentary troops, who were forced to fall back along the street. Then having secured an entrance into a royalist house, they took the defenders in the rear. One Parliamentary officer, Serg.-Major Leigh, had his horse shot under him, and was himself wounded in the arm while mounting another. Finally, however, two of the garrison forced an entrance into the royalists' houses, and Captain Ashhurst with 16 men breaking in from the side, the town was gradually cleared of the royalist troops. While the fight lasted their horse within the town had prevented reinforcements from coming in, but now hearing the shouts of approaching troops they hastily retreated towards Wigan. Captain Radcliffe arrived with 20 fresh soldiers from Manchester, but too late to take part in the battle.

1. ("Special Passages and Certain Information from several Places" (C.W.T., p.77), "A punctual relation, etc"; C.W.T., p.79. The former tract gives the defenders' losses five, the latter as eight or ten; and it is stated that 100 of the Royalists were either killed or mortally wounded. These numbers must be received with considerable reservation.

The first royalist attack on Bolton was one of the hardest fought encounters of the whole war. Colonel [Ralph] Assheton [he was to become the commander-in-chief of all the Parliamentary forces in Lancashire] himself is said to have showed much bravery, and the hand to hand fighting was severe.

During the months of March and April [1643] there was almost incessant fighting in Lancashire with varying fortune. At the end of February the Parliament held both Preston and Lancaster, and Blackburn and Bolton besides, the royalists still keeping possession of Wigan, Warrington and Liverpool; and repeated attempts were now made by each party on the positions of the other side.

The Earl of Derby captured Lancaster on 18th March and the town was thoroughly plundered and sacked. Colonel Ralph Asheton, having collected what men he could from Salford hundred, reached Preston on the same day in his efforts to intercept him, but by the time he arrived at Lancaster the Earl had gone back to re-take Preston, which he easily did, while taking many prisoners, as it had been left only lightly garrisoned.

The royalists were now in the ascendancy and Derby made a second attack on Bolton on 28th March, but his forces was beaten off and soon afterwards, the Parliamentary leaders, who seem to have restored the morale of their troops, mounted an attack of their own. Under the command of Colonels Holland and [Ralph] Asheton, with 2000 foot, mostly musketeers, and 200 or 300 horse, with 8 guns, they besieging Wigan. After an hour's fighting [Ralph] Asheton's musketeers forced an entrance at the south-east end of the town and the garrison of 1,400 men broke and fled in disorder. The town was thoroughly plundered by the Parliamentary soldiers who were said to have taken goods to the value of £20,000: Wigan being described as 'the only place of receipt for Papists' goods and treasure. [43]

The Parliamentary forces, elated with their success in taking Wigan 'that impregnable piece the enemy's pride and presumption our fear and despair', now assaulted weaker Warrington on 5th April; but the royalists garrison there, commanded by the Earl of Derby in person, defended with great determination, and in spite of their superior numbers the Parliamentarians under the command of Sir William Brereton of Cheshire and Col. Holland of Manchester, were unable to gain an entrance to the town." [44]

These then were the two main battles which took place in Lancashire during the spring of 1643, with many other smaller battles and skirmishes being fought in between; mainly in the west and middle of the county, and with Richard Brearley being fatally wounded, probably a matter of days before he made his will on the 9th April, perhaps

Warrington on the 5th April or Bolton on the 28th March are the two most likely places where, in one of which, he fought and received his mortal wound.

It is just possible that Richard Brearley of Paulden, agreed with the Parliamentary cause and therefore decided to revoke his agreement with his master Edmund Ashton Esq., as did the Earl of Derby's tenants of Bury and Pilkington, who refused to join his forces and fought for the Parliament. [45]

However, as a comfortably off yeoman with a vested interest in supporting his master and landlord, we would expect Richard Brearley, to honour his leasing agreement and follow Edmund Ashton of Chadderton Esq. in support of the King. Confirmation that Edmund Ashton Esq. did take part in the civil war struggle in Lancashire, before he left the north to became part of the King's main army and later the Oxford garrison, is obtained from the Earl of Derby's 'Orders', dated at Wigan 30th December 1642.[46]

The 'Orders' enumerate the garrisons to be stationed in the various Lancashire towns and include:

'At Warrington 300 men...Captain Ashton's company be also armed...'
And near the end he is included in a list of Commissioners for the county: '
That upon occasion the General Maior may call to his assistance in Counsell the Maior of Wigan...Mr. Anderton of Lostock... [and seven more Lancashire gentry including] 'Mr. Ashton of Chadderton,'

[Autograph signature] Derby. [47]

So we do know that Captain Edmund Ashton's company was at Warrington just before the town suffered but withstood, the severe Parliamentary attack, on 5th April. Thus fitting in perfectly with Richard Brearley's wound, sustained before he made his will dated 9th April, and allowing 3-4 days for him to return home to Paulden, perhaps on one of the 'two mares' listed in his Inventory as being worth the valuable sum of £5 10s.

This John Brearley was said by Butterworth in 1825, to have been a very eccentric character and rustic wit who was a carrier to London. He had long associations with Paulden but I have as yet to discover his relationship, if any, to the family above.

I have not, so far, been able to discover any deeds relating to Paulden Farm and the Brearly family but I have been fortunate to discover the next best thing: the deeds for the period almost immediately following the end of the eighty year Brearley lease which extended from 1582 to 1662.

Judging by other leases granted by Edmund Asshton of Chadderton Esq. to his tenants, including the example already given, of the one granted to Robert Taylor of Horsedge, Oldham, in 1622, then it seems very likely that the following one granted to Joseph Twedall, who succeeded the Brearleys at Paulden, would be identical in all conditions to theirs except that it was granted for three lives instead of a period of years.

I find the two most extraordinary features of Edmund Asshton's leases are firstly the acceptance of following the master in military service (or paying for a man to serve in his place) and secondly the menial boon services which still have to be rendered

The Brearley/Brierley Family of Paulden

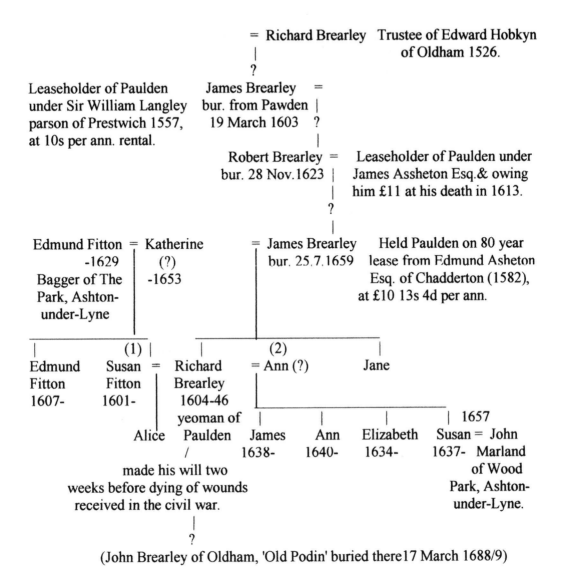

(John Brearley of Oldham, 'Old Podin' buried there 17 March 1688/9)

(although with the option of money payments in each case). Other conditions giving the landlord free access to any part of the land, at any time, for all aspects of mining, quarrying and hunting &c appear to give the leaseholder little control over the property. In fact, apart from a condition obliging them to grind their corn at his mill, (which his tenants in Chadderton had to do) Edmund Ashton's leaseholders appear to be little better off than their tenants-at-will ancestors who rendered suit and service to Edmund's ancestor Sir John Assheton, as described in his 1422 rental.

Despite the apparently feudal conditions the Asshtons of Chadderton appear to have been on the best of terms with their leaseholders as we learn from John Taylor, gentleman and freeholder of Horsedge Hall, (great grandfather of John Taylor killed at

Newbury) who in making his will on 8th May 1574, bequeaths to his second son Henry a lease of 'Church Cross' held off James Asshton son & heir of Edmund Asshton Esq. of Chadderton...he leaves his eldest son & heir Edmund Taylor his own 'demesne lands, lying south & south west of Oldham church and he desires 'my trusty and well-beloved Master Edmund Asshton of Chadderton Esq. to be supervisor of this my will' bequeathing him '13s 4d for his paynes'. [48]

A lease of Pawden for three lives - Edmund Asshton Esq. to Joseph Twedall yeoman 6 June 1666, includes much fascinating detail and also confirmation of the leaseholder's military tenure:-

> ...And the said Joseph Twedall his heires and assignes shall and will finde a sufficient man to serve in the Warres with a Musket when and so often as the said Edmund Asshton or his heires shall serve and if the said Edmund Ashton or his heires do make forth a foot man or horseman and do not go in their owne person or persons then to be contributarie thereunto as other Tenants of the like tenements have beene and are used to do...(for full details see appendix).[49]

The one disappointing feature of the foregoing lease is the lack of detailed information regarding the actual extent of the lands, which are included and taken to be part of Paulden Farm. Some years later however, in a document dated 1700, we are delighted to find the omission of land details rectified.[50]

A Schedule of deeds for a messuage in Pawden in Oldham 1666-1738,[51] reveals further splendid details of the farm's history.

Paulden, and part of a close called Four Acres in Saddleworth, was purchased by Joseph Tweedale from Edmund Asshton Esq. on 18 May 1671 for £4. He sold it on 13 June 1682 to John Arnfield for £300 but held it on a 200 year lease from Arnfield at a rent of £5 a year. On 25 Aug 1685 all Tweedale's interest in 'one messuage, 2 Gardens, 15 acres of Land, 10 acres of Meadow, 15 acres of pasture, 8 acres of Wood, 20 acres of ffurze & Comon of pasture for all Catle & Comon of Turbary with app's in Oldham' passed to Arnfield and soon afterwards he conveyed it to his son-in-law James Marlor, yeoman/innkeeper of Failsworth, as a marriage portion with his daughter Mary. Marlor mortgaged it and then sold it on 29 July 1718 to Thomas Drinkwater, of Ancoates, Chapman (yarn whiter).

In 1685 then, the Paulden messuage and tenement consisted of 48 acres plus 2 gardens (these very likely being Lancashire acres would be about 74 statute acres) and right of pasture on twenty acres of common (?Sholver Moor). Shaw quotes Butterworth as saying Paulden Wood was the largest wood in the parish but he (Butterworth) does not hazard a guess as to its whereabouts. The 1848 6" O.S. map shows Paulden Wood Colliery to be on the Lancashire Yorkshire boundary at the bottom of Strinesdale, which confirms my idea that the 'eight acres of Wood' referred to in 1685 was almost certainly close to or actually in that same area.

Thomas Drinkwater died unmarried in 1723 having made his will dated 8 October 1712. His two sisters, as heirs at law inherited all his property: Mary wife of Samuel Barnes and Hannah wife of James Holt. Hannah Barnes in her will of 14 Aug 1729 bequeathed her interest in Pawden to her son Samuel and Arthur Holt and his mother held the other half interest Pawden. On 24 July 1731 Arthur Holt and his mother Mary purchased Samuel Barnes' interest in Pawden for £257 10s and then they mortgaged it to Joseph Byrom for £260.

In articles of Agreement dated 18 Aug 1732, The Rev'd Samuel Sidebottom, rector of Middleton and Arthur Holt of Pawden, yeoman - for the rebuilding of two adjoining messuages in Oldham: very likely at Paulden.

Samuel Sidebottom bought an interest in Paulden sometime after the death of Thomas Drinkwater and the Holts lived on the property there with three families living in adjoining cottages as undertenants. On 25 November 1735 Mary Holt of Pawden, widow, made her will bequeathing 'my best bedstead with all the bedding thereon hangings matt & cord thereto belonging' and 1/4 part of her estate to her daughter Elizabeth and to her only son Arthur she bequeathed 'my best horse, mare or gelding to be chosen by him.' An endorsement on the will declares that on 17 March 1740 Arthur Holt acknowledges it to be his mother's last will.

On 8 July 1738, Arthur Holt, yeoman of Paulden, finally sold out to Samuel Sidebottom for £685; the undertenants at that time being Phineas Wrigley, Abraham Wrigley & John Dronfield.[52]

The tenant of Paulden for most of the period of Twedale and Arnfield's ownership appears to have been John Lees, who may have held it by a lease dated 13 June 1684. In a deed dated 30 June 1691 John Lees of Paulden clothmaker, granted a right of way across a field called Ley Close to Ralph Sandiford. One of the Overseers of the Poor for the year 1696, was John Leese of Paulden.[53] Lees of Paulden and Dronfields of Paulden were Woollen cloth manufactures in 1724.[54] And in the will of Hannah Barnes dated 14 Aug 1729 she mentions Edm'd Lees as being in late possession of Paulden. John Lees of Paulden junior married Mary Milne of Stampstone at Saddleworth church on 17 October 1710.

In the Window Lay, dated 4 June 1730, Francis Clegg of Paulden is said to be a proper person for collecting for ensuing year.[55] John Wyld of Palden, Weaver married Sarah Anneley of Huddersfield at Saddleworth 1st November 1734. Thomas Cheetham of Paulden and John Wrigley of Paulden were woollen cloth manufactures between 1742-1762.[56]

Many other references to Paulden, including the census, reveal its inhabitants during the late 18th and 19th centuries. In 1785 John Dunkerley, probably a cottager, of Paulden paid 1s 2d Church Rate and the family were residents for a hundred years or more [57] The old corn mill at Waterhead had been converted for cotton and the days of domestic and small time industries was coming to a close with the advent of the Industrial Revolution. Large woollen mills and cotton mills were being built especially in the Yorkshire and Lancashire Pennine region, which was plentifully supplied with water-power to drive the machinery.

Religious Connotation

Although the old Paulden farm house was 'taken down' in May 1876 [58] there still remains a building used as a stable cum shippen, situated in between a terraced row of cottages, and a large barn, yet quite incongruent and distinct from them in appearance. The line of arched windows appears incongruous and lends support to the theory that it was used as a chapel in the 17th century. Was this a continuation of a history of Christianity in the district from the very earliest times?

Trevlyan in his History of England and Winfred M Bowman tell us: `when the Romans withdrew it was said that 'the Christian missionaries...did not desert the Britains in their day of troubles, It is well known that refugees cling more firmly to their traditions and creeds that do those who have no need to preserve them. Certainly the Britons who fled to Brittany did so. We cannot say, therefore, for how long after the coming of the heathen Angles Christianity survived in this district. The West Riding of Yorkshire remained in Celtic (British) hands until A.D. 616. Saddleworth, on our north and eastern border, shows signs of 'more than usual survival of Britons' (2) W.G.C.). All about the countryside, encircling the lands which became the parish of Ashton-under-Lyne, there may have existed descendants of a people given that Christian teaching which was brought here from Rome even before the establishment of the Primacy of the Roman See. Theirs was the early Christian Church - similar to that founded in Celtic Gaul, where St. Patrick (himself a Romanised-Briton) gained his learning, and whence he brought the word on which he founded the Celtic Church in Ireland. Of the group of missionaries originally spreading out from this Church, early in the 7th century came Aden, whose labours succeeded the brief work of Paulinus in converting, or reconverting, the people in the lands north of the Humber and Mersey. But it is well within the bounds of possibility that the Christian doctrine, which first took rout in our district, never entirely died, and was that sown here long before the time of King Edward's conversion. .[59] (If, as is stated, Ecclesley near Halifax was the site of a British church which Angles later used as a 'ley', then Eccles near Manchester, so early associated with the landowning families of our own manor and area, may also derive its name from Roman days; Eccleston, too, may mean an Anglian tun on the site of an early Celtic church.

Speculation?

The Place names of Lancashire gives Palden/Polden as originating from pole, but offers little evidence to support this view; which may or may not be true, but I would contend that Palden/Polden/Paulden is just as, if not more, likely to have been originated from the name of the dene [deep wooded valley] where Paulinus laboured to convert the local population to Christianity. This may sound far-fetched but we have at least the postulation of Winifred M. Bowman, quoted above, to give support to our speculation! Strinesdale, a steep valley with a stream down the middle forms the boundary between Oldham, in Lancashire and Saddleworth, in Yorkshire. In the 16th century, and no doubt long before, Paulden bestrode this boundary (see James Brearley &c in Saddleworth church history) and I believe Strinesdale, well-wooded in the middle-ages could well have been coterminous with Palden Wood.

And if so, could it not possibly be the place where Paulinus preached to local people who, venerating the place, gave to it the name of Paulinus's dene, over the years to became 'Paul's dene' and then Paulden?

It seems strange that we have so many people in the 14th and 15th century Assheton Rental, who's descendants continued to live in the area down the centuries, who became known by the name of their original place of residence such as Lees, Knolles, Aspenhalgh, Bardsley, Hollinworth etc. and yet there appears never to have been anyone living in the area at any time recorded known by the name of Palden/Paulden. We have one example in the 1422 rental who just could be an example to contradict this statement:

'Alys, that was Pole wife, the same service for a cottage, [less than 4 days shearing, which was 'a whole service'] and shall pay 12d., and a present at the value of 4d.'

Was Alice's, apparently deceased husband Paul, connected in any way with Palden? Or does his name give support to the 'Place name of Lancashire' the name Palden comes from pole! I suspect neither is the case.

In my theory we can take some satisfaction, however, from the fact that though many of the 1422 tenants held land in Alston londs (still existing today as Austerlands) no-one of that name (just like Palden) has ever been found recorded and even the local place name of Alt, taken by an important landowning family does not appear to have survived past the early 14th century.

In researching Paulden Farm, I read Winifred M.Bowman's excellent book 'England in Ashton-under-Lyne' and found much fascination information about Palden and its history, but more than this I was also quite amazed to discover her well documented proof that the earliest lords of Ashton-under-Lyne were the Kirkby family of Kirkby-in-Furness, the very parish in Furness, north Lancashire where my own Postlethwaite ancestors lived in the 16th and 17th centuries and who themselves were connected to the Kirkby of Kirkby-in-Furness family. I knew the Kirkbys to be one of the earliest families recorded in Furness but I was completely unaware of their land ownership outside Furness, let alone that in Ashton-under-Lyne.

Mrs Bowman tells us that...Between 1154 and 1189, William de Kirkby-Ireleth (Kirkby-in-Furness) held a large amount of land, as 'demesne' or unlet territory, which constituted the greater part of Ashton-under-Lyne. This he placed in Orm's hands as his sub-tenant. So began the development of the greater manor of Ashton-under-Lyne. Roger son of Orm I was well known as 'de Eston' and of other landed titles in his possession. In some way the charter from Albert Grelley III, Lord of Manchester, confirming the lands of Ashton to Roger son of Orm, had come into the possession of Sir John de Kirkby, probably whilst he was guardian to Sir John de Ashton II during the years of his minority, after his father's death. The Covenant giving the right to hold a Court Leet in Ashton-under-Lyne, dated 21st September, 1413, tells us that John de Asheton, chevalier, has held the manor of Assheton subtus lymam in Com. Lancs. of Richard de Kirkby knight, by fealty and service, paying yearly one penny for all services [whilst] Richard de Kirkby holds the aforesaid manor of Thomas la Warre, lord of Mamcestrem, by fealty and service and paying yearly twenty shillings and a hawk. When Sir John de Assheton III died on 8th September 1428, his Inquisition Post Mortem showed that he held the manor of Assheton subtus lyman (of the yearly value of £40) of Robert de Ogull, Armiger, and Isabella his wife - in her right as heiress of Sir Richard de Kirkby, her grandfather, and daughter of Alexander de Kirkby, his son - by the payment of one penny per annum. There is no evidence to show when these payments to the Kirkby family ceased but they were still being paid in the 17th century.

Our earliest proven Postlethwaite ancestor is John (c1640-1678) yeoman of Yeathouse, Woodland, Kirkby-in-Furness, North Lancashire. John Postlethwaite, who was living at Yeathouse in 1623 and died there c1643, was almost certainly his father and I believe John Postlethwaite (c1550-1604) of Bankend & Wellhouse in Kirkby, to be the grandfather. Great grandfather was another John (c1515-1587) Tanner of Gargrave in Kirkby, who had married Jane daughter of Henry Kirkby Esq. of Cross House, Lord of Kirkby, and was his Bailiff. The will of Ann, widow of Henry Kirkby Esq.(1566) confirms this relationship.

The origin of the name Postlethwaite although unconnected with our subject nevertheless bears a theme similar to the postulated origin of Paulden. The earliest recorded instance of the name Postlethwaite is in 1272, when it is given as the name of a sub-manor in Mirehouse near Millom, in south Cumberland (adjacent to Kirkby-in-Furness). The Postlethwaite settlement itself has long disappeared but the name survives today as 'Great Postlethwaite', an 18 acre field, part of Mirehouse Farm. Thwaite was the Scandinavian name for a clearing in the 'forest' i.e. a settlement, and Postlethwaite is said to have been the place where an early Christian Apostle preached the gospel.

It is of interest to discover, in a numerous list of free tenants in the rent roll of Sir John Assheton 1379-1422, that they almost all, derived their names from the paternal lands that they occupied: Adam de Tetlawe, John of the Highrode &c whereas the tenants-at-will had a mixture of place names plus occupational names such as:- Robbin the Cropper, Roger the Baxter &c patronymics: Tomlyn Diconson, Dycon Wilkynson &c and others such as Hobbe the King (who performed the office and kept order at manorial court festivals).

If, as seems likely then, Captain Thomas Paulden's ancestor who took his name from the land he had occupied would be a freeholder in Palden/Paulden, when he decided to take up his residence in Halifax and this would also account for his right to exercise his freedom and, if he departed after the twelfth century when surnames had begun to be assumed, leave the constraints of the manorial system under the Asshetons.

Sir John Assheton III is said to have married (as his first wife) Isabella Ellend of Brighouse on the outskirts of Halifax and there would no doubt be regular social contact between the two families and their retainers, and perhaps Thomas Paulden's ancestor was a regular go-between which allowed him to learn the advantages of inhabiting that growing town; or perhaps like his descendants he got involved in transporting his own and neighbours' wool to the market there and so became a chapman an occupation carried on by his descendant Gregory Paulden.

In a growing centre of the wool and clothing trade which Halifax was from the earliest time, there would be far more opportunity and freedom for a young man to improve himself, as opposed to life in the rural area of Palden Wood or Paldon Ley, in Ashton-under-Lyne, still strictly under the control of its manorial lord.

My friend Mr. Fred Lees, in his writings notes 'a "rumour" present in the neighbourhood for at least a hundred years that 'the first church at Waterhead was at Paulden'. The 17th century barn/shippon at Paulden has eight rustic 'arched' windows, which feature on its own would be sufficient cause and is perhaps the only source of the 'church' rumour. A detailed drawing of one of the Paulden rough 'arched' windows, by Mrs. Dora Birkhead has been reproduced in 'Home in Waterhead', together with a conventional church arched window for comparison. The classical (professionally designed and built) embellished lines and mouldings of the latter leave Mr. Lees (a lecturer on architecture) in no doubt about the former, and he states 'Quite simply: there NEVER was a church at Paulden.'

I feel sure that Mr. Lees' assertion is perfectly correct, but although there never was a church at Paulden, I find it difficult to accept that 'arched' windows being introduced without a good reason. From my own farming background and experience, I know that farmers, and landlords, never spend a penny where a halfpenny will do. All farmers have had to endure hard times, poor harvests often brought about by bad weather; anthrax, foot and mouth disease or cattle plague as it was called; sheep rot/scab to name but a few of their perennial problems. Farmers were always thrifty, having to save for a 'rainy day' and being careful with their money was inbred, especially in the shrewd and canny farming community of the Pennines. If the barn/shippon at Paulden required windows to give more internal light, then I feel sure that square/rectangular practical windows, like all the others in the neighbourhood, would have been fitted. 'Arched' windows, which required even a little more effort / time / money to construct / build / repair, would not be undertaken without a purpose.

The stonework surrounding the 'arched' windows at Paulden looks to have been roughly hacked into to make space for the windows and they do not appear to have been originally built into the structure. An 'independent' nonconformist farmer used to repairing walls and buildings would see no reason to employ an expensive professional architect/builder to convert his barn/shippon into a practical place for worship.

Whether one of Paulden's later tenants or even one of the Brearley family was responsible for making his cowshed look more suitable for worship, it is not yet possible to say; perhaps the person responsible was the very eccentric rustic wit, and London carrier, John Brearley, (buried at Oldham on 17 March 1689) and known as 'Owd Poden' from his long association with the place.

Eccentric it may seem to use a cowshed as a place of worship but it was not an unusual occurrence in 17th and 18th century England when thousands of houses and barns &c were utilised for that purpose and there were several instances in Oldham itself.

After the Toleration Act of 1689 when dissenters could worship as they pleased, many houses were licensed for worship and one in Oldham was licensed as a Quaker meeting house in that same year. James Lees, Quaker, paid 2s for his seven windows in the window laye of 4th June 1730.

Mr Robert Constantine ejected puritan 'independent' minister of Oldham, (vigorously persecuted by the patron, Mr James Asshton of Chadderton, Esq., J.P. for refusing to sign the engagement of 1650) in 1673, took out a licence to preach and rented a thatched cottage on Greenacres Moor. Exactly where I have still to discover. When his wife died in 1695 he returned to Manchester where he died in 1699. After his departure the congregation at Greenacres converted an old barn into a chapel which satisfied them until 1783 when new Congregational Chapel was built in 1785. Thomas Brierley a weaver of Oldham petitioned for a licence to use his house as a Protestant nonconformist meeting house in 1765.

I haven't, so far, been able to prove that the arched window building at Paulden is connected with any of the religious centres in its neighbourhood referred to above but I hope I have shown that the speculation is a distinct possibility.

Whatever future research may decide on my religious speculations, I will never forget my excitement at first discovering Paulden and then later all its wonderful associations to complement, not only the name, but also the story, of my Royalist hero.

APPENDIX 1

THE PAULDEN FAMILY & OUR CONNECTIONS

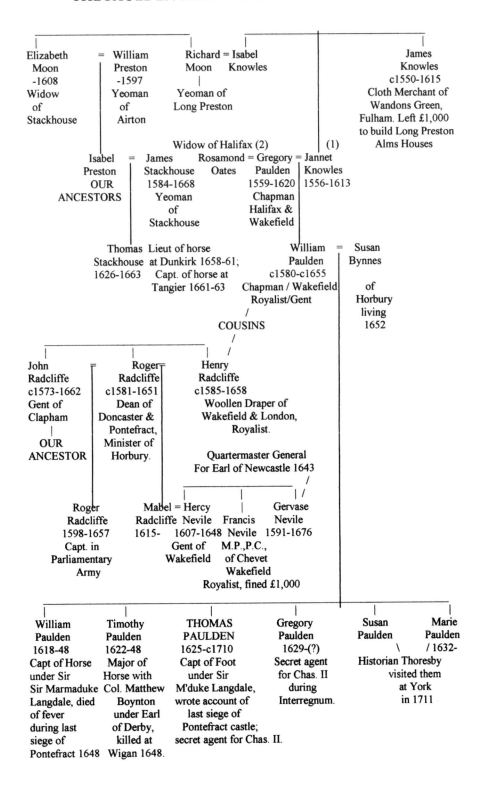

Elizabeth Moon -1608 Widow of Stackhouse = William Preston -1597 Yeoman of Airton

Richard = Isabel Moon Knowles Yeoman of Long Preston

James Knowles c1550-1615 Cloth Merchant of Wandons Green, Fulham. Left £1,000 to build Long Preston Alms Houses

Isabel Preston OUR ANCESTORS = James Stackhouse 1584-1668 Yeoman of Stackhouse

Widow of Halifax (2)
Rosamond = Gregory = Jannet
Oates   Paulden   Knowles
          1559-1620 1556-1613
          Chapman
          Halifax &
          Wakefield

(1)

Thomas Stackhouse 1626-1663 Lieut of horse at Dunkirk 1658-61; Capt. of horse at Tangier 1661-63

William = Susan
Paulden   Bynnes
c1580-c1655
Chapman / Wakefield of
Royalist/Gent   Horbury
                     living
                     1652

COUSINS

John Radcliffe c1573-1662 Gent of Clapham

OUR ANCESTOR

Roger Radcliffe c1581-1651 Dean of Doncaster & Pontefract, Minister of Horbury.

Henry Radcliffe c1585-1658 Woollen Draper of Wakefield & London, Royalist.

Quartermaster General For Earl of Newcastle 1643

Roger Radcliffe 1598-1657 Capt. in Parliamentary Army

Mabel = Hercy Radcliffe Nevile 1615-   1607-1648 Gent of Wakefield

Francis Nevile M.P.,P.C., of Chevet Wakefield Royalist, fined £1,000

Gervase Nevile 1591-1676

William Paulden 1618-48 Capt of Horse under Sir Sir Marmaduke Langdale, died of fever during last siege of Pontefract 1648

Timothy Paulden 1622-48 Major of Horse with Col. Matthew Boynton under Earl of Derby, killed at Wigan 1648.

THOMAS PAULDEN 1625-c1710 Capt of Foot under Sir M'duke Langdale, wrote account of last siege of Pontefract castle; secret agent for Chas. II.

Gregory Paulden 1629-(?) Secret agent for Chas. II during Interregnum.

Susan Paulden

Marie Paulden / 1632- Historian Thoresby visited them at York in 1711

APPENDIX 2

FAMILY LINKS

John Radcliffe = Hester Armitstead   James Stackhouse = Isabel Preston
c1580-1662   c1582-1668
Gent of Light Birks,   Yeoman of
Austwick, Clapham   Stackhouse, Giggledswick

Robert Radcliffe = Isabel   William Brown = Ellen Stackhouse
1637-1716   c1625-1683
Yeoman of Austwick   Yeoman of Stackhouse

John Radcliffe   =   Mary Brown
1658-1695   1660-
Gent of Austwick

Thomas Sergeantson = Hellen Radcliffe
Husbandman of Rathmel   1689-1749

Margaret Sergeantson = Nathaniel Armitstead
1717-1790   1715-1801
                      Husbandman of Milldam, Bentham

Ruth Armitstead = Christopher Bateson
1745-1831   1752-1842
                Farmer of Mewith

Robert Bateson = Mary Howson
1777-1858   1779
Farmer of Croasdale Grains

William Gornall = Ruth Bateson
1803-1859   1802-1869
Farmer of Dovenanter, Keasden

(1 ?) = Alice Gornall = (2) William Shepherd
          1827-
Sunny Bank, Bentham   Farmer of Austwick

William Gornall = Rebecca Johnson
1850-1920   1856-1933
Farmer of Rantree, Keasden   Israel, Keasden

Ruth Annie Gornall = Thomas Jackson
1880-1961   18876-1947
            Farmer Smalden House, Grindleton

OUR GRANDPARENTS

APPENDIX 3

OTHER EXAMPLES OF RECLAMATION OF THE
SEA SHORE - IN LINCOLNSHIRE. [1]

Some notes relating to land reclamation further down the east coast in Lincolnshire gives us a good idea of what Thomas Paulden's task involved at Holy Island.

Page 19. The low lying sea-coast of Lincolnshire was subject to great changes from time immemorial, especially when high tides were accompanied by storms during winter time. The worst recorded occurred on 5 October 1571 when all sea walls were breeched and thousands of acres were flooded, whole villages and churches were lost (some of this land was never recovered), and 20,000 head of cattle, and 4,000 sheep were lost between the Humber and the Wash. A Mr Spicer lost 1,100 sheep between Humberston and Grimsby. Other lesser inundations continued spasmodically and in 1637 the inhabitants of Sutton who had suffered destruction of their church and lands, petitioned the Privy Council, complaining that the Commissioners of Sewers for the province of Lindsey, had failed to provide a new sea bank to protect them from the ravages of the sea. 'The Sea looseth and gaineth considerable in this county' wrote Christopher Merret in 1696.

"The method of sea bank repair, or the construction of a new bank...was to dig clay from in front, or behind, the bank line and move it by horse and sled to where the 'bankmen' or 'spademen' were working. The main season for this work was May and early June (between seed-time and haymaking) as the demand for labour was considerable. A new bank might require a work force of over 300 men. There was also carpentry work in building sluice-gates (gouts or gotes), piles and 'jetty work' (groynes),...Brushwood 'hedges' or kidding were set in the seaward side of the banks to trap blown sand.

The instructions of the Commissioners of Sewers to the dikereeves for the repair of two-thirds of a mile of sea bank at Theddlethorpe in 1571 were that it was to be 13 or 14 feet high when wet 'so that when it is thoroughly settled it remain 12 feet plum high, and to batter to the seaward 30 foot from the top to the skirt without any hollowness; and to be 6 foot broad in the top and to batter to the land 10 foot... And to be made only with clay, and all sand to be clean rid at the foundation, that clay may be laid on clay'.

The costs of work in the Lindsey coastal parishes were met by assessing 'acresilver', a rate calculated on the number of acres a man owned. When work on a drainage outfall was required or there was a serious emergency due to damage to sea banks, inland parishes also had to pay a levy...

When danger threatened, the whole community was there, 'when the north-easter is blowing above, the spring tide roaring outside, the brimming tide-way laping up to the dyke top, or flying over in sheets of spray; when round one fatal thread which is trickling over the dyke, or worse, through some forgotten rat's hole in the side, hundreds of men are clustered...The sheep have been driven off the land below; the cattle stand ranged shivering on the higher dykes inland: they will be moved by punts if the worst befall, but a hundred spades, wielded by practiced hands, cannot stop that tiny rat hole. The trickle becomes a rush, the rush a roaring waterfall. The dyke top trembles - gives. The men make efforts, desperate, dangerous...with faggots, hurdles, sedge turf; but the bank will break... through the breach pours a roaring cataract'."

In the New Lands. Intermittent inundations continued in the 17th century; sea-walls were erected and later breached during storms but reclamation work began to increase, 400 acres of marsh south of Skegness was reclaimed in 1616 followed by a further 400 acres in 1627, were typical.

As a result of law suits in the 1560's about reclaimed marsh, it was established that 'if...the sea abandon the...salt shore, whereby it became of value, then the King's right prevails'. To assert this right James I offered villagers… the right to buy their common marsh. On the north-east coast London courtier Endymion Porter (Gentleman to the Royal Bedchamber) was granted about 2,000 acres of commoners' marsh in north and south Somercoates in 1632. The local inhabitants refused to supply lodging and food for the imported labour force, but five miles of embanking and draining were completed by 1636. Although a first crop of oats and barley was harvested in 1638, the commoners took advantage of the Civil War to throw down the banks and retake possession.

In south Yorkshire the Dutch engineer Cornelius Vermuyden had, says Prymne, to the great surprise of the whole nation expending £400,000, in dis-chasing and draining 24,000 acres of Hatfield Chase by 1626. In 1639 he was in gaol for debt- caused by the flooding of Fishlake, Sykehouse and Snaith. Despite his enterprise, indeed because of it, he died miserably poor in the south – owing to unforeseen expenses.

The Participants for draining The Isle of Axholme in the summer 1642: included Sir George Saville, Mr Richard Burdett, Lady Ramsden, Lady Saville and Mr Neville. The original Commission of 1620's 'for draining and reclaiming Axholme' included Sir John Saville.

APPENDIX 4

Coffee Houses (Extracts from *A History of London* Mitchell and Leys, 1958)

In one sense the coffee-houses were the inheritors of the news and gossip disseminated in Paul's Walk; in another they were forerunners of the London clubs. Club life, with its amenities and its concentration of people with over-riding interest within a single group, was foreshadowed by the coffee-houses that soon became adopted by a particular sort of customer.

They were a specially 'London' institution: as Macaulay pointed out in his famous third chapter 'the coffee-house was the Londoner's home, and...those who wished to find a gentleman commonly asked, not whether he lived in Fleet Street or Chancery Lane, but whether he frequented the Grecian or the Rainbow'. The Rainbow was one of the earliest - if not the earliest - if not the very first - of London coffee-houses; it was opened in 1656 by James Farr, a barber.

Within a very few years, every shade of opinion was catered for by one or other of the coffee-houses: here you would go if you wanted to consult a medical man, there if you wanted witty conversation... At Will's, which stood at the north-west corner of Russell Street and Bow Street, it was possible to meet all the luminaries of London's literary world. Dryden frequented Will's and later Steele, Addison, Swift and the great Dr. Johnson himself.

Stock jobbers and financiers foregathered at Jonathan's in Change Alley, and here the talk was all of speculation and visionary projects. At the time of the South Sea Bubble many other strange schemes were launched and some of these had their inception in this house, where fortunes were lost and won by rumour and by credulous cupidity. At nearly all the coffee-houses newspapers and journals were displayed, so that it was possible to go the round the houses and acquire information of many different kinds.

...A Swiss traveller in the late seventeenth century was quick to recognise the value of the coffee-houses. 'These houses', he said 'are extremely convenient. You have all Manner of News there: You have a good Fire which you may sit by as long as you please; you have a Dish of Coffee, you meet your Friends for the Transaction of Business, and all for a Penny, if you don't Care to spend more.'

The coffee-houses were a delightful institution and filled a very real need. Good conversationalists could sharpen their wits and speech; those who enjoyed an argument could always find one to their taste; writers found encouragement, politicians enlightenment; the lonely found solace; and everyone enjoyed good company, warmth and comfort, stimulation refreshment, in the place of his own choice - in short, all the amenities of a London club - without the entrance fee.

Several fire insurance companies had been formed within a few years of the Great Fire; the Phoenix was established in 1682 and the Friendly Society began only two years later. By 1710 the Amicable Contributors had completed its first fifteen years and secured 13,000 members; at this point it changed its name to the well-known one of the

Hand-in-Hand. Like the other societies it was based on the principle of mutual contributions with the sole object of protection for its members. The Hand-in-Hand took to
meeting at Tom's Coffee-house in Westminster and built a strong-room there for its
assets....The deposit was reckoned as 12s for every £100 of the buildings value which
was assessed by the company's own surveyor. There were a hundred and fifty of them,
mostly craftsmen and small trade's people living in Westminster, but also a few who
had thrown in their lot with the Hand-in-Hand and although they owned property in
the city preferred to insure it in Tom's Coffee-House. These were minor gentry and professional men.

Charles II saw the multitude of coffee-houses, 'lately set up', as the meeting places
for the supporters of Shaftsbury, opposed to Catholicism, the Queen, the Duke of York
and France, and on 20 December 1675 he issued a proclamation for their suppression,[1]
but with little apparent effect as we read just four years later that when Samuel Pepys
was sent to the Tower on a charge of treason, during the Popish Plot of 1679, he wrote
about one of his false accusers '...This onely I can tell you, that hee gives out in his
Coffee-house talke, that hee has Eleven Witnesses to bring...against us...'[2]

Pepys himself had been asked by the authorities to spread stories (i.e. lies) of Dutch
maltreatment of English seamen in the coffee houses where it would 'spread like the
leprosy'.

APPENDIX 5

LORD LANGDALE

Sir Marmaduke Langdale 1598-1661, 1st Lord Langdale of Holme-on-Spalding-Moor,
Yorkshire, Colonel-General. (From biography by Frederick Harold Sunderland. (1926)

An event of importance in the career of Sir Marmaduke Langdale was the arrival in this country of Rupert, the son of the Elector Palatine of Bavaria and his wife Elizabeth Stuart, elder daughter of James VI of Scotland (James I of England), a sister of King Charles I.

Rupert, then in his seventeenth year of age, visited England in 1636. In 1633 he had accompanied the Prince of Orange during his campaign, and was present at the siege of Rhynberg. In 1635 he served as a volunteer in the Life Guards of the Prince of Orange during the invasion of Brabant. So fascinating was young Rupert, a scheme was proposed for the establishment of an English colony in Madagascar, of which Rupert was to be made governor. The King seriously considered the project, and asked the advice and assistance of the East India company. Rupert's mother did not favour the idea, and wrote with some wisdom:

"As for Rupert's conquest of Madagascar, it sounds like one of Don Quixote's conquests, where he promised his trusty acquire to make him king of an island," and told Rupert that such a scheme was "neither feasible, safe, nor honourable for him"

She pressed for his return to Holland, saying, "though it be a great honour and happiness to him to wait upon his uncle, yet his youth considered, he will be better employed to see the wars."

During his stay in England Rupert earned the good opinion of the King and the Court, and when the King dismissed him, in July, 1637, to return home, he granted him a monthly pension of eight hundred crowns.

Sir Marmaduke Langdale met Rupert during his visit, and conceived a warm regard for him. It is quite possible that he may have accompanied the young prince back to the Hague. In the autumn of 1637 Rupert took part in the siege of Breda, at which sir Marmaduke Langdale may have been present. It is evident from a letter written by Rupert's mother that Sir Marmaduke Langdale had been abroad about this time and that there existed a ripe friendship and regard by the Queen of Bohemia for Sir Marmaduke Langdale. Written in 1638 to Sir Marmaduke Langdale she writes from the Hague:

"I ame verie glade to know by your letter that you are so well arrived in England, and that the King doe still continue his affection to Rupert, I have sent him your letter he had not yett had answere from the Emporour for his leave but looked for it everie day, he meant in the meane time to goe to Berlin to visit the Electour of Brandebourg where I beleeve my letter will finde him, I assure you I cannot be in England sooner then I wish myself, and when the King shall please to send for me I shall goe verie willinglie. I may remember him of it when you finde a fitt time, the weather is so hott I can say no more."

1 Elizabeth Stuart, Queen of Bohemia, was granddaughter of Mary Queen of Scots. The Queen of Bohemia was great-grandmother of King George II, whose daughter Louisa became Queen of Denmark. King Christian IX, the late Queen Alexandra's father, was Queen Louisa's great-grandson. H.M. the King is therefore descended on both the maternal and paternal side from Elizabeth Stuart, Queen of Bohemia, as King Edward VII was also directly descended from that Queen.

Again in July of the same year the Queen writes from the Hague, twitting Sir Marmaduke on the dignity of addressing his friend as "madame" and "majesty" for which if she had him with her she would "jeer him to some tune for it."

"julie 5/15, Hagh. I send you your letter againe where you will see how you mistooke the superscription. I beleeve those you sent my letter to were as much surprised to se Madame and Majestie upon it, as I was to see gentleman, if I had you heere I woulde jeere you to some tune for it, but now I ame mercifull to you, and onlie assure you that I ame still extremelie your friend. There is no news stirring heere, your friend Rupert has not bene well since he came into his quarters, he had like to have had a feaver, but he writes to me it had left him, onlie he was a little weak; as soone as he can he will be in England where I wish myself to, for this place is verie dull now, for there is verie little companie."

Sir Marmaduke Langdale evidently wrote apologising for his mistake in addressing his friend the Queen in so formal a manner, and that he did so without delay after receipt of the queen's letter is evident from the reply he received the same month. The Queen wrote:

"You need make no excuse for your mistake for I comitted the like manie times. Rupert has bene ill, but is now recovered and gone to Rostok to change aire. I have written to him to come hither to goe for England as soon as he can, I heere there be some new prisoners, I hope they shall have what they deserve, it is so hott that I can write no more."

In the same year Rupert, instead of coming to England, accompanied his father, who had raised a small army to invade Wesphalia. On 17 October the Elector Palatine's little army was defeated on the banke of the Weser, and Rupert after performing prodigies of valour was taken prisoner. Thus the desire expressed by his friend Sir Marmaduke Langdale that he should return to England was in consequence delayed by a three year' imprisonment at Linz.

With truth could the Queen of Bohemia state that she was "born to so much affliction."

Elizabeth Stuart, Queen of Bohemia, was born at Falkland Castle in Fifeshire on 19 August, 1596, the elder daughter of James VI of Scotland by his consort Ann of Denmark. In 1613 she married the young Elector Palatine Frederick V. Rupert, her third son, was her favourite child. He was born at Prague on 17 December, 1619, about six weeks after his father's coronation as King of Bohemia. On 8 November, 1620, the battle of the White Mountains obliged his parents to fly from Prague, and Rupert accompanied his mother first to Berlin, and finally to Holland in April, 1621. This brief reign earned for the King and Queen of Bohemia the sobriquet of "the Winter King." Elizabeth Stuart, a very amiable princess, bore her misfortunes with dignity and even magnanimity. So engaging was her behaviour, she was known as the "Queen of Hearts" in the Low Countries where she lived in exile many years.

My Lord you need make no
excuse for your mistake for I
have comitted the like manie
times, Rupert has bene ill
but is now recovered and
gone to Bristol to change
aire. I have written to him to
come hither to goe for England
as soone as he can, I heare there
be some new prisonners, I hope
they shall have what they de-
serue, it is so hott that I can
write no more but rest euer

Your verie affectionat
frend

Elizabeth

Elizabeth Queen of Bohemia to Lord Langdale.

APPENDIX 6

SLAIN AT THE SIEGE OF PONTEFRACT

These are to Certifie unto your Worships pleasure that the petitinor here of Allice Earneshaw of Ratchdale in the Countie of lankastor widdow haveing hir husband Sleane in the wares att the Seige against poumfret Castle who beeing then under the Command of Captaine Robert Sanders wich said Captaine was in the Regement under the Command of Collonel Sir Charles ffairfax then beeing the 12th day of ffebruarie bearing date in the yeare of our lord god one Thousand six hundreth fortie and eight for & Never as yett Resseved any releife for the want of hir husband hee beeing theire Shot wth a Cannon bullett and his harmes taken away from his body wich was pressent death unto him for the wich which said Allice his wife and Child'n have Sustained Long wth much greefe and sorowshee remaining Still his wife theare fore this is to dessire your worship pleassure to Consider my Case in this my nessecitie and this your poore pettitinor will and ever bee in dutie bound to pray for you and remaine

> Your Servant Allice
> Earenshaw the wife of
> Johnathan Earenshaw

dated att Ratchdall
this 24 day March 1651

> to incert her in the list

> Lancashire Quarter Sessions Papers.98

N.B. Johnathan Earnshaw may have been recruited when General Lambert and his troops were in Rochdale on 1st September,1648.

APPENDIX 7

CIPHER WITH `MR. SYMSON' 100

Two letter from the King to the agent `Symson' in May, 1654, contain passages in numerical cipher. Symson and Plant were two of the aliases used by Thomas Paulden and in the spring of 1654 he was appointed to maintain contact between the Sealed Knott (a group of only six high ranking Royalists) and a group of north country Royalists.

1. Hyde to `Symson' May 12/22, 1654:- `Mr. Atkinson

(obviously the King)is resolved to have n o - g e n
                            45 5 43 21 12 22

e r a l l but him s e l e nor l t g
1 26 11 23 51   53 20 51 1   23 1 43

but Mr. Brook' (the Duke of York).

2. The King to`Symson' May, 1654:- `I must requyre you to communicate freely as well as the business of -(?)
Emstede (Ely?) as a l l o t h e r s t o Mr. Drayton
                  2 23 51 9 8 29 1 3 27 44 32

(Charles Davison?) or to someone of t h e - k n o t
                                    44 29 20   43 18 31 44

and I would have   N. - A r m o r e r   to do the
                22 43 32 3 30 31 26 1 3
like, by himselfe or through you.'

Many of the Royalists had their own cipher and in John Cooper's Thomas Paulden is given as Mr. Roberts.

The solution was obtained by a comparison of the two letters with similar passages in the draft instructions to the Sealed Knot: Cl.Ms.48,fol.215. The principle on which the cipher is constructed is not obvious, but the numbers used give the following key:

1:E 2:A 3:R 5:O 8:T 9:O 11:A 12:E 16:F 17:Blank? 18:K 20:E 21:G 22:N 23:L 26:R 27:S 29:H 30:M 31:O 32:A 43:Blank 44:T 47:N 51:L 53:S.

APPENDIX 8

MARTIN CLIFFORD (*c.*1624–1677),
MASTER OF CHARTERHOUSE AND AUTHOR SEE D.N.B.

Extracts from the biography of the celebrated author / poet *Abraham Cowley The Muse's Hannibal*, by Nethercot, (1931) reveal the circle of friends of Thomas Paulden's partner in the crystal glass patent and fellow servant of the Duke of Buckingham Martin Clifford; particularly those in the Royal Society.

It was probably through Mr Thomas Fotherby of Canterbury Esq., too, that Cowley became the friend of young Martin Clifford, the former's nephew, who entered Trinity in 1640 from Westminster and soon insinuated himself into the attentions of Buckingham as well as of other members of the 'society'.

Just prior to the Restoration 'Not only do the names of Charles and Jermyn figure conspicuously therein, but the glittering title of the Marquis of Ormond adds itself to the list, and Mart Clifford appears as a messenger and intermediary.'

Letter from Cowley in Paris the day after Christmas 1659 to Ormond, at the royal headquarters at Brussels: 'My Lord: Having been told by Mr. Clifford of the favourable impressions your Excellency was pleased to make concerning me [about Charles' displeasure].

1662/3 *The Rehearsal* written by seven or eight persons as a satire against Buckingham's enemies:

> Intelligence was brought, the Court being set,
> That a Play Tripartite was very near made;
> Where malicious Mart Clifford and spiritual Sprat
> Were joined with their Duke, a peer of the trade.

Lost letters from Sprat to Mart Clifford saying he had suppressed 'private' letters i.e. satires.

In Sprat's History of the Royal Society –he mentions meetings at Gray's Inn of Mr. Cowley, Dr. Sprat, Mr. Waller, the D of Buckingham, Mart. Clifford, Mr. Dryden and some other promoters of it –an English organisation to standardize the language of the British (but the death of Cowley saw it crumble to nothing).

Cowley's epistle 'A.C. Cliffordo, S.D.' his poetry always turning Latin into English and vice versa. Dr. Thomas Sprat (Bishop of Rochester, Dean of Westminster): 'An Account of the Life and Writings of Mr. Abraham Cowley, Written by Mr.M. Clifford' In the Works of Mr. Abraham Cowley. London 1668.

Cowley's body was taken from Chertsey to Buckingham's Wallingford House, Whitehall…to Westminster Abbey…on his tombstone the most florid of Latin exequial eulogies, composed, according to various guesses, by Sprat, Clifford, Scarborough, or even Dr. Thomas Gale…King Charles remarked that Mr. Cowley had not left a better man behind him in England. Clifford was left £20 in Cowley's will.

APPENDIX 9

ABSTRACTS OF TWO INDENTURES

Lease of Pawden for three lives - Edmund Asshton Esq. to Joseph Twedall yeoman 6 June 1666

INDENTURE Sixth day of June 1666 BETWEEN Edmund Asshton of Chaderton in the County of Lancaster Esq. and Joseph Twedall of Powden in the Township of Ouldham, the said Edmund Ashton for Twentie seaven pounds paid by Joseph Twedall, HATH demised that Messuage or tenament in the occupation of Joseph Tewdall called POWDEN With the houses edifices buildings outhouses barnes Stables Orchards Yards gardens Lands Meadows Closes ffields Pastures Parcells of land comon of pasture and turburie (so long as the same shall Lie open and uninclosed and not taken in and n£ longer) ways waters watercourses liberties easments profitts and comodities whatsoever unto the said Messuage and tenement in any wise belonginge or appurtaineinge or to or with the same occupied used and enjoyed or reputed or taken as parte parcell or member of the same EXCEPT and always reserved unto the said Edmund Asshton All Timber trees and other trees hedgroves & springes of wood now growinge or at any time dureinge the terme hereafter menconed may grow upon the premises And also all mines of Coales Cannell and Stone whatsoever And also except free Libertie or Royaltie for him the said Edmund Asshton his heires and servants or workemen or any other person whatsoever authorized by the said Edmund Ashton at his will and pleasure to g£ ride or drive in or through the said premises with Cart Waine and horses or otherwise to cut Square Shredd Myne digg and cary away the said trees mynes quarries and Coales or for the doing of any other thinge or thinges whatsoever And also to ffishe foule hunt and hauke in through and upon or on the same & the game there taken and found to take and cary away TO HAVE AND TO HOULD the said Messuage and Tenement dureinge the time of the naturall lives of Jacob Twedall John Twedall his Sonnes and Timothie Goddard the sonne of William Goddard of Raworth in the County of Derby yeoman - and for and dureinge the naturall life of the Longest Liver of them, paying yearly unto the said Edmund Asshton the Annual rent of Eleven Shillings and six pence And also yeildinge and payinge doinge performeinge unto the said Edmund Asshton yearely where it shall be required Two days Harrowing or two shillings six pence in money two days sheareinge or reapeinge of Corne in harvest or one shilling in money and two hens at Christmas or one shilling in money Together with the best beast or best good of every one dyeinge tenant or three pounds in money at the eleccon and choyce of the said Edmund Asshton in the name of a Herriot together also with all other Boones services duties and customes as heretofore have beene due and accustomed to bee done yielded and paid for the said premises yearely dureinge the said terme And if it happen the said Boones services herriot or herrriots duties or customes or any of them unpaid and not done then it shall bee lawfull for the said Edmund Ashton to enter the premisses and distraine of goods untill such time as hee the said Edmund Ashton is satisfied of the customes And two shillings six pence for every such distresse bee fully satisfied contented and paid AND if the yearely rent of Eleven shillings and six pence to be unpaid by the space of Ten dayes and if n£ Sufficient distresse can be found upon the premises That then it shall be lawfull for Edmund Asshton to reenter the same and every part and parcell thereof with the appurtences to retaine have and repossesse and reenjoy as in his and their first and former state right and title And the said Joseph Twedall doth covenant grant promise and agree with Edmund Asshton by these presents that he will at all times hereafter repaire and maintaine all the Messuage tenement and fermehould, at the end of the said terme to deliver up PROVIDED that Joseph Twedall d£ grant Set Let alien or passe over all or any part of the premises unto any person whatsoever (except to the use of the wife child or children of him the said Joseph Twedall without the assent and consent of Edmund Asshton in writinge it shall bee lawfull for Edmund Asshton to reenter the same and repossesse AND Joseph Twedall doth covenant grant promise and agree with Edmund Asshton by these presents that hee shall at the request of Edmund Asshton in Space of six monthes next after the death of any of Jacob Twedall John Twedall and Timothie Goddard pay unto Edmund Asshton Twentie and fife pounds And then also surrender upp unto Edmund Asshton this present Indenture of Lease to bee cancelled Soe upon payment of the sume and Surrender of this Indenture Joseph Twedall shall upon his owne part cost have a sufficient Lease of the premisses for the two surviveing lives and one other life to be therein menconed by Joseph Twedall after the life clawse therein for reneuinge of the terme upon the death of the Three lives to be therein menconed and upon payment of Twentie fife pounds at the request Edmund Asshton within the terme time and space of six monthes next after the deathe of any of the three lives PROVIDED if Joseph Twedall shall make default of the payment of the Twentie and five pounds then it shall lawfull for Edmund Asshton to reenter and repossesse - And the said Joseph Twedall his heires and assignes shall and will finde a sufficient man to serve in the Warres with a Musket when and s£ often as the said Edmund Asshton or his heires shall serve and if the said Edmund Ashton or his heires d£ make forth a foot man or horseman and d£ not g£ in their owne person or persons then to be contributarie thereunto as other Tenants of the like tenements have beene and are used to d£ AND Edmund Asshton doth grant and agree with Joseph Twedall that Edmund Assheton demise the said Messuage and tenement unto Joseph Twedall.

EDMUND   ASSHETON [47]

Arnfield to Marlor 1700

[Abstract]: INDENTURE made the thirtieth first day of December 1700 BETWEEN Thomas Arnfield of Dinting in the parish of Glossop and County of Derby yeoman And James Marlor of ffailsworth in the County of Lancaster yeoman in consideration of a Marriage already had & solemnized between the said James Marlor and Mary daughter of the said Thomas Arnfield And a portion given by the said Thomas Arnfield with the said Mary now wife of the said James Marlar. Thomas Arnfield GRANTED his Messuage and tenement with Appurtenances situate lying and being in Powden in the Parish of Ouldham and County of Lancaster And now or late in the tenure holding or occupation of him Thomas Arnfield and Commonly Called by the name of Powden And all those Closses Clausures and parcels of land meadow and pasture lying & being in Powden aforesaid and Commonly Called the great meadow, the meadow head, Crooked acre with the Clough thereunto adjoyning Called the Acre clough the High field the Leg close the Ley close meadow the Over Bowden the Lower Bowden and the two little Crofts or by what other name or names soever the same & every or any of them now are heretofore have beene or hereafter shall bee called or known And also one parcell of ground already enclosed or to bee enclosed ffrom a certain Commom or Waste Called Sholver Moore within Ouldham aforesaid And Also the Moyety and one halfe of all that Close Clausure and parcell of land meadow and pasture with their Appurtenances situate lying & being in Saddleworth in the County of York called or known by the name of the ffower Acres AND all houses Edifices Buildings Barns Stables Shippons and other outhouses Orchards gardens tofts Crofts ffoulds Lanes ffields meadows pastures Closses Enclosures Leasses Commons Common of Pasture and turbury ways waters woods underwoods Moores Mosses Mossroomes Mosse doles Mines of Coals Connell Slate or Stone quarries liberties privileges profits Commodities and hereditaments whatsover to the said Messuage and tenament Closses Clausures parcells of Land and premisses and every or any part and parcell thereof belonging.

APPENDIX 10

FRIENDS DIVIDED BY THE WAR

Sir William Waller 1597-1668   *Sir Ralph Hopton 1598-1652*

`Certainly my affections to you are so unchangeable that hostility itself cannot violate my friendship to your person. But I must be true to the cause wherein I serve - I should most gladly wait on you according to you desire, but that I look upon you as you are engaged in that party beyond a possibility of retreat, and consequently uncapable of being wrought upon by any persuasion. And I know the conference could never be so close between us, but that it would take wind and receive a construction to my dishonour. That great God which I is the searcher of my heart knows with what a sad sense I go upon this service, and with what a perfect hatred I detest this war without an enemy; but I look upon it as Opus Domini, which is enough to silence all passion in me. The God of peace in his good time send us peace, and in the meantime fit us to receive it. We are both upon the stage, and must act our parts that are assigned us in this tragedy. Let us do it in a way of honour and without personal animosities.'

This is an excerpt taken from a letter written by the Parliamentarian Sir William Waller, one of the most brilliant Parliamentary commander, to his Royalist friend and opponent Sir Ralph Hopton - It exemplifies the highest and noblest feelings between friends of different loyalties as shown in the splendid civil war film *By TheWar Divided* [before much death and destruction, immorality and recrimination had occurred -it has to be said] and what I judge must have been the feelings between our relatives Royalists William Paulden / Henry Radcliffe and his Parliamentarian nephew Captain Roger Radcliffe.

From The Lord Savile, C.St.J., J.P., D.L.

GRYCE HALL,
SHELLEY,
VIA HUDDERSFIELD. HD8 8LP.

TELEPHONE:
HUDDERSFIELD 602774.

22nd December 1993

Dear Mr Postlethwaite,

I do apologies for the very long delay in replying to your interesting letter. I have been in London a lot lately so am therefore rather behind with my correspondence.

I shall be delighted to give you permission to use the photographs of my ancestors, Sir William Savile, 3rd Bart. and his wife Anne who was the daughter of Lord Coventry. I knew Barbara Nuttall well and am, of course, completely clued up with my family history and in particular with the Civil War around Sheffield, Pontefract and Thornhill.

I am most interested to hear you are a distant relative of Captain Thomas Paulden and know of his connection with Thornhill.

It is very kind of you to suggest sending me a copy of your biography which I am sure would be very interesting. I am, however, worried about finding time these days for the reading material that I would like to pursue!

With every good wish.

Yours sincerely
Savile

R. H. Postlethwaite Esq.,
Vice-Chairman; Cumbria Family History Society.

GRYCE HALL,
SHELLEY,
VIA HUDDERSFIELD. HD8 8LP.

TELEPHONE:
HUDDERSFIELD 602774.

4th February 1994

Dear Mr Postlethwaite,

How very kind of you to send me a copy of your intended work; "Captain Thomas Paulden, a True Cavalier". I certainly will and must have time to read it and I think I will take it on holiday with me, when I go to Mauritius on March 1st. I know I will find it extremely interesting.

Meanwhile, every good wish and much gratitude for your gift.

Yours sincerely
Savile

APPENDIX 12

from Lady Craven
Peelings Manor
Nr. Pevensey
East Sussex
BN24 5AP

Feb. 12th 92

Dear Mr Postlethwaite

                    I am writing to
Thank you for your letter & to explain
that my grandson the present Earl of
Craven is only two & a half, sadly his
father my son, was killed in a
car accident a year & a half
ago.
All you have written about the Craven
family is of immense interest
while knowing a fair amount
of the past history you have
been able to add to it considerably
To my knowledge no biography has
ever been written of the 1st Earl
or of his father, he is mentioned
of course in many books
of which we have quite a collection
I've always thought that his life
should be written, he was such
a colourful exceptional man
& his devotion to the Winter Queen
was touching
There are family archives on loan
at the Bodleian Library in Oxford
which you could always have
access to.
Should you ever get as far as
Oxford my daughter Lady Ann
Tarrassenko (husband half Russian) & a
Don at St Hughes College would be
delighted to meet you, they live at
Cummor just 5 miles S. W. of
Oxford.
When she & her two brothers were
young they were members of the
Sealed Knot & fought with The
Earl of Craven's Artillery Company!
We were living at Hampstead Marshall then
Coombe Abbey was sold in 1922 after
the death of the 4th Earl, sadly
all the family homes have gone
with the deaths of 5 Earls this
century you can imagine what
the capital transfer Taxes have
been like.
If ever you find yourself in this
part of the world, do look us up

            Yours sincerely
            Elizabeth Craven

(Typescript of longhand letter.)

REFERENCE NOTES

Introduction

1   *Royalist Composition Papers*, PRO. Record Society of Lancashire & Cheshire, Vol. XXIV, Second Series, Vol. VII, No. 344, (1891) fols. 594-95.

2   Hist. Mss. Comm. Dunkirk was under the nominal command of Sir William Lockhart but the actual commander was Colonel Tobias Bridge who was later knighted and presented with a gold chain for saving Tangier from the Moors; he became Col. of the Barbados Regt. of Foot & member of Council there in 1674. Bridgetown, capital of Barbados is named after him. Captain Thomas Stackhouse bequeathed him 'my best horse and furniture' (1663).P.C.C.

3   Routh, E.M.G., *Tangier 1661-1684* (1912); and (Colonial Office:279,1-49).

4   Firth,C.H. & DAVIES G., *The Regimental History of Cromwell's Army*, Oxford, (1940).

5   Paulden, Thomas. *Letter*, first published at The Savoy,1702; London,1719 (for benefit of his widow); Oxford,1747; and in *Somer's `Tracts, 1812 vii, 3-9*; included in *The Sieges of Pontefract Castle* ed. Richard Holmes(1887) reprinted 1985; and separately, by Old Hall Press in 1986. A different version from Clarendon Mss. 1648, 2978, is in Archaologia XLVI, 48, Appendix A, pp. 46-63, *Notes on Thomas Rainsborough*.

6   See Paulden Family & our connections p.167.

7   Underdown, David, *Royalist Conspiracy in England 1649-1660*, not only gave me vital references to follow up but also outlined Thomas Paulden's part in Royalist Conspiracy.

Chapter 1. Radcliffe, Paulden and Knowles

1   Radcliffe, Henry, his will proved at PCC, London, by widow Dorothy 9th Feb.1658/9.

2   *Royalist Composition Papers*, PRO., No. 370. 5th Sept.1650.

3   Paulden. Probably taking its name from a small settlement of that name near Oldham, Lancashire, adjacent to the Yorkshire border.

4   Chetham Society Vol. CXII (1884); *The Great De Lacy Inquest 1311*.pp.xxvi, 156.

5   Record Society of Lancashire & Cheshire *Lay Subsidies*.

6   Yorkshire Archaeological Society Journal,Vol.7, p.168.

7   Will at York

8   Halifax Antiquarian Society (1930); *Rentals of Halifax 1587-88*. Also Thoresby Society Miscellaneous.Vol.15; *Yorkshire Lay Subsidies 1588*; and will of William Paulden of Halifax, father of Gregory, proved 13th Feb.1570/71, at York.

9   Peacock, M.H., *The History of the Free Grammar School of Wakefield* (1892), Edward Watkinson 1605-09; Christopher Naylor 1610-38; and Daniel Oley 1649-73 were governors related to Gregory's son William Paulden.

10 Temple-Newsham Mss. Tn/wk II,/10; III.2,2B,17,20B, at Leeds Ref. Lib. Archives, Sheepscar.

11 Prestwich, M., *Cranfield, 1st Earl of Middlesex* (1966). He was supported by the Duke of Buckingham.

12 Upton, A., *Sir Arthur Ingram* (1961). Ingram was the most shameless. In another of his contemporary satirical plays *The Devil Is An Ass* Ben Jonson's con-man Meercroft sucks gullible Norfolk squire Fabian Fitzdottrell into investing in a giant land draining project on the east coast with the promise of a dukedom.

13 Harford, C.H., (D.N.B.).

14 Cust, L., (D.N.B.).

15 Wakefield Old Park was sub-let to tenants by the lease holders. Hist.Mss.Com. *The Cranfield Papers, Sackvile of Knole.*

16 Rosamond bapt.1559 dau. of Robert Oates & Sybil nee' Lister, and grand daughter of Gilbert Oates of Shibden Hall, Halifax.

17 Proved at York 19th January 1613/14.

18 His signature appears on the leases Tn/wk.

19 P.R.O. Chancery C2/26/1 James I, Bill dated 24 Nov 1614.

20 Y.A.S. Journal, Vol. XI, Paver's Marriage licences 1615-1616.

21 Proved at York, 9th June 1620.

22 Drake's journal is used extensively by George Fox in *The Three Sieges of Pontefract Castle* (1987).

23 Clode, W., Craven Sir William, (c1548-1618) from Appletreewick, just ten miles from Long Preston, was sent by the common carrier to London, at the age of 13-14 to be apprenticed to a merchant tailor; he rose to be master of the Merchant Taylors Company, was knighted in 1603, became Lord Mayor in 1610-11 and his eldest son William became the Earl of Craven and friend of the Royal family. Burnsal Grammar School was founded by him. (D.N.B.)

24 James Knowles's will, proved in London by his executor nephew William Paulden.

25 Saint Stephen's Coleman St. London: Parish Registers.

26 Prior Richard Moon's family belonged to Long Preston: Richard Moyn [Moon] died vicar there in 1456; see his will at York.

Chapter 2 The English Civil War 1642-49

1   He was elected a governor two years earlier on 6 Nov 1622 but for some reason refused to take office.

2   Venn, J., *Alumni Cantabrigienses*, ed. 1922). *Matriculations and Degrees 1544-1659*, p.514.

3   By Vice-Chancellor, Dr. Comber.

4   It is not surprising therefore that the Duke of Buckingham often thought his opinion as good as and sometimes better than the King's.

5   Porter, Miss, His courage and loyalty to his friends, the King and the Royalist cause made him justly famous. (D.N.B.).

6   He appears to have received some employment from the Duke at the Restoration.

7   Courtney, W.P., P.C.C. will of Barnabus Oley,16 March 1685/86.

8   Originals in Wakefield R.O., D3/1.

9   Yorkshire Archaeological Society, Vol. LIV, *Q.S. Records of West Riding,1611-1642*, p.126.

10 Wakefield R.O., Z125, *1641 Protestation Returns*, p.175.

11 *Wakefield Its History and its People* p.431. Mr P Nevile & Reynor.

12 *Yorkshire Archaeological Society, Record Series, Vol. XX; Vol. II* (1896). No.332, 22 July. He was described as a *Chapman*.
13 Hodkin Mss, Hist. Mss. Commission, T. P's letter Oct 52.
14 Firth, C.H.,(D.N.B.) and *Royalist Conspiracy*. It is stated in Surtees Soc. II (1861) *Depositions from York Castle that* 'The original commission to Capt. William Paulden by Marmaduke Langdale is now at Sledmere'. But it is now lost.
15 *Naseby* by Peter Young

Chapter 3 The Siege of Sandal Castle

1   *The True Informer, Aug. 2,1645*; p.182.
2   Walker J.W. *Sandal Castle* Journal of Y.A.S. Vol.13 (1895).
3   Clarendon Mss. 1648, 2978, in Archaeologia XLVI,48, pp.55 & 63.
4   *Victoria County History of Yorkshire,Vol.3*, p.431

Chapter 4 The Third, and last, Siege of Pontefract Castle

1   *Cheshire in the Civil Wars* p.138
2   Fox, George,*The Three Sieges of Pontefract Castle* (1987); p.119.
3   *A Full and Exact Relation of the Horrid Murder of Col. Rainsborough*, London: Printed for R.A., 1648 - A Letter from J. Barnard, Doncaster Oct 30 1648. This calumny was again presented as fact in the recent civil war film *The Devil's Whore*.
4   *Notes on the Life of Thomas Rainsborough* Archeologia XLVI, 48; p.53.
5   Ibid. Thomas Paulden's report in Clarendon MSS. 1648, 2978, pp.55-63.
6   The Life of John Barwick, p.51.
7   *Royalist Composition Papers*, No. 333, Barnabus Oley is described as of Chevet July 1649 Nr. Wakefield: home of the Neviles. See p.59, q.v.
8   Fox, George,*The Three Sieges of Pontefract Castle* (1987).
9   Ibid.
10   *Life at Thornhill Hall in the Reign of Charles I* Barbara C. Nuttall.
11   Fox, George,*The Three Sieges of Pontefract Castle* (1987).
12   C.S.P. Dom 1660, p153.
13   Fox, George,*The Three Sieges of Pontefract Castle* (1987).
14. *Notes on the Life of Thomas Rainsborough*, Clarendon Mss. 1648, 2978, in Archaologia XLVI,48, pp.55 & 63.
15   Fox, George,*The Three Sieges of Pontefract Castle* (1987), p.132.
16   Ibid.p.132.
17   Ibid.p.107.
18   Ibid. p.126.
19   Taylor, K., *Wakefield District Heritage Vol. II*; (1979). `Sir John Bright was a Civil War Stalwart, great man of repute. His marvellous tomb in Badesworth Church. A suit of armour said to be his is in Wakefield museum.' He mediated in the surrender of Pontefract Castle.
20   Fox, George,*The Three Sieges of Pontefract Castle* (1987), p.144.

Chapter 5 Thomas as Secret Agents

1   Hist.Mss.Com. Hodkin Mss., p115.
2   Underdown, D., *Royalist Conspiracy in England 1649-1660.*
3   Letter, Ms Fairfax 32. Bodleian Library.
4   *Clarendon State Papers, Vol.2,1649-54,* p.168 - received 100 livres. Sir Nicholas Armorer of Belford (close to Holy Island) was an active plotter, well known to Thomas Paulden, and responsible for shooting of one of Thurloe's agents on the Continent. A close confederate of Edward Hyde in his dealings with Ralph Hopton. In Jan 1672 he was 'master of horse' in the Royal household. On'18 Jan 1678, said to have eminently served the king. To Secretary of State Sir Joseph Williamson, after taking up his appointment as Captain in Dublin he writes '…God keep thee; and, as my predecessor Sancho says, 'Let sin be deaf'.To Sir Nicholas Armourer, in full satisfaction made for building ships for his said Ma'tie in Ireland, and for buying timber for the said use £300.00.00, c.1683. He died Captain in Dublin in 1686.
5   Vigur, C. Corker: *Cambridge Admissions*: Corker, Francis admitted sizar at Jesus Ap. 24 1626, of Yorks. Matric 1626 B.A.162-30, Vicar of Bradford 1642-3, 1662-7. Buried Bradford Mar 29 1667 (A. Gray).
6   Vigur C. Corker *Francis Corker, Vicar of Bradford,* Bradford Antiquary Society.
7   Thurlow's State Papers, Vol.1.
8   Vigur C. Corker *Francis Corker, Vicar of Bradford,* Bradford Antiquary Society
9   *State Papers of John Thurloe Esq.,* ed. Thomas Birch (1742).

Chapter 6 Events Leading to the Restoration

1   Barwick,Peter *The Life of John Barwick.*
2   Redman's memorial, with reference to his Irish estate, received for capturing a castle at Ballinabola, near Lilkenny, stands in Kirkby Lonsdale church.
3   Clobbery did good service against the Dutch and again in the following reign, in Monmouth's rebellion, at the battle of Sedgemoor. He died at Winchester in 1687 and was buried in the cathedral, and honoured as he deserved with a copious Latin inscription.
4   LRO. DDPd/41/1, Pedder Mss. Copy of John Barwick's will.

Chapter 7 The King Restored to his Own again

1   Clarendon *Rebellion,* xvi. 246.
2   John Otway D.N.B. & LRO *News Cuttings 1880-82 Preston Guardian.*
3   Employed in 1660 with Martin Clifford and others as agents by the Duke of Buckingham.
4   S.P.Dom. 1661-62,100, Petition; p.528.
5   Ibid., Greg 1661-62, Oct. 27; Entry Book 9, p.22. £500 was the market price for a baronetcy at the Restoration.
6   Ibid., Greg 1661-62,Oct.29, London.112. p.530.
7   Ibid.
8   *A List of Officers Claiming to the Sixty Thousand Pounds'(granted by King Charles II) for the Relief of his truly Loyal and Indigent Party.* P.R.O. S.P. 29, Vol.68, (1663).

9 *John Evelyn's Diary.*
10 Woodcroft, Bennet, *Alphabetical Index of Patentees 1617-1852-1854*; (1969): 90 Paulden, Thomas, Progressive No.134, Date 10th Nov.1661, Subject Matter, Making Crystal Glass.(Ditto for Martin Clifford). And (f) 1663-64, p.229, Aug.4,1663.
11 Harrison M., & O.M.Royston: *How They Lived 1450-1700* (1965).
12 D.N.B. Goodwin, G., M. Clifford was elected master of the Charterhouse, a post which he doubtless owed to his friendship with the Duke of Buckingham.
13 D.N.B. Cooper,T..
14 S.P.Dom., 4 April 1668.
15 Hatton Correspondence, Camden Society, n.s. Vol. (1878).
16 Thoresby, Diary II.p.62, 18th July 1711.
17 Royalist Composition Papers, 26th July 1649.

Chapter 8 Further Exciting Discoveries
1 P.C.C.
2 PRO.
3 PCC.
4 Lang, R.G. *Greater Merchants of London in the Early 17C* (1963).
5 *The Striding Dales*, p.85.
6 Will of Queen of Bohemia (Latin translated by my friend Tony Gould).
7 Yorkshire Deeds - Thorpe/884.

Chapter 9 Thomas' Dream of becoming 'Governor' of Holy Island
1 John Evelyn, in his Diary records six occasions, between 3 Feb 1684 & 23 April 1702, when he attending the excellent preaching of 'that incomparable Devine' Dr. John Sharp, Dean of Canterbury (11 April 1690), Archbishop of York April 1 1694, at St. Martins and; 'His prayer before sermon was one of the most excellent and comprehensive I have heard.' At the Middle Temple.
2 Names of those fit and qualified to be made knights of the Royal Oak, with the value of their estates. AD 1660. Northumberland: Daniel Collingwood Esq. £600; George Collingwood Esq. £800. George, of Easington, married Agnes daughter of John Fleming of Rydal. Son or grandson of same name attainted and executed 1715. The Flemings in Oxford, Vol. 1, pp10 & 516, Ed. J.R. Magrath, 1904.
3 I am indebted to Maurice McDougall of Cullercoats for this reference.

Chapter 12 'I Despise Wealth but not Honour' says Don Quixote
1 Shakespeare has the Fool addressing King Lear as 'nuncle'. Which appears to be a name for someone humouresly claimed as an uncle.

Chapter 13 Paulden and its Origins
1 Lancashire Record Office, DDX 228/251/8D; DX228/251/12; DDX228/271/1-39; DDX228/273.
2 26th August 1968; & Vol.34 1973-74, p.110, *Oldham Weekly Chronicle, 22 Dec.1973.*

3   Oldham Library Local Studies Collection.
4   Chetham Society Vol.103, Misc., *Langley Notes*, pp.10-11.
5   Bowman,W.M., *England in Ashton-under-Lyne*, p.22.
6   Brownbill & Farrer, *Victoria County History of Lancashire,Vol.4.*
7   Ibid.
8   Bowman, W.M., *England in Ashton-under-Lyne*, p.22; Ass.R.405m,1.
9   Brownbill & Farrer, V.C.H.L.Vols. 4 & 5.
10 Ibid, p.24.
11 LRO. W/C/W.
12 Ibid., V.C.H.L.Vol.5; (Lich. Epis. Reg. i fol. 23).
13 L.T.R. Mem. R. 163, XIIII (21 Richard II) and 169, XII (5 Hen. IV).
14 Brownbill & Farrer, V.C.H.L.Vol.5.
15 Ibid., V.C.H.L.vol.5, p.217,
16 D/L Pleadings, R.S.L.& C, Vol.35, (1897).
17 *Raine mss., deeds bundle 418*; (V.C.H.L.Vol.5).
18 *Raine mss.Vol.22, p.523, Chetham Library.*
19 *Yorkshire Fines Michaelmas Term, 23 Eliz.*
20 *D/L Inq. P.M. xvi, 22.*
21 *Raine mss.Vol.22, p.523, Chetham Library.* Disputed lands in Quick D/L Pleadings vol. ii, p.145.
22 Ibid. vol. iii, p.328.
23 *Inq. P.M., 2 Oct.10 Jac. 1613.*
24 Chetham Society, Misc.
25 *Raine Deeds. Bdle.4. No. 484.*
26 Chetham Society.
27 *Raine Deeds.*
28 Cheshire Wills.
29 *S.P.Dom.1623-26*, pp.31, 35, 36, 40 & 44.
30 *S.P. Dom. 1627-28*, pp.133, 134, 146 & 201.
31 Ibid.
32 Ibid.
33 *History of Horsedge Hall* by Bateson.
34 Ormerod, G., Ed., Chetham Society, Vol.2, *Tracts relating to Military Proceedings in Lancashire during the Civil War.*
35 *History of Horsedge Hall* by Bateson.
36 H.M.S.O., *Committee for Compounding Cases*, p.1466.
37 L.R.O. Cheshire Wills (WCW).
38 *Raine Deeds.*
39 Ormerod, G., Ed., Chetham Society, Vol.2, *Tracts relating to Military Proceedings in Lancashire during the Civil War.*
40 LRO. QSB/1/107/20.
41 *Royalist Composition Papers*, R.S.L & C.
42 Broxap, E., refers to Civil War Tracts, 67 & 79.

43 Transactions of The Lancashire & Cheshire Antiquarian Society, Vol.47.

44 *Wigan's Part in the Civil War, 1639-1651*, by Arthur J. Hawkes, pp.84-138.

45 L.R.O. DDK 12/7, Knowsley Deeds. Clubmen of Oldham came to aid of Bolton.

46 Blackwood B.G., *Parties and Issues in the Civil War* p.112.

47 Wigan R.O. Anderton D & P, 16/23.

48. LRO W.C.W John Taylor's will 1574.

49 L.R.O. Preston, DDX 439/23/1? (1666 lease).

50 L.R.O. Preston, DDX 439/24/6.

51 L.R.O. Preston, DDX 439/23/13.

52 L.R.O. Cheshire Wills

53 Shaw, G., *Annals of Oldham & Distric.*

54 Butterworth, E., 'Historical Sketches of Oldham', (1856), reprint (1981).

55 Shaw, G., *Notes & Gleanings of Oldham & District.*

56. Ibid.

57 Church Lay.

58 *Local Almanac* issued in 1878.

59 *Wakefield Court Rolls*: p.164. Hyperum 13 Edw I, 1286. John son of John de Quermeby, drew blood from John son of <u>Paulinus</u> of the same, Let him be distrained to answer therefore – 6d.

Appendix 3 Other Examples of Reclamation of the Sea-Shore.

1   Robinson David N. *The Book of the Lincolnshire Seaside*, 1981.
     Ivan & Broadhead *The Yorkshire Ouse*, 1982. p160.
     Stonehouse Revd W.B., *The Isle of Axholme*, 1939.

SELECT BIBLIOGRAPHY

Acton, Lord, *Secret History of Charles II*, 1907.

Akerman, J.W., *Secret Service Money*, Camden Soc. 1851.

Baker L.M. *The Letters of Elizabeth Queen of Bohemia* (1953).

Browning, A. *Thos Osborne, E of D*, 3 vols. Glasgow, 1944-51.

Chappell, E., Ed., *Tangier Papers of Samuel Pepys*, Navy Records Society, 1935.

Grosman, Edith, *Don Quixote* by Miguel de Cervantes; London, 2004.

Haythornthwaite, Philip J. *The English Civil War 1642-1651 An Illustrated Military History* Colour illustrations by Jeffrey Burn (1983).

Historical Mss. Commission - *The Cranfield Papers*, Sackvile of Knole.

Kendall, James, *Acct of Warrington Siege A.D. 1643* H S L C, Vol. V 1851-2.

Prestwich, Menna. *Cranfield, 1st Earl of Middlesex* Clarendon Press (1966)

Tanner, J.R. (Ed). *Private Corresp. & Misc Papers of Sam.P.1679-1703*, 1926.

Thompson, E.M. *Hatton Corresp*, Camden Soc. 1876-78.

Tupling, G.H.Lancashire and Cheshire Antiquarian Soc Vol. 65 – *Causes of the Civil War in Lancs*.

Upton, Anthony .*Sir Arthur Ingram,* Oxford (1961)

Mss Sources

Pepysian Mss in Pepys Library, Magdelene College, Cambridge.

My Two Volumes of Mornamont, Pepysian mss.no.2881-2.

Pepys Letter Book 1679-83, Rawl. Mss,A.194, (Bodleian).

The Royalist Army in Northern England 1642-45 by P.R. Newman; unpublished thesis D23378/78 (2 Vols.).

INDEX